Human Relations
Career, Relationships, and You
Version 3.1

Laura Portolese

978-1-4533-3576-5

Human Relations: Career, Relationships, and You
Version 3.1

Laura Portolese

Published by:

FlatWorld
175 Portland Street
Boston, MA 02114

Gen: 202006021308

Brief Contents

Contents

About the Author

Laura Portolese holds a master of business administration from City University of Seattle and a doctorate of business administration from Argosy University Seattle. Laura is an Associate Professor at Central Washington University in the Department of Information Technology and Administrative Management, part of the College of Education and Professional Studies.

Before beginning her teaching career, Laura worked for several organizations in management and operations. She's also an entrepreneur who has performed consulting work for companies such as Microsoft. She is the author of *Human Resource Management; Consumer Behavior Today; The Art of Leadership and Supervision;* and *Entrepreneurship* with FlatWorld and two other textbooks with McGraw-Hill.

Laura lives in Ellensburg, Washington, a farming and ranching town, with her husband Chris and mischievous black lab Finley. She is an active traveler, camper, and scuba diver.

Acknowledgments

I'd like to thank Nikki Ross, Senior Associate Digital Editor at FlatWord. I greatly appreciate working with Nikki. Her attention to detail, lightning-fast responses, advice, and insight helped make this edition what it is. I'd also like to thank the entire team at FlatWorld, including Sean Wakely, for creating fantastic products, and saving our students money!

Mary Rucker, Wright State University

Greg Watson, Arizona College

Laura Riolli, California State University, Sacramento

Greg Richards, Spokane Community College

Irene Z. Church, Muskegon Community College

Dedication

This book is dedicated to my husband, Chris, for his unwavering support.

Preface

Knowing how to get along with others, resolve workplace conflict, manage relationships, communicate well, and make good decisions are all critical emotional intelligence skills that students need to succeed in careers and in life. Our *Human Relations: Career, Relationships, and You* book will address all of the critical topics to obtain career success. This book isn't an organizational behavior (OB) text, which is too theoretical for many of our students' needs. While this book will focus on some of the theories you might find in an OB book, the focus is a direct benefit to students in their current and future careers.

This book also isn't a professional communications, business English, or professionalism book, as the focus is much broader: it focuses on general career success and how to effectively maneuver in the workplace.

The core concept in the book is emotional intelligence and how these skills carry over into career success, such as through ethics, communication, diversity, teamwork, conflict, good decision making, stress management, motivation, and leadership.

This book's easy-to-understand language and tone is written to convey practical information in an engaging way. Plenty of examples are included in each chapter so students understand the concepts and how the concepts can benefit their careers. This book will meet the needs of a course in the business department or will be offered to professional technical students in any number of career fields, such as automotive, dental hygiene, culinary, or technology. In addition, this book would be a great addition to any school offering human relations courses for teacher certification.

This book could be used in the following courses:

- Human relations
- Psychology
- Career-focused courses
- Professionalism
- Business communications
- Teacher/education certification

Features

Each chapter opens with a realistic example that introduces a concept to be explained in detail later. Each chapter contains relevant examples, YouTube videos, figures, learning objectives, key takeaways, Why Human Relations? boxes, exercises, and a chapter-ending case that offer different ways to promote learning.

What's New in Version 3.1?

The COVID-19 global pandemic that appeared in early 2020 impacted every aspect of the organization—large and small, profit and nonprofit. Productively handling stress, maintaining productive relationships with work colleagues, resolving unexpected ethical dilemmas, communicating clearly in times of uncertainty, providing strong leadership, and showing empathy and patience with others are just a few of the skills we particularly need to uncover and develop in times of crisis. While the full implications of the pandemic are yet to be clear, our experience thus far has pointed out the many ways in which we can grow as individuals, colleagues, and leaders. Version 3.1 of *Human Relations: Career, Relationships, and You* reflects our earliest experiences with the current pandemic as reflected in coverage of stress, maintaining positive attitudes, and working from home. It also builds upon the many revisions reflected in Version 3.0 that brought this book fully up to date just a few months before this Version 3.1 update was published.

Version 3.1 of *Human Relations: Career, Relationships, and You* comes complete with new figures and graphics in every chapter, new examples, and a variety of new videos to demonstrate concepts. In addition, new "What's in It for Me?" features explain the importance of key topics and how they directly relate to career success. Each chapter has been reviewed and updated to keep pace with changes in the field and to keep student informed of the latest thinking in human relations. Specific chapter updates include:

Added "Why Human Relations?" boxes, as well as "What's in it for me?" boxes throughout the text

Chapter 1: Revised discussion of empathy and compassion. Added information on personality tests and how knowing your personality can help you succeed at work.

Chapter 2: New emotional intelligence quizzes.

Chapter 3: New chapter covers self-esteem and how to increase self-esteem to achieve better productivity in the workplace.

Chapter 4: New content on "selling yourself" and persuasion.

Chapter 7: New presentation of the team building process, team dynamics, and how to handle difficult team members.

Chapter 8: New content on how to make good decisions using a variety of decision-making models.

Chapter 10: Revised coverage of unions relocated to this chapter and combined with information on conflict and negotiation.

Chapter 11: New coverage of the competitive advantages gained from diversity. Extensive new information on cultural intelligence and how to develop cultural intelligence.

Chapter 13: New discussion on resume writing and interviewing.

CHAPTER 1
Human Relations in a Nutshell

I present myself to you in a form suitable to the relationship I wish to achieve with you.
—*Luigi Pirandello*

If you don't like something, change it. If you can't change it, change your attitude.
—*Maya Angelou*

No One Wants to Work with Her

At work, Jenny avoids interpersonal relationships and small talk because she is uncomfortable revealing too much of herself. When Jenny attends meetings at work, she sighs impatiently when someone is late and when people veer too far from the topic, and she makes sure to bring people back to reality. When choosing project teams, people rarely want to work with Jenny, even though she is very competent at her job. Some of the people from the office get together for lunch on Tuesdays, but Jenny is never invited. Needless to say, Jenny isn't well liked at work because she comes across as disagreeable and unfriendly.

We have all met someone like Jenny, who is seemingly uncomfortable with herself and unpleasant. We may even try to avoid the Jennys we know. Despite Jenny being good at her job, no one wants to work with her. You would think that success at work only takes talent at job-specific tasks. However, this isn't the case. As we will discuss throughout this chapter and the book, successful people have the skills to do the job, but they also have the human relations skills to get along with others. The focus of this chapter will be personality (and tools you can use to measure personality), attitudes, empathy, self-esteem, and perceptions—all of these topics and more impact our ability to get along with others.

1.1 Why Study Human Relations?

Learning Objectives

1. Define human relations.
2. Discuss why human relations skills are necessary in your future workplace.
3. Explain how the progression of human relations studies relates to today's human relations in your life.

The study and understanding of human relations can help us in our workplace and, as a result, assist us in achieving career success. The better our ability to relate to others, the more likely we are to grow both professionally and personally. Knowing how to resolve workplace conflict, manage relationships, communicate well, and make good decisions are all skills we will discuss throughout the book.

Why Human Relations?

human relations

Relations with or between people, particularly in a workplace or professional setting.

So, what is human relations? We can define **human relations** as relations with or between people, particularly in a workplace or professional setting.[1] From a personal perspective, there are many advantages to having good human relations skills. First, several of the top reasons people lose their job relate back to a lack of human relations skills—for example, the inability to work within a team, insubordination, or poor performance.[2] Other reasons, perhaps not directly related to human relations, include absenteeism, stealing, political reasons, downsizing, and sabotage. Second, people who communicate goals, take initiative, and show leadership potential are more likely to be promoted.[3] In fact, according to personal development guru Brian Tracy, 85 percent of your success in life is determined by how well you communicate and inspire others to take action.[4] Another reason to develop good relationships with others relates to your own personal happiness. A lot of joy can come from having positive, happy relationships with others.

Consider John, a very talented project manager but lacking in human relations skills. While he is easily able to plan and execute the finest details for a project, no one likes to work with him. He doesn't make an effort to get to know his team members, comes across as unapproachable, and people are afraid to ask him questions. How successful do you think John will be in his workplace? While he has the skills necessary to do the job, he doesn't have the people skills that can help him excel at it. One could say he does not have emotional intelligence skills—that is, the ability to understand others—therefore, he may always find himself wondering why he isn't more successful at work (we will discuss emotional intelligence in Chapter 2). While project management skills are something we can learn, managers find it difficult to hire people without soft skills, or human relations skills. We aren't saying that technical skills are not important, but human relations skills are equally as important as technical skills to determine career and personal success. Consider human relations skills in your personal life, as this is equally important. Human relations skills such as communication and handling conflict can help us create better relationships. For example, assume Julie talks behind people's backs and doesn't follow through on her promises. She exhibits body language that says "get away from me" and rarely smiles or asks people about themselves. It is likely that Julie will struggle with the human relations aspect at work and in her personal relationships. If Julie had positive human relations skills, there is a much better chance she could be more successful.

organizational structures

Refers to the way a company arranges people, jobs, and communications so that work can be performed.

empowerment

When an organization gives the employees freedom in making decisions about how their work gets done.

We can benefit personally and professionally from good human relations skills, but how do organizations benefit? Since many companies' organizational structures depend upon people working together, positive human relations skills reduce conflict in the workplace, thereby making the workplace more productive. **Organizational structures** refers to the way a company arranges people, jobs, and communications so that work can be performed. In today's business world, teams are used to accomplish company goals because teamwork includes people with a variety of skills. When using human relations skills in a team, a better product and better ideas are usually produced. In most businesses, to be successful at our job, we need to depend on others. The importance of human relations is apparent in this setting. If people are not able to get along and resolve conflicts, the organization as a whole will be less productive, which could affect profitability. Many organizations **empower** their employees; that is, they give employees freedom in making decisions about how their work gets done. This can create a more motivated workforce, which results in more positive human relations. We will explore this topic further in Chapter 7.

Most organizations employ a **total person approach**. This approach recognizes that an organization does not just employ someone with skills, but rather, the whole person. This person comes with biases, personal challenges, human relations skills, and technical skills, but also comes with experiences. By looking at a person from this perspective, an organization can begin to understand that what happens to an employee outside of work can affect his or her job performance. For example, assume Kathy is doing a great job at work but suddenly starts to arrive late, leave early, and take longer lunches. Upon further examination, we might find that Kathy is having childcare issues because of her divorce. Because of a total person approach, her organization might be able to rearrange her schedule or work with her to find a reasonable solution. This links to human relations because we are not just people going to work every day, we are people who live our personal lives, and one affects the other. Because of this, our human relations abilities will most certainly be affected if we are experiencing challenges at home or at work.

> **total person approach**
>
> This approach recognizes that an organization employs not just someone with skills but rather the whole person.

FIGURE 1.1 Getting People to Like You
Joan Harrington, a blogger and life coach, says there are a few key things to getting people to like you.

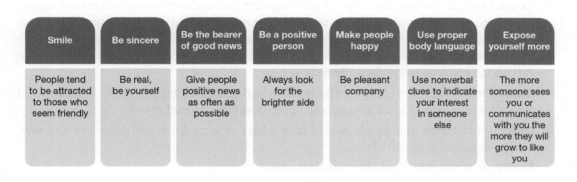

Smile	Be sincere	Be the bearer of good news	Be a positive person	Make people happy	Use proper body language	Expose yourself more
People tend to be attracted to those who seem friendly	Be real, be yourself	Give people positive news as often as possible	Always look for the brighter side	Be pleasant company	Use nonverbal clues to indicate your interest in someone else	The more someone sees you or communicates with you the more they will grow to like you

Data from: http://m.ibosocial.com/joantruesuccess/pressrelease.aspx?prid=58768

Evolution of Human Relations Study

Human relations, however, was not always central to the conversation on organizational success. In fact, until the 1940s, little thought was given to the human aspect of jobs. Many of the jobs in the early 1900s were focused on production and located in factory-like settings where the jobs themselves were repetitive. The focus in these types of work environments was on efficiency. We can call this time period of human relations studies the **classical school of management**. This school of thought took place from 1900 to the early 1920s. Several theories were developed, which revolved around the idea of efficiency, or getting a job done with the least amount of steps.

> **classical school of management**
>
> A time period relating to the research of human relations that focused on efficiency. The time period for this school of thought took place from 1900 to the early 1920s.

Frederick W. Taylor was an engineer who today is known as the father of scientific management. He began his career in a steel company and, because of his intimate knowledge of the industry, believed that organizations could analyze tasks to make them more efficient.

Following his work, Frank and Lillian Gilbreth performed numerous studies on physical motions workers took to perform specific tasks and tried to maximize efficiency by suggesting new ways to perform the tasks, using less energy and thereby being more efficient.

While Taylor and Gilbreth's research was more focused on physical motions and tasks, Henri Fayol began looking at how management could improve productivity instead of focusing on specific tasks and motions. Fayol created the Fourteen Principles of Management, which focused on management but also hinted, at the importance of human relations:[5]

1. **Division of work.** Work should be divided in the most efficient way. Fayol believed work specialization, or the focus on specific tasks for teams or individuals, to be crucial to success.

2. **Authority.** Authority is the right to give orders and accountability within those orders. Fayol believed that along with giving orders and expecting them to be met, that the person in authority also assumed responsibility to make sure tasks were met.

3. **Discipline.** Discipline is the practice of applying penalties to encourage common effort, as a successful organization requires the common effort of all workers.

4. **Unity of command.** Workers should receive orders from only one manager. In other words, reporting to two or more managers would violate Fayol's Fourteen Principles of Management.

5. **Unity of direction.** Everyone in the organization should move toward a common goal and understand how the team will achieve that goal.

6. **Subordination of individual interests to general interests.** The interests of one person shouldn't have priority over the interests of the organization as a whole. This focuses on teamwork and the importance of everyone acting to achieve the same goal.

7. **Remuneration.** Many things should be considered when paying employees, including cost of living, supply of qualified people, and business success.

8. **Centralization.** The degree of importance in the subordinates' (employees') role in their organization and the amount of decision making that occurs at a central versus a decentralized level. For example, in many organizations decisions are made centrally (i.e., in the "corporate office"), which does not allow as much flexibility as decentralized decision making; this would mean each individual area can make its own decisions.

9. **Scalar chain.** This refers to how authority is divided among managers. Specifically, Fayol said lower-level managers should always keep upper-level managers informed.

10. **Order.** All materials and people related to one kind of work should be organized and neat. Things should be easy to find.

11. **Equity.** All employees should be treated equally.

12. **Stability of tenure of personnel.** Retention of employees should be a high management priority. The cost of hiring a new worker is expensive, so efforts should be maintained to keep current employees.

13. **Initiative.** Management should take steps to encourage workers to take initiative. In addition, workers should be self-directed and not need a lot of management control to accomplish tasks.

14. **Esprit de corps.** Managers should encourage harmony among employees. This harmony creates good feelings among employees.

Fayol's research was some of the first that addressed the need for positive human relations in a work environment. As further research was performed into the 1920s, we moved into a new period of human relations studies called the **behavioral school of management**. During this time period, employees had begun to unionize, bringing human relations issues to the forefront. Because workers demanded a more humane environment, researchers began to look at how organizations could make this happen.

One of the more notable researchers was Elton Mayo, from the Harvard Business School, and his colleagues. They conducted a series of experiments from the mid-1920s to early 1930s to investigate how physical working conditions affected worker productivity. They found that regardless of changes such as heat, lighting, hours, and breaks, productivity levels increased during the study. The researchers realized the increased productivity resulted because the workers knew they were being observed. In other words, the workers worked harder because they were receiving attention and felt cared about. This phenomenon is called the **Hawthorne effect** (named for the electrical plant where the experiments were conducted).

behavioral school of management

During the 1920s when employees had begun to unionize, researchers began to look at the human aspect of workers.

Hawthorne effect

Coined during the 1920s during a series of experiments where workers had higher productivity because they were being watched by researchers and felt cared about.

In the 1950s, researchers began to explore management techniques and the effect on worker satisfaction. This was called the **behavioral science approach**. These techniques used psychology, sociology, and other human relations aspects to help researchers understand the organizational environment.

Since the 1960s, research on human relations has been much easier to assimilate because of technology and a focus on statistical analysis. Hence, this is called the **management science school**. So, while research today focuses on the human relations aspect, we are now able to use complex statistical models to improve efficiency and productivity while still focusing on the human relations component.

Human Relations, Technology, and a World View

While we discuss the impact of technology on human relations throughout the book, it is important to mention the immense impact technology has had on this field of study. The inability to see body language indicators can make it more difficult to communicate using traditional methods, but software options like Zoom, GoToMeeting, and Skype, as face-to-face but virtual communication can help alleviate some of these issues. Also, consider that through globalization, we are working with people from all over the world in many time zones who have different perspectives. Between technology and globalization, humans have never had to work with such a diverse group of people—using various methods of communication—than at any time in history.

Many organizations today are focusing on how to use technology to save workers time commuting to work. In fact, an estimated 25 percent of workers **telecommute** at least two days per month.[6] Global Workplace Analytics cites the following benefits to telecommuting:

1. Improved employee satisfaction
2. Reduced unscheduled absences
3. Increased productivity

However, Global Workplace Analytics also says there are some key drawbacks:[7]

1. Social needs may not be met
2. People must be self-directed
3. Employees must be comfortable with technology or it won't work

While technology has greatly impacted human relations at work, there are some common denominators for human relations success in today's workplace—whether or not technology is used. These factors will be discussed throughout this book:

- Chapter 1 Understanding how personality, attitudes, self-esteem, and perception impact human relations. How we are, how we behave, and our belief systems all impact how we view ourselves and others.
- Chapter 2 Understanding the components to personal success, such as goal setting and emotional intelligence skills. Being able to achieve personal success is the first step in attaining career success.
- Chapter 3 This chapter will address how to recognize low self-esteem and provide strategies on how to increase self-esteem for career success.
- Chapter 4 Managing stress and understanding how too much stress can negatively impact our human relations.
- Chapter 5 Communication abilities. Everything we do at work and in our personal lives involves communication. Understanding how to communicate effectively is the cornerstone of positive human relations.

behavioral science approach

During the 1950s when researchers began to explore management techniques as opposed to earlier years where the focus was more on productivity.

management science school

During the 1960s when the research on human relations was more focused on statistical aspects, due to the increase in technology.

telecommute

The practice of working from a remote location.

- Chapter 6 Ethical decision making is necessary because ethical decisions must be made all the time in our personal and work lives. Understanding how to make an ethical decision can help us become better employees and human beings.

- Chapter 7 Understanding what motivates you can help you know the right career path and can assist you in guiding your supervisor. Without an understanding of our own motivations (our own self-knowledge) we may not be able to complete tasks as efficiently. Of course, this skill is the key to successful human relations.

- Chapter 8 Working in teams has become necessary in most every work environment. Understanding how teams work and how they achieve success together will provide you with the tools to be an effective team member.

- Chapter 9 Good decision making, both personally and professionally, can help our human relations in that it provides a framework to make sure we are thinking about all aspects of the decision. We tend to be happier when we make better decisions, which means we relate better to others.

- Chapter 10 The ability to manage conflict is necessary in today's workplace. Not everything will work exactly as we planned, nor will we get along with everyone we meet. Learning how to work through these challenges can help us become better at human relations.

- Chapter 11 In a globalized, diverse workforce, we will work with people from all cultures and backgrounds. Understanding how to effectively work with people different from us can help us be more successful at work.

- Chapter 12 Leadership and management skills can assist us in understanding how we can be leaders in our workplace, even if we do not have a formal title.

- Chapter 13 Managing one's own career success, and discussing strategies such as etiquette, dealing with change, and networking. This capstone chapter will relate our discussion back to these key components to human relations.

We will focus on human relations in a work setting, but many examples will also relate to personal settings. The examples provided will give you tools to have positive relationships with coworkers, supervisors, and people in your personal life. These positive relationships—both at home and at work—help us become more rounded, happier individuals. This is good for everyone, including the company you work for.

Key Takeaways

- *Human relations* is an important part of our career success. It is defined as relations with or between people, particularly in a workplace setting. Because a company depends on good human relations throughout its organizational structure, developing these skills is important.

- Technology has allowed for virtual workplaces, where you can have live meetings using technology. Using the phone or texting can be a challenge, as lack of seeing body language can result in miscommunications. Many workers *telecommute* to work. There are advantages and disadvantages, more notably a disadvantage being the lack of human, face-to-face contact.

- There was an evolution in human relations study. In the *classical school of management*, the focus was on efficiency and not on human relations.

- Employees began to unionize in the 1920s due to lack of positive human relations, and therefore the *behavioral school of management* was created. During this time period, researchers began to focus on the human relations aspect of the workplace. One of the major theories developed was the *Hawthorne effect*, which determined that workers were more productive when they were being watched and cared about by researchers.

- During the 1950s, the *behavioral science approach* looked at management techniques as a way to increase productivity and human relations.

- In the 1960s and beyond, sophisticated tools allowed researchers to analyze more data and focus on the statistical aspects of human relations and management data.

Exercises

1. Have you ever worked with anyone like Jenny (in the opening case), either in school or at a job? Discuss your experiences and how you handled working with this person. How could they have benefited from an understanding of human relations?
2. Discuss two advantages to learning about human relations skills. Why do companies value good human relations skills?
3. Would you be interested in telecommuting for work? What are the advantages and disadvantages to the employee? Discuss in small groups.
4. Draw a timeline of human relations research. On the timeline, indicate the events that changed human relations thinking. Bring your timelines to class and discuss in small groups.

1.2 Human Relations Skills

Learning Objective

1. Explain the skills needed for effective human relations.

Now that we know the reasons why we should study human relations, let's talk a bit about some of the skills needed to be successful in human relations.

There is much discussion about the critical skills needed for human relations. In this section, we'd like to discuss a few of them, with the understanding that an entire book could be written about one particular human relations skill!

First, communication is a key component in human relations, which we will address at length in Chapter 5. It is important from the perspective of conveying clear messages and being a good listener, but it is also key in building trust, making connections, and working effectively with others. Like everyone, I'm sure you've experienced both miscommunication as well as communication that brought about a good connection with someone else. This shows the power of communication in human relations. Consider our opening situation, where Jenny was unable and/or unwilling to make connections with others. Her body language, attitude, and overall message to others is "stay away." This type of person can be difficult to communicate and work with, as well.

Besides communication, empathy is an important aspect in positive human relations skills. **Empathy** is defined as the ability to understand and share the feelings of others. With empathy, we are able to understand how someone feels when they are experiencing disappointment, happiness, sadness, anger, and stress, to name a few. Empathy is one way we can connect with others, because we've likely experienced these emotions, too, so we know how it feels. Assume you receive a phone call from a friend who just found out he didn't get a job he had interviewed for. He really wanted the job, and you knew he was really excited about it. Empathy is what allows you to say something like, "I understand how disappointed you must feel, I am so sorry." In saying that, you genuinely feel bad for the person, because you know what they are feeling right now isn't positive.

empathy

The ability to understand and share the feelings of another.

 **WATCH THIS!**

Helen Riess discusses the power of empathy.

View the video online at: http://www.youtube.com/embed/baHrcC8B4WM?rel=0

The ability to manage stress is also an important human relations skill. Everyone experiences stress in their life, and understanding how to best handle stress can be key to ensuring stress doesn't negatively impact your ability to interact with others. We will discuss stress and ways to manage it in detail in Chapter 4.

Conflict is a healthy and normal part of life. A conflict can be as simple as being upset at your roommate for not doing the dinner dishes, or it could be a work conflict with your supervisor about your work schedule or expectations. We will address the types of conflict and ways to manage conflict that may occur in our personal and work lives in Chapter 10.

What's in it for me?

Conflict is a normal part of life, and learning to manage conflict with others has many benefits! When conflict is discussed and resolved,[8] it is easier for people to meet goals, and it can help strengthen relationships, and create better understanding for others. On the other hand, if conflict isn't handled or handled inappropriately, it can be damaging to relationships. So, what's in it for me? Understanding the key human relations skills—and making an effort to improve them can help YOU build healthy relationships personally and professionally!

All of the skills we addressed in this section, combined with our personality, values, and perceptions, can determine how well we connect with others in our personal life and at work. In the next section and throughout this book, we will address some of these factors, and how we can continually improve these skills.

1.3 Personality, Values, and Attitude Affect Our Human Relations

What Determines Our Personality?

Our **personality** is defined as a set of traits that can explain or predict a person's behavior in a variety of situations. In other words, personality is a set of characteristics that reflect the way we think and act in a given situation. Because of this, our personality has a lot to do with how we relate to one another at work. How we think, what we feel, and our normal behavior characterize what our colleagues come to expect of us, both in behavior and the expectation of their interactions with us. For example, let's suppose at work you are known for being on time but suddenly start showing up late daily. This directly conflicts with your personality—that is, the fact that you are conscientious. As a result, coworkers might start to believe something is wrong. On the other hand, if you did not have this characteristic, it might not be as surprising or noteworthy. Likewise, if your normally even-tempered supervisor yells at you for something minor, you may believe there is something more to his or her anger since this isn't a normal personality trait and you also may have a more difficult time handling the situation since you didn't expect it. When we come to expect someone to act a certain way, we learn to interact with them based on their personality. This goes both ways, and people learn to interact with us based on our personality. When we behave differently than our normal personality traits, people may take time to adjust to the situation.

Personality also affects our ability to interact with others, which can impact our career success. In a study by Sutin and Costa,[9] it was found that the personality characteristic of neuroticism (a tendency to experience negative emotional states) had more effect than any personality char-

personality

A set of traits that can explain or predict a person's behavior in a variety of situations.

acteristic on determining future career success. In other words, people with positive and hopeful personalities tend to be rewarded through career success later in life.

Although there is debate between whether or not our personalities are inherent when we are born (nature) versus the way we grew up (nurture), most researchers agree that personality is usually a result of both nature and our environmental/education experiences. For example, you have probably heard someone say, "She acts just like her mother." She likely behaves that way because she was born with some of her mother's traits, and because she learned some of the behaviors her mother passed to her while growing up.

FIGURE 1.2 Personality
Nurture and nature factors determine our personality.

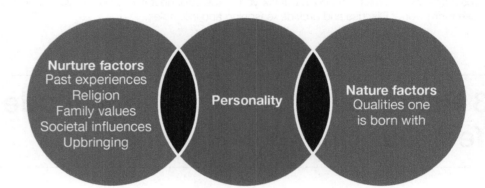

Another example might be someone who grows up in a family that cooks a lot—chances are, the person will probably learn to cook and focus on that within his or her own family. This could also have the opposite effect, in that the person is tired of always eating at home and ends up eating out a lot. These environmental and educational experiences can create positive or negative associations, which results in how we feel about any situation that occurs in our lives.[10]

Personality Tests

There are many types of "tests" to help determine personality. In fact, some organizations use personality tests as a way to determine if a person is a good fit for their organization. Let's talk about some of these personality tests next.

The Meyers-Briggs Type Indicator (MBTI) may be one of the most popular tests to determine personality. The MBTI focuses on several main characteristics. First, preference for introversion (I) or extroversion (E). The second part of the test determines if there is a preference to focus on basic information or if a person takes in information and then adds meaning to it. This is called sensing (S) or intuition (N). Third, the test focuses on how a person prefers to make decisions. Does someone prefer to look at logic first, or people and circumstances first? This is called thinking (T) or feeling (F). Finally, the MBTI looks at whether or not someone likes to get things decided, or stay open to new information. This is called judging (J) or perceiving (P). MBTI then combines each of these to give a person a four letter personality type.[11] For example, an Extroversion, Sensing, Feeling, and Judging person would be a ESFJ. The MBTI then states that there are certain characteristics shared with all persons of this type.

What is your MBTI?

Take this quiz (note, you may need to sign up for free to receive the results): https://psychcentral.com/quizzes/personality/start.php

What is your MBTI? Do you find it accurate? Why or why not?

© Shutterstock

Another popular personality test is the DISC profile. The DISC profile looks at four main personalty traits: Dominance (D), Influence (I), Steadiness (S), and Conscientiousness (C). Dominance refers to the tendency of a person to focus on results and self confidence. Influence refers to the ability to handle and influence relationships. Steadiness refers to the extent of a person's focus on relationships and cooperation. Finally, conscientiousness refers to a person's emphasis on quality, accuracy, and expertise.[12]

What is your DISC Profile?

Take this quiz (note, you may need to sign up for free to receive the results):

https://www.123test.com/disc-personality-test/

What is your DISC profile? Do you find it accurate? Why or why not?

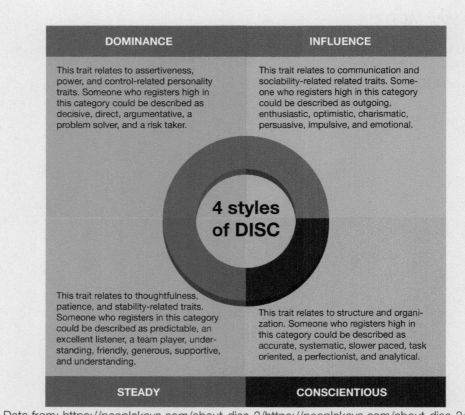

Data from: https://peoplekeys.com/about-disc-2/https://peoplekeys.com/about-disc-2/

There are many other types of personality tests. One thing to keep in mind about personality tests is their reliability. There is extensive research stating that personality tests are not reliable;[13] however, it can serve as a good starting point to understanding your personality, reactions, and the personality of others. Next, we will address personal values, which are an important part of personality.

Values

values

The things we find most important to us.

Our values help determine our personality. Our **values** are those things we find most important to us. For example, if your value is calmness and peace, your personality would show this in many possible ways. You might prefer to have a few close friends and avoid going to a club on Saturday nights. You might choose a less stressful career path, and you might find it challenging to work in a place where frequent conflict occurs.

 **WATCH THIS!**

How to take stock of your personal values.

View the video online at: http://www.youtube.com/embed/Lp_GOrM16Xc?rel=0

We often find ourselves in situations where our values do not coincide with someone we are working with. For example, if Alison's main value is connection, this may come out in a warm communication style with coworkers and an interest in their personal lives. Imagine that Alison works with Tyler, whose core value is efficiency. Because of Tyler's focus, he may find it a waste of time to make small talk with colleagues. When Alison approaches Tyler and asks about his weekend, she may feel offended or upset when he brushes her off to ask about the project they are working on together. She feels like a connection wasn't made, and he feels like she isn't efficient. Understanding our own values as well as the values of others can greatly help us become better communicators.

Examples of Values

What are your top five values? How do you think this affects your personality?

Accomplishment, success	Ease of use	Meaning	Results-oriented
Accountability	Efficiency	Justice	Rule of law
Accuracy	Enjoyment	Kindness	Safety
Adventure	Equality	Knowledge	Satisfying others
All for one & one for all	Excellence	Leadership	Security
Beauty	Fairness	Love, romance	Self-givingness
Calm, quietude, peace	Faith	Loyalty	Self-reliance
Challenge	Faithfulness	Maximum utilization	Self-thinking
Change	Family	Intensity (of time, resources)	Sensitivity
Charity	Family feeling	Merit	Service (to others, society)
Cleanliness, orderliness	Flair	Money	Simplicity

Collaboration	Freedom, liberty	Oneness	Skill
Commitment	Friendship	Openness	Solving problems
Communication	Fun	Other's point of view, inputs	Speed
Community	Generosity	Patriotism	Spirit, spirituality in life
Competence	Gentleness	Peace, nonviolence	Stability
Competition	Global view	Perfection	Standardization
Concern for others	Goodwill	Personal growth	Status
Connection	Goodness	Perseverance	Strength
Content over form	Gratitude	Pleasure	A will to perform
Continuous improvement	Hard work	Power	Success, achievement
Cooperation	Happiness	Practicality	Systemization
Coordination	Harmony	Preservation	Teamwork
Creativity	Health	Privacy	Timeliness
Customer satisfaction	Honor	Progress	Tolerance
Decisiveness	Human-centered	Prosperity, wealth	Tradition
Determination	Improvement	Punctuality	Tranquility
Delight of being, joy	Independence	Quality of work	Trust
Democracy	Individuality	Regularity	Truth
Discipline	Inner peace, calm, quietude	Reliability	Unity
Discovery	Innovation	Resourcefulness	Variety
Diversity	Integrity	Respect for others	Well-being
Dynamism	Intelligence	Responsiveness	Wisdom

Source: http://www.gurusoftware.com/GuruNet/Personal/Topics/Values.htm

What About Our Attitudes?

Our **attitudes** are favorable or unfavorable opinions toward people, things, or situations. Many things affect our attitudes, including the environment we were brought up in and our individual experiences. Our personalities and values play a large role in our attitudes as well. For example, many people may have attitudes toward politics that are similar to their parents, but their attitudes may change as they gain more experiences. If someone has a bad experience around the ocean, they may develop a negative attitude around beach activities. However, if that person has a memorable experience seeing sea lions at the beach, for example, then he or she may change their opinion about the ocean. Likewise, someone may have loved the ocean, but if they have a scary experience, such as nearly drowning, they may change their attitude.

The important thing to remember about attitudes is that they can change over time, but usually some sort of positive experience needs to occur for our attitudes to change dramatically for the better. We also have control of our attitude in our thoughts, and if we constantly stream negative thoughts in our own minds, it is likely we may become a negative person.

In a workplace environment, it is obvious that attitude is important. Someone's personality may be cheerful and upbeat. These are the prized employees because they help bring positive perspective to the workplace. Likewise, someone with a negative attitude is usually someone that most people prefer not to work with. The problem with a negative attitude is that it has a devastating effect on everyone else. Have you ever felt really happy after a great day and when you arrived home, your roommate was in a terrible mood because of her bad day? In this situation, you can almost feel yourself deflating! This is why having a positive attitude is a key component to having good human relations at work and in our personal lives.

But how do we change a negative attitude? Because a negative attitude can come from many sources, there are also many sources that can help us improve our attitude.

Changing Your Attitude

On the Motivation123 website, they describe the three things to consider when trying to change your attitude.

Reams are written about improving your attitude; not so when it comes to defining that thing you're trying to improve. In this checklist, we're going to fix that.

Though there are many ways to define attitude, I find the three checkpoints below to be the most helpful. They make it clear not only what your attitude is made of but also how it affects what you do.

1. How You Enter

Before heading down South for a vacation, I expected a relaxing and enjoyable time. This is the first piece of your attitude: it is what you expect before something happens.

For me, I expected good things. Someone with a more negative bent—at least in relation to traveling—would predict rough times ahead.

2. How You Live through It

The second piece of your attitude is the way in which you gauge progress. Do you notice what is going wrong? Going well? Somewhere in between?

I went to dinner the other night with a few friends. I'm always on the lookout for stories to use on the site, so when they started to comment on the place, I was drawn in. One friend noticed how noisy the restaurant was, how grumpy the waiter seemed, and how bad the food tasted.

On the heels of this cheery testimonial, the friend sitting next to me said she loved the atmosphere, the style of the tables, and her dinner. Two attitudes looking for very different things.

3. How You Exit

The last role your attitude plays happens at the end of a situation or experience. At this point, your attitude affects the way you sum things up.

I was watching a competition-based reality show the other night and, when two people were sent home, they were given the chance to talk to the camera one last time.

They were asked what they would take away from the experience. The first reflected on the friendships he had made and the good times he had had. The second was angry and vengeful. To her, the experience was a waste of time. Attitude strikes again.

Reprinted with permission: Motivation123.com. Get hundreds of simple motivation tips, along with your free Motivation123 Welcome Kit, at the Motivation123.com website. Visit http://www. motivation123.com today.

As many sources point out, our attitude is ultimately about how we set our expectations; how we handle the situation when our expectations are not met; and finally, how we sum up an experience, person, or situation.[14] When we focus on improving our attitude on a daily basis, we get used to thinking positively and our entire personality can change. Consider the COVID-19 crisis of 2020. While this situation was challenging for most, trying to see the positive, such as, "I am able to spend more time at home with my dogs," makes it easier to handle quarantine and other negative aspects associated with the pandemic. It goes without saying that employers prefer to hire and promote someone with a positive attitude as opposed to a negative one. Other tips for improving attitude include the following:

1. When you wake up in the morning, decide you are going to have a good day! Ultimately, it is your choice how you handle setbacks.

2. Be conscious of your negative thoughts, and try to avoid negative thinking.

3. Spend time with positive people.

4. Spend time in a comfortable physical environment, such as a work space or office space you feel comfortable in.

Self-Assessment: What's My Attitude?

1. People would describe me as unhappy.
   - True
   - False

2. I complain right away if there is something I don't like.
   - True
   - False

3. Being positive most of the time is far too unrealistic.
   - True
   - False

4. If I have a bad morning, the rest of my day is sure to be ruined.
   - True
   - False

5. I tend to think more about my weak points than my strong points.
   - True
   - False

6. I don't give out compliments because I don't want someone to get a big ego.
   - True
   - False

7. In the past two weeks, I have called myself depressed.
   - True
   - False

8. I worry too much about things I can't control.
   - True
   - False

9. It takes a lot to make me happy.
   - True
   - False

10. When I experience a failure, I usually just stop trying.
    - True
    - False

Now, count the number of true and false answers. The more false answers you have, the better attitude you tend to have. If you have many true answers, what are some ways to help you change to a more positive attitude?

When considering our personality, values, and attitudes, we can begin to get the bigger picture of who we are and how our experiences affect how we behave at work and in our personal lives. It is a good idea to reflect often on what aspects of our personality are working well and which we might like to change. With self-awareness (discussed further in Chapter 2), we can make changes that eventually result in better human relations.

Why Human Relations?

Our personality traits, attitude, and self-esteem have everything to do with human relations. When you are planting a vegetable garden, you wouldn't fill the new garden with old soil that no longer has nutrients in it. Doing this will result in your plants not growing as large as they can, or could even result in them not growing at all. If we look at our human relations ability, the same idea applies. **Personality, attitude, and self-esteem comprise the nutrient-rich soil required for our human relations skills to grow.** Our personality is how we see the world, either positive and full of hope or negative and full of despair. **Without a positive attitude, it can be difficult to relate to others—because they may not want to be around us!** Likewise, having a positive self-image can give us the confidence to nurture relationships, resulting in positive human relations as well. **Just like the garden that needs soils rich in nutrients, our human relations skills are the same.** To make our human relations skills grow, we need to look at our underlying personality characteristics, attitudes, and self-esteem that could be helping—or hindering—our ability to relate to others.

Key Takeaways

- *Personality* is defined as a set of traits that predict and explain a person's behavior. Values are closely interwoven into personality, as our values often define our traits.
- There are many personality tests to help determine the type of person you are. The MBTI and DISC profiles are just two of many examples you can use as a starting point to understanding your personality.
- Our personality can help define our *attitudes* toward specific things, situations, or people. Most people prefer to work with people who have a positive attitude.
- We can improve our attitude by waking up and believing that the day is going to be great. We can also keep awareness of our negative thoughts or those things that may prevent us from having a good day. Spending time with positive people can help improve our own attitude as well.

Exercises

1. Visit http://www.colorcode.com. Find the section that allows you to take the personality test for free, take the test, and then review the results. What color are you? How does this impact how you relate to others either at school or at work?
2. The Big Five refers to a popular personality test. Visit this website, https://psychcentral.com/quizzes/personality/start.php take the free test, then analyze your results. What is correct? What is not?
3. Looking at "Examples of Values", which five are most important to you? Connect two to three personality traits you possess as a result of these values. For example, if you value practicality you might see this manifested through the importance placed on goods purchased or the type of wardrobe you have.
4. In two or three paragraphs, discuss your attitude and name four specific strategies you will use to improve your attitude.

1.4 Perception and Effect on Human Relations

Learning Objective

1. Explain influencers of perception that impact your ability to relate to others.

Why Does Perception Matter to Human Relations?

As we have discussed so far in this chapter, many things impact our human relations with others. Perception is no different. **Perception** is the recognition and interpretation of sensory stimuli based upon our memory. In other words, it is the way you interpret data around you. The data could come from sight, smell, touch, taste, and hearing. For example, if you wake up in the morning to the smell of coffee, your perception is likely correct that your roommate is already awake. The challenge with perception in human relations is that we may not always understand someone else's perception and/or assume their perception is our own. This is where disagreements and other communication issues can occur. In a workplace setting, perceptions can cause miscommunications. For example, you may perceive your coworker to be lazy because he always arrives to work at 8:15 a.m. when the start time is 8 a.m. Suppose he has a child with a medical condition who needs special schooling, and the school doesn't open until 8 a.m.? Perhaps he has made arrangements with your supervisor of which you are unaware. We need to handle and be aware of our perceptions, especially if we do not have all of the facts.

perception

The recognition and interpretation of sensory stimuli based upon our memory.

How many legs does this elephant have? This section on perception is going to address the many ways we perceive things—and how these perceptions impact our ability to relate to others.

Source: http://www.moillusions.com/2006/05/elephant-optical-illusion.html

 WATCH THIS!

Researcher and professor Dan Simons provides a short video that looks at our own perceptions.

View the video online at: http://www.youtube.com/embed/IGQmdoK_ZfY?rel=0

What Influences Our Perception?

We have defined perception and given some examples to show how perceptions can be incorrect—negatively impacting relationships. But where do our perceptions come from? There are a number of things that influence our perception. First, our heredity can be major influencers of our perception. Height, skin color, and gender influence the way we see the world. For example, someone who is 5'2" may perceive an object to be stored too high, while someone who is 6'2" may not have that same perception.

Our needs impact our perception as well. Physiological needs, such as food and water (or lack thereof), can influence how we feel about certain situations. Have you ever been in a social situation where you were very hungry? If so, you know this impacted your ability to socialize with other people. You may have found yourself less patient to listen because you were concerned about when you were going to eat! Or, if you have ever taken a road trip and needed to use the restroom, your perception may be that the highway lacks a sufficient number of rest areas.

Our peer group can also impact our perception. Our peers tend to determine what is desirable or undesirable, thereby giving us information on how to interpret data around us. You have experienced this personally, no doubt. If you perceive a brand of clothing desirable, it is more likely your friends also feel similarly. The same thing happens at work; for example, suppose a supervisor uses Skype to conduct meetings because her perception is that it is an efficient way to do business. It is highly likely that others in your workgroup will also perceive it as a useful tool.

Our interests impact our perception. If you like running marathons, your perception on how much to spend on running shoes will be different from someone who prefers kayaking for fun and needs a pair of athletic shoes for walking. Assume your interest at work is to be promoted. Your perception of work is very different than that of someone who can't stand the job and is looking for a position with a different company.

Our expectations are another driver of our perceptions. For example, research performed by Ronald Melzack[15] suggests that our expectations about how much something will hurt alters our perception after the fact. For example, if you are dreading getting a flu shot because you believe it will hurt a lot (expectations), but once you actually have it done, you may say, "That didn't hurt at all" (perception), because your expectation prepared you beforehand. In other words, our expectations affect our perception after the fact. In this example, our expectation was extreme pain, but when that didn't occur, our perception was quite the opposite. Our expectations and resulting perception can also be looked at in a work setting. For example, if you have high expectations that your workgroup will win the annual chili cook-off at your company picnic, but you don't win, your perception could be one of unfairness: "The judges like the marketing department better." Likewise, if your team wins the chili cook-off and you expected to win, your perceptions may be, "Of course we won, we knew ours was the best."

A **halo effect** or **reverse halo effect** can also alter our perceptions. The halo affect assumes that if a person has one trait we like, then all traits must be desirable. The reverse halo effect is if we find an undesirable trait in someone, we assume all traits are undesirable. Assume you don't like the way your coworker, Mariette, speaks. You may then make an assumption that all of Mariette's traits are negative. Likewise, if you believe Rhonda is a great dental hygienist, you may promote her to manage the other dental hygienists. Later, if the other hygienists complain about her management style, you may realize you promoted her because you thought her skill as a dental hygienist meant she also had good management skills. In this case, the halo effect occurred.

Awareness of our own perceptions and what drives those perceptions is a key component to being successful at work. If we know why we believe something to be good, right, fair, negative, or unfair based on our perceptions, we can begin to let go of some of our misperceptions. As a result, developing good relationships at work, respect, and mutual understanding can create a better workplace.

halo effect
Assumes that if a person has one trait we like, that all traits must be desirable.

reverse halo effect
If we find an undesirable trait in someone, we assume all traits are undesirable.

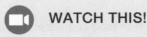

WATCH THIS!

The classic optical illusion that shows our perceptions can be very different from other's perceptions. Do you see an old woman or a young woman in this picture?

View the video online at: http://www.youtube.com/embed/G9gPFVreivk?rel=0

Key Takeaways

- *Perception* refers to how we interpret stimuli such as people, things, or events. Our perception is important to recognize because it is the driving force behind our reaction to things.
- Heredity, needs, peer group, interests, and expectations all influence our perception. A *halo effect* or *reverse halo effect* can also influence our perception.

Exercises

1. In groups, discuss a situation where you have experienced the halo or reverse halo effect. What was the outcome of the situation?
2. Think of at least five perceptions you had today. What influenced those perceptions? Were your perceptions correct?
3. In groups, discuss a school, personal, or work situation where your perception was wrong. What was the outcome?

1.5 Chapter Summary and Exercise

Chapter Summary

- *Human relations* is an important part of our career success. It is defined as relations with or between people, particularly in a workplace setting. Because a company depends on good human relations throughout its organizational structure, developing these skills is important.

- Technology has greatly impacted human relations because so much of our communication occurs without the advantage of seeing body language. This can result in miscommunications. Many workers *telecommute* to work. There are advantages and disadvantages, a more notable disadvantage being the lack of human, face-to-face contact.

- There was an evolution in human relations study. In the *classical school of management*, the focus was on efficiency and not on human relations.

- Employees began to unionize in the 1920s due to a lack of positive human relations, and therefore the *behavioral school of management* was created. During this time period, researchers began to focus on the human relations aspect of the workplace. One of the major theories developed was the *Hawthorne effect*, which determined that workers were more productive when they were being watched and cared about by researchers.

- During the 1950s, the *behavioral science approach* looked at management techniques as a way to increase productivity and human relations.

- In the 1960s and beyond, sophisticated tools allowed researchers to analyze more data and focus on the statistical aspects of human relations and management data.

- *Personality* is defined as a stable set of traits that can explain or predict a person's behavior in a variety of situations. Our personality affects the way we interact with others. Our personality comes from both environmental factors and some factors we are just born with (nature).

- The four main human relations skills include: communication, empathy, stress management, and conflict resolution.

- *Values* are the things we find important to us. If our values conflict with another's, there may be a miscommunication or other issues.

- *Attitudes* can be favorable or unfavorable feelings toward people, things, or situations. Our attitudes have a great impact on each other. If one person has a bad attitude, it is likely to be contagious. We can do many things to change our attitude, but they all include making a conscious effort to be aware of our negative thoughts and feelings.

- *Perception* refers to how we interpret stimuli such as people, things, or events. Our perception is important to recognize because it is the driving force behind our reaction to things.

Chapter Exercise

1. Visit the following website and take at least three of the personality quizzes located there. Expect this to take 1–2 hours. Then, answer the following questions:

   a. Which tests did you take? Provide the link to the tests.

   b. What were the general results of each of the quizzes?

   c. Were the quiz results similar?

   d. What can you learn from these results to engage in better human relations?

Endnotes

1. Merriam Webster Dictionary, (n.d.) Retrieved from https://www.merriam-webster.com/dictionary/human relations

2. Doyle, A. (24 April 2019). 10 Reasons for Job Termination. Retrieved from https://www.thebalancecareers.com/top-reasons-for-getting-fired-2060732

3. Thiefels, J. (5 February 2018). 8 Habits of employees that get promoted. Retrieved from https://www.glassdoor.com/blog/8-habits-of-employees-that-get-promoted/

4. Brian Tracy International. (n.d.) Retrieved from https://www.briantracy.com/success/effective-communication/op/getting-your-ideas-across.html

5. Sharmaa, G. (n.d). Henri Fayol's Principles of Management. Retrieved from http://www.publishyourarticles.org/knowledge-hub/business-studies/henry-fayols-principles-of-management.html

6. Guta, M. (7 March 2018). Up to 25% now work occasionally from home. Retrieved from https://smallbiztrends.com/2018/03/2017-virtual-vocations-year-end-report-and-telecommuting-statistics.html

7. Global Workplace Analytics, (July 2018). Latest teleworking trends. Retrieved from https://globalworkplaceanalytics.com/

8. Conover Company. (n.d.). Conflict resolution: An important life skill. Retrieved from https://www.conovercompany.com/conflict-resolution-an-important-life-skill/

9. Sutin, A.R. & and Costa, P.T. (March 2009). Personality and Career Success, *European Journal of Personality* 23, no. 2: 71–84.

10. Lupu, A. (2 July 2009) Personality: Is It Genetically Inherited or Determined by the Environmental Factors? Retrieved from, http://news.softpedia.com/news/Our-Personality-Is-It-Genetically-Inherited-or-Determined-by-The-Environmental- Factors-28413.shtml

11. The Myers & Briggs Foundation. (n.d.). Retrieved from https://www.myers-briggs.org/my-mbti-personality-type/mbti-basics/

12. DISC Profile. (n.d.). Retrieved from https://www.discprofile.com/what-is-disc/overview/

13. Chen, A. (10 October 2018). How accurate are personality tests? Retrieved from https://www.scientificamerican.com/article/how-accurate-are-personality-tests/

14. James, G. (n.d.). 8 ways to improve your attitude. Retrieved from https://www.inc.com/geoffrey-james/8-ways-to-improve-your-attitude.html

15. Ronald Melzack et al., "Central Neuropasticy and Pathological Pain," *Annals New York Academy of Sciences 933* (2001): 157–59.

CHAPTER 2

How To Be Your Best Self

Once you are in the field, emotional intelligence emerges as a much stronger predictor of who will be most successful, because it is how we handle ourselves in our relationships that determines how well we do once we are in a given job.

—Daniel Goleman

If you want to be successful, it's just this simple. Know what you are doing. Love what you are doing. And believe in what you are doing.

—Will Rogers

Developing Emotional Intelligence

Reegan is highly committed to her company but is having trouble getting along with two of her coworkers. They just don't seem to like her, even though she has a lot of good ideas to contribute to the team. While she wants to stay with the company, she just doesn't see that happening with the current work environment. Reegan schedules a meeting with her manager, Lynn, hoping she will have some ideas on how to improve the situation.

Lynn listens intently to Reegan's concerns and says, "Reegan, you are an asset to this organization, with all of your abilities and skills. But as of right now, you are lacking in some areas we should discuss." Reegan is very upset with this reaction; she expected Lynn to talk with the others in her department and force them to be easier to work with. "First, the perception is that you are not a team player. You spend time in meetings talking about your ideas, but you don't ask others what they think of those ideas, nor do you seem to notice body language that indicates someone might have something to say," says Lynn. "Another thing I have noticed is your seemingly unwillingness to engage your coworkers in anything besides work-related tasks. Remember, this team has worked together for over eight years and they have built personal relationships. You don't seem to be interested in anyone you work with."

Reegan, defensive, says, "No one will say anything when I mention my ideas! It isn't my fault that they don't care about bettering this company. They need to speak up if they have comments or ideas of their own. As far as personal life, I am here to work, not make friends."

Lynn sits back in her chair and asks Reegan if she has ever heard of emotional intelligence skills. Reegan hasn't, so Lynn gives her some websites to check out, and then schedules a meeting to talk in two days about emotional intelligence.

This workplace situation is not uncommon yet causes thousands of lost work hours and frustrations on the part of managers and employees. Emotional intelligence skills (sometimes referred to as EQ or EI), as we will discuss in this chapter, can help people be aware of their own emotions, manage those emotions, and work better with others. These skills can be developed over time and are an important part of career success.

Before we begin this chapter, it is important to distinguish between personal and professional success, because personal success does not always mean professional success and the other way around. In addition, personal and professional success means different things to different people. For example, having a nice car, a beautiful home, and a fancy job title could be considered professional success. On the other hand, personal success may include the ability to travel, interpersonal relationships, friendships, and other factors that have little to do with professional success. Consider Desiree—she does not earn large sums of money and does not have a fancy job title. She has never been promoted and has worked as an administrative assistant for twelve years for more or less the same salary. However, she does not have the goal of being promoted and prefers to leave the office at 5 pm and not have to think about work beyond that. She has a rich life full of friends and travel and often takes classes to learn new skills such as pottery and kickboxing. One would not argue that Desiree has achieved success and happiness personally. For her, achieving this is far more important than achieving what many would call professional success. However, we know there is much crossover between skills that can help us achieve both professional and personal success or happiness. Emotional intelligence is one of those skills, which we will discuss in greater detail throughout this chapter.

2.1 Emotional Intelligence

Learning Objective

1. Understand how emotional intelligence can impact your career success.

emotional intelligence (EQ)

A form of social intelligence that involves the ability to monitor one's own and others' feelings and emotions, to discriminate among them, and to use this information to guide one's thinking and actions.

intelligence quotient (IQ)

The measure of intelligence based on a score derived from an intelligence test.

Emotional intelligence is a topic that has been researched since the early 1990s and has been found to be an important indicator of life and career success. In fact, this book is written around the ability to develop emotional intelligence skills. **Emotional intelligence (EQ)** refers to a form of social intelligence that involves the ability to monitor one's own and others' feelings and emotions, to discriminate among them, and to use this information to guide one's thinking and actions.[1] This is different from **intelligence quotient (IQ)** in that IQ measures intelligence based on a score derived from intelligence tests. The other main difference between the two is that IQ is stable over a lifetime, while EQ can grow and develop over time as we continue to learn about ourselves.

The original researchers of EQ, John Mayer and Peter Salovey,[2] provided the first hint of emotional intelligence in their research, but much of the later research on emotional intelligence was done by Daniel Goleman.[3] According to Goleman, there are four main aspects to emotional intelligence, which we will discuss later in this section. But first, why is emotional intelligence necessary for success?

To start, different from what was previously thought, IQ is not a good predictor of job performance, happiness, or success. Goleman points out that if this myth were true, everyone who graduated at the top of their class with honors would be the most successful people. Because we know this isn't the case, we know qualities other than just IQ can help predict success. Research by Travis Bradberry and Jean Greves has shown that EQ makes up 58 percent of job requirements and is the single biggest predictor of performance in the workplace and the strongest driver of leadership and personal excellence.[4] Their research also showed that 90 percent of high performers at work had high EQ, while 20 percent of low performers had low EQ. In other words, you can be a high performer at work without EQ, but the chances are slimmer with low EQ.[5] EQ research by Bradberry and Greves shows a link between higher EQ and higher salary. In fact, for every point increase in EQ, there is a $1,300 per year increase in salary.[6]

Test your EQ!

Take the short quiz listed here: https://www.mindtools.com/pages/article/ei-quiz.htm and here: https://www.ihhp.com/free-eq-quiz/ to help determine your emotional intelligence levels.

Didn't get the results you wanted on your EQ? Here are some ways to improve your EQ:[7]

- Reflect on your emotions
- Ask people close to you about their observations on your EQ
- Become more observent
- Pause before acting or speaking
- Always put yourself in someone else's shoes
- When you're given feedback from someone, instead of being defensive, ask, "what can I learn from this?"

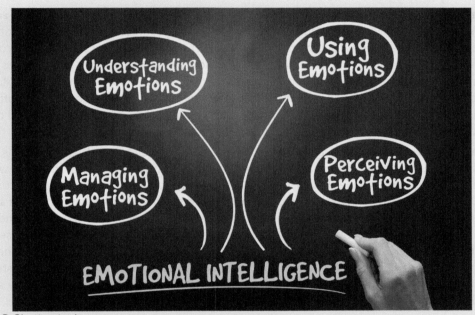

© Shutterstock

In one study performed by Virginia Tech,[8] six hundred undergraduate computer science students and twenty institutions participated in a survey that measured emotional intelligence and the ability to handle demanding curriculum. Although emotional intelligence was not directly linked to academic success in the study, students with higher levels of emotional intelligence had more self-efficacy (belief in one's own ability), which allowed them to handle problems better—creating higher academic success. For example, the ability to read body language and understand when someone is sad or mad and needs to talk is an emotional intelligence skill. These skills enable us to interact with others successfully. Consider a person who does not have a "filter" and continually puts down others and says exactly what is on their mind, even if it is hurtful. This clear lack of emotional intelligence affects this person's ability to have good, healthy relationships, both at work and in their personal life.

So, we know that emotional intelligence is important for success at work, at school, and in our personal lives. Let's discuss the four main components of EQ:

1. **Self-awareness** refers to a person's ability to understand their feelings from moment to moment. It might seem as if this is something we know, but we often go about our day without thinking or being aware of our emotions that impact how we behave in work or personal situations. Understanding our emotions can help us reduce stress and make better decisions, especially when we are under pressure. In addition, knowing and recognizing our own strengths and weaknesses is part of self-awareness. Assume that Patt is upset about a new process being implemented in the organization. Lack of self-awareness may result in her feeling angry and anxious, without really knowing why. High self-awareness EQ might cause Patt to recognize that her anger and anxiety stem from the last time the organization changed processes and fifteen people got laid off. Part of self-awareness is the idea of positive **psychological capital**, which can include emotions such as hope; optimism, which results in higher confidence; and resilience, or the ability to bounce back quickly from challenges.[9] Psychological capital can be gained through self-awareness and self-management, which is our next area of emotional intelligence.

2. **Self-management** refers to our ability to manage our emotions and is dependent on our self-awareness ability. How do we handle frustration, anger, and sadness? Are we able to control our behaviors and emotions? Self-management also is the ability to follow through with commitments and take initiative at work. Someone who lacks self-awareness may project stress on others. For example, say that project manager Mae is very stressed about an upcoming Monday deadline. Lack of self-management may cause Mae to lash out at people in the office because of the deadline. Higher EQ in this area might result in Mae being calm, cool, and collected—to motivate her team to focus and finish the project on time.

3. **Social awareness** is our ability to understand social cues that may affect others around us. In other words, understanding how another person feels, even if we do not feel the same way. Social awareness also includes having empathy for other people, recognizing power structure, and unwritten workplace dynamics. Most people high on social awareness have charisma and make people feel good with every interaction. For example, consider Erik's behavior in meetings. He continually talks and does not pick up subtleties, such as body language. Because of this, he can't understand (or even fathom) that his monologues can be frustrating to others. Erik, with higher EQ in social awareness, may begin talking but also spends a lot of time listening and observing in the meeting, to get a sense of how others feel. He may also directly ask people how they feel. This demonstrates high social awareness.

4. **Relationship management** refers to our ability to communicate clearly, maintain good relationships with others, work well in teams, and manage conflict. Relationship management relies on your ability to use the other three areas of EQ to manage relationships effectively. Take Caroline, for example. Caroline is good at reading people's emotions and showing empathy for them, even if she doesn't agree. As a manager, her door is always open and she makes it clear to colleagues and staff that they are welcome to speak with her anytime. If Caroline has low EQ in the area of relationship management, she may belittle people and have a difficult time being positive. She may not be what is considered a good team player, which shows her lack of ability to manage relationships.

 **WATCH THIS!**

Emotional Intelligence for Success: Author and Pulitzer Prize nominee Daniel Goleman discusses the importance of emotional intelligence in career success.

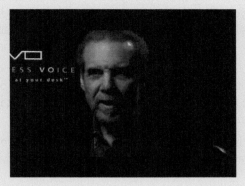

View the video online at: http://www.youtube.com/embed/wJhfKYzKc0s?rel=0

To increase our self-awareness skills, we should spend time thinking about our emotions to understand why we experience a specific emotion. We should look at those things that cause a strong reaction, such as anger, to help us understand the underlying reasons for that reaction. By doing this, we can begin to see a pattern within ourselves that helps explain how we behave and how we feel in certain situations. This allows us to handle those situations when they arise.

To increase our self-management skills, we can focus on the positive instead of the negative. Taking deep breaths increases blood flow, which helps us handle difficult situations. Although seemingly childish, counting to ten in our head before reacting can help us manage emotions such as anger. This gives us time to calm down and think about how we will handle the situation. Practicing positive **self-talk** can help increase our self-management. Self-talk refers to the thoughts we have about ourselves and situations throughout the day. Since we have over 50,000 thoughts per day,[10] getting into the habit of managing those thoughts is important. By recognizing the negative thoughts, we can change them for the positive. Table 2.1 shows some examples.

self-talk

Refers to the thoughts we have about ourselves and situations throughout the day.

TABLE 2.1 Examples of Positive and Negative Self-Talk.

Positive	Negative
I made a mistake.	I am, or that was, dumb.
I need some work on xx skills.	I am an idiot.
It may take a bit more effort to show them what I have to offer.	They will never accept me.
I need to reprioritize my to do list.	I will never be able to get all of this done.
Let me see what seminars and training is available.	I just don't have the knowledge required to do this job.

Using the "stoplight" approach can help us increase our self-management skills. Red means stop, think, and calm down. Yellow means to think of possible solutions, consider feelings of those affected, and make sure you understand how you feel. Green means to proceed with our best possible action.

© Thinkstock

Increasing social awareness means observing others' actions and watching people to get a good sense of how they are reacting. We can gain social awareness skills by learning people's names and making sure we read body language. Living in the moment can help our interactions with others as well. Practicing listening skills and asking follow-up questions can also help improve our social awareness skills.

Strategies for relationship management might include being open, acknowledging another's feelings, and showing that you care. Being willing to listen to colleagues and employees and understanding them on a personal level can help enhance relationship management skills. Being willing to accept feedback and grow from that feedback can help people be more comfortable talking with you.

The importance of emotional intelligence, as we noted at the start of this section, is imperative to being successful at work. Figuring out a plan on how we can increase our emotional intelligence skills can also benefit us personally in our relationships with others.

Emotional intelligence is the key to everything we will discuss throughout the book, and each aspect of our discussion relates back to emotional intelligence, as you can see from Figure 2.1.

FIGURE 2.1 Emotional Intelligence Aspects

Emotional intelligence applies to all areas of our lives, both professionally and personally. We will be discussing each of these emotional intelligence aspects throughout the book.

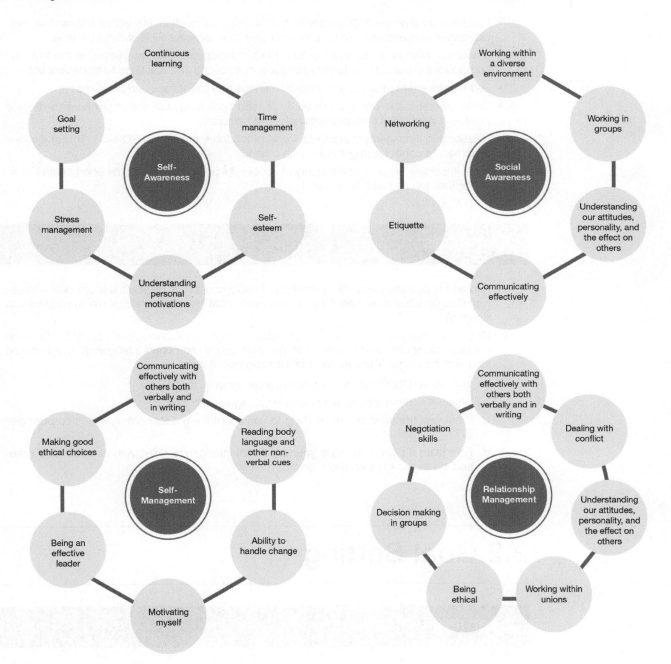

Key Takeaways

- Emotional intelligence (EQ) is different from intelligence quotient (IQ) in that EQ can help predict career success and can be improved over time, whereas IQ is stable over time.
- Emotional intelligence consists of four main components. Self-awareness is the first and comprises the ability to understand one's own emotions and reactions to those emotions.
- Self-management refers to the ability to manage one's reactions and emotions.
- Social awareness refers to one's ability to read body language and social cues to develop positive relationships both professionally and personally.
- Relationship management skills require all of the three mentioned EQ skills. This skill allows us to handle conflict and get along with others.
- EQ is important because the majority of successful people have both the appropriate IQ levels for their job and also EQ skills.

Exercises

1. Reread the opening case. What emotional intelligence issues do you think Lynn will address with Reegan when they meet? If you were Lynn, what recommendations would you make to Reegan?
2. Visit http://www.queendom.com/tests/access_page/index.htm?idRegTest=3037 (you do not need to register) and take the 146-question quiz on emotional intelligence, which should take about an hour. Then answer the following questions:
   a. Why do you think EQ predicts more career success than IQ?
   b. What were the results of the quiz? Do you agree with them?
   c. What was the most surprising thing to you about the results? What wasn't surprising at all?
   d. Formulate a plan to improve your emotional intelligence skills, with at least three goals and strategies to reach those goals.

2.2 Goal Setting

Learning Objectives

1. Explain strategies you can use for goal setting.
2. Implement personal strategies on how to effectively deal with change.

Goal Setting

As we discussed, our emotional intelligence is the cornerstone for career success. Part of self-management is knowing ourselves and being able to set goals based on understanding our own needs and wants.

Many people end up adrift in life, with no real goal or purpose, which can show lack of self-management. Some people are happy this way, but most people would prefer to have goals that can set the direction for their life. It is similar to going on a road trip without a map or GPS. You might have fun for a while, going where the wind takes you, but at some point you may like to see specific things or stop at certain places, which creates the need for GPS. What happens if you have been driving aimlessly for a while but decide what you want to see is five hundred miles back the other way? A goal would have helped you plan the steps along the way in your trip. Goals are the GPS for your life. Research done by Locke et al. in the late 1960s shows a direct connection between goal setting and high achievement.[1] One of the most popular methods to setting goals is called the **SMART philosophy**. This includes the following "steps" or aspects to goal setting:

1. **Specific.** First, the goals need to be specific. Rather than saying, "I want to be a better person," try a goal such as "volunteer two hours per week." The more specific the goal, the more we are able to determine if we were successful in that goal. In other words, being specific allows us to be very clear about what we want to achieve. This clarity helps us understand specifically what we need to do in order to achieve the goal.

2. **Measurable.** The goal must be measured. At the end of the time period, you should be able to say, "Yes, I met that goal." For example, "increase my sales" isn't measurable. Saying something such as, "I will increase my sales by 10 percent over the next two years," is very specific and measurable. At the end of two years, you can look at how well you have performed and compare your goal with the result.

3. **Attainable.** The goals should be something we can achieve. We must either already have or be able to develop the attitudes, skills, and abilities needed to achieve the goal. This doesn't mean you need these skills right now, but it does mean over time you should be able to develop them. For example, if my goal is to become a light aircraft pilot, but I am afraid of flying, it may mean I am not willing (or able) to develop the skills and abilities needed to achieve this goal. So this goal would not be attainable and I should choose another one.

4. **Realistic.** The goal that is set must be something you are willing *and* able to work toward, and cannot be someone else's goal. For example, earning a business degree because your parents want you to may not be compelling enough to follow through with that goal. The goal should be realistic in terms of your abilities and willingness to work toward the goal. Being a WNBA player is probably not a realistic goal for me. I am too old, I am five feet two inches, and not really willing to put in the time to get better at basketball. So, as a result, I would likely not achieve this goal. This isn't to say we shouldn't have goals that are challenging, but we do want to avoid goals that may be nearly impossible!

5. **Time-oriented.** There should always be a timeframe attached to a specific goal. Most individuals will have longer-term and shorter-term goals. For example, a long-term goal might be to manage a medical lab. In order to meet this longer-term goal, shorter-term goals might include the following:

   - Earn a medical lab technology degree
   - Obtain employment as a medical lab tech
   - Develop skills by attending two conferences per year
   - Develop positive relationships with coworkers and supervisor by using emotional intelligence skills

Within all of our goals, there are shorter-term objectives. **Objectives** are the shorter-term goals we must do in order to accomplish our larger goals. For example, possible objectives for two of the goals mentioned previously might be the following:

- Earn a medical lab technology degree
  - Take three courses per quarter to finish in two years
  - Study at least three to six hours per day to earn a 3.5 GPA or higher

SMART philosophy
A strategy to use when setting goals; includes goals being specific, measurable, attainable, realistic, and time-oriented.

objectives
The shorter-term goals we must do in order to accomplish our larger goals.

- See my advisor once per quarter
- Slot one night per week for social time, but focus on studies the rest of the time
- Obtain employment as a medical lab tech
  - Do an internship in the last quarter of school
  - Create a dynamic resume
  - Obtain recommendations from instructors
  - Attend the quarterly medical lab networking event while in school
  - Research and attend career fairs

Another effective strategy in goal setting is writing goals down.[12] Why is this so important? First, you are forced to clarify and think about specific goals using SMART objectives. Second, writing goals down can turn your direction into the correct one, and you will be less likely to be sidetracked by other things. Writing goals down and revisiting them often can also provide an outlet for helping you celebrate meeting a certain objective. In our previous example, by writing these things down, we were able to celebrate smaller successes such as earning a 3.7 GPA or finishing an internship.

Research performed by Shalley also suggests that goals are much more likely to be met if the goal is set by the person attaining the goal.[13] For example, if Sherry's parents want her to become a dental hygienist, but she really wants to become an automotive technician, achieving the goal of dental hygienist may be more difficult, because it's not her own. While this may seem obvious, we can easily take on goals that other people want us to achieve—even well into our adult life. Expectations from our partner, spouse, friends, and social group can influence our goals and make them not our own. For example, if your group of friends all have the goal of becoming lawyers, we can assume this should be our goal, too. As a result, we may try to meet this goal but be unsuccessful or unmotivated because it isn't truly what we want.

Another thing to consider about goal setting is that as we change, and situations change, we need to be flexible with them. For example, let's say Phil has a goal of earning a degree in marketing. Suppose Phil takes his first marketing class but creates a great idea for a new business he would like to start once he graduates. At this point, Phil may decide earning an entrepreneurship degree instead makes the most sense. It is likely, as a result, that since Phil's goal has changed, his objectives and timelines may need to change as well.

Revisiting our goals often is an important part of goal setting. Checking on your goals to see what progress you are making toward them—and making revisions based on that progress, is a final important step to goal setting.

WATCH THIS!

Goal setting tips: This video discusses goal setting and gives tips on how to set goals that are more achievable.

View the video online at: http://www.youtube.com/embed/TQMbvJNRpLE?rel=0

Why Human Relations?

In a 2005 study[14] that compared violence and emotional intelligence, inmates were divided into nonviolent offenses and violent offenses. When emotional intelligence was measured, there was a clear difference between emotional intelligence deficiencies and violence as a vehicle to act out emotions. This, of course, is an extreme example, but it proves the point: **the ability to understand our emotions allows us to be better prepared to handle those emotions appropriately, which in turn can create success personally and at work**. It allows us to create coping tools to deal with emotions such as anger and frustration.

The ability to manage ourselves helps us handle our emotions but also allows us to handle ourselves in other ways. For example, **practicing self-management can teach us how to forgo immediate gratification to meet our goals, a necessary skill to create the kind of life you want**. Time management, handling change, and other skills allow us to be successful personally and professionally.

Social awareness is a skill that helps us see how we are affecting others. Often, we can get too tied up with ourselves and we fail to notice how another person is feeling. Someone who "gets" the social cues, for example, **can develop positive working relationships and motivate people**.

Relationship management can help us foster skills that help us maintain good working relationships with others. Learning how to handle conflict and communicate well are necessary skills to have a successful marriage, relationship, friendship, and work relationships.

All of these skills are part of every chapter in this book because emotional intelligence skills are the core of a successful career and a happy work life.

Time Management

Part of reaching goals also refers to our ability to manage our time. This is also part of emotional intelligence, specifically, self-management—the ability to understand what needs to be done and appropriately allot time to achieve our goals. **Time management** refers to how well we use the time we are given. In order to meet our goals, we must become proficient at managing time. Common tips include the following:

time management

Refers to how well we use the time we are given.

- Learning how to prioritize. Develop the skills of making sure the most important things are done first (even if they are less fun).
- Avoid multitasking. Focus on one task and finish it before moving on.
- Don't get distracted—for example, with e-mails, text messages, or other communications—while working. Set time aside to check these things.
- Make to-do lists. These lists can be daily, weekly, or monthly. Organizing in this way will help you keep track of tasks and deadlines. However, note that a study by the *Wall Street Journal* suggested 30 percent of people spend more time managing their to-do list than actually doing the work on them.[15] To-do lists can help manage time but should not be a hindrance to actually getting things done!
- Don't overwork yourself. Schedule time for breaks and spend time doing things you enjoy.
- Be organized. Make sure your workspace, computer, and home are organized so you can find things easily. Much time is wasted looking for a file on a computer or a specific item you misplaced.
- Understand your work style, a self-awareness skill. Some people work better in the morning, while others work better at night. Schedule important tasks for times when you are at your peak.
- Don't say yes to everything. Everyone has a limit, and being able to say no is an important part of managing time.
- Find ways to improve concentration. Learning how to meditate for twenty minutes a day or exercising, for example, can help focus your energy.

Effective time management can help us manage stress better but also ensures we can have time to relax, too! Making time management a priority can assist us in meeting our goals. The ability to deal with change—another aspect of emotional intelligence and an important part of career and personal success—will be addressed next.

Dealing with Change

As we discussed, the ability to set goals is part of emotional intelligence. Perhaps equally as important, being flexible with our goals and understanding that things will change—which can affect the direction of our goals—is part of being emotionally intelligent.

Dealing with change can be difficult. Since most businesses are always in a state of flux, it is important that we learn how to handle change effectively for career success. But first, why do people tend to resist change? There are many reasons why:

1. **People are afraid the change will affect the value of their skills.** For example, if someone avoids using a new computer program, it could be because they are nervous their skills with the older technology will no longer be useful to the company. To combat this concern, use a can-do attitude and be the first to sign up for training, since we know technological change is a constant.

2. **People are concerned about financial loss.** Many people worry about how the change will affect them from a financial perspective. Will the change result in lost hours or income? If a change is introduced and you aren't sure how it will affect these things—and it is not effectively communicated—the best course of action is to talk with your supervisor to clarify how exactly this change will affect you.

3. **Status quo is easier.** People get comfortable. Because of this comfort level, change and the unknown seem scary. Try to always look for new ways to enhance and improve the workplace. For example, revisiting and improving business processes can help us avoid becoming stagnant.

4. **Group norms exist.** Sometimes team members are happy to change, but the company does not have a culture that embraces change. Listening to people's ideas and reacting positively to them can help create a climate of change. Avoiding defensiveness and "going along with the crowd" can help combat this reason for not embracing change.

5. **Leadership is required.** The leadership in our organizations may not provide all of the information we need, or we may not trust them enough to lead us through a change. Despite this, change is inevitable, so obtaining clarification around the change expectations can be an important step to not only understanding the change, but helping the leader become a better leader.

When a change occurs or is occurring, people are likely to experience four phases associated with that change. First, they may experience denial. In this phase, they do not want to accept the change nor do they want to move on to the future. In the resistance phase, people may feel angry or hurt. They may wistfully think about how great things were before the change. In the third phase, exploration, the person may begin to accept the change but with some reservations. In this phase there may be confusion as people start to clarify expectations. In the commitment phase, people have accepted the change, understand how they fit in with the change, know how the change will affect them, and begin to embrace it. For example, assume Alan is an expert on the company's most popular product offering, a special computer program used for accounting purposes. He is the organization's top seller, with many of his commissions coming from this product. However, the company has just developed new accounting software, which has much better features for customers. He might find this adjustment difficult because he is comfortable with the current software, and it has been lucrative for him to sell it. Here is how he might go through the phases:

1. **Denial.** Alan does nothing. He continues with his job and ignores e-mails about the new product.

2. **Resistance.** Alan tells his coworkers that the change is unnecessary and wonders why they can't continue selling the old product. He discusses why the old product is much better than the new one. He may complain to his manager and find reasons why the change is a bad idea.

3. **Exploration.** Alan is still nervous about the change but begins to use the new software and realizes it may have some worthwhile features which will actually help him sell better. He wonders how that affects his ability to sell the product, and he begins to think about how he might sell the new software.

4. **Commitment.** Alan takes some training classes on the new product and realizes how much better it is. He talks with his coworkers about the new product and helps them understand how it works. He sends an e-mail to his customers introducing the new software and all of its benefits.

As you can see in this example, Alan's resistance to the change was because he didn't understand the need to change at first and he was worried about how this change would affect the value of his skills.

Because of technological changes, the fact that many companies have global operations, and the need for businesses to be agile, change is a constant force affecting business. Be positive about change and accept it as a necessary part of our work life. We cannot expect things to stay the same for very long. The better we can get at accepting change, the more successful we will likely be in our career.

FIGURE 2.2 Phases of Change
This figure depicts the common process people go through when experiencing change. At each phase, the employee will have a different set of feelings. Leadership can go a long way to helping people understand the need for change, the reason for change, and explaining how the change will affect the employee.

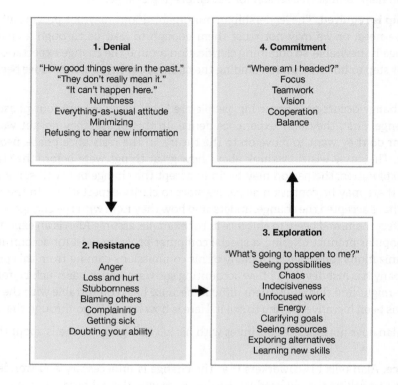

Many a theory has been written about how people undergo change, but one of the more popular models is Lewin's Model of Change.[16] His model proposes three main phases in handling change:

1. **Unfreezing.** Friction causes change and reduction of forces cause a change to happen. For example, suppose Gillian has been unhappy in her job for three years. She recently gets a new manager who she doesn't like, and a friend tells her about a job at a competing company. In this case, friction occurred (the new manager). In addition, Gillian was worried she wouldn't be able to find another job, but now that she knows about a new job, that reduces the forces that prevented her from changing to begin with.

2. **Change.** Now that motivations to change have occurred, the change needs to actually occur. Change is a process, not one event at one time. For example, assume Gillian realized taking the new job makes sense, but even though she knows this, accepting the offer and going to her new job on the first day is still scary!

3. **Refreezing.** Once the change has been made, the refreezing process (which can take years or days, depending on the change) is where the change is the new "normal." People form new relationships and get more comfortable with their routines. Gillian, for example, likely felt odd taking a different way to her new job and didn't know where to have lunch. Gradually, though, she began to meet people, got used to her new commute, and settled in.

FIGURE 2.3 Lewin's Change Model
Lewin's Change Model suggests there must be a motivation to change before a change can take place.

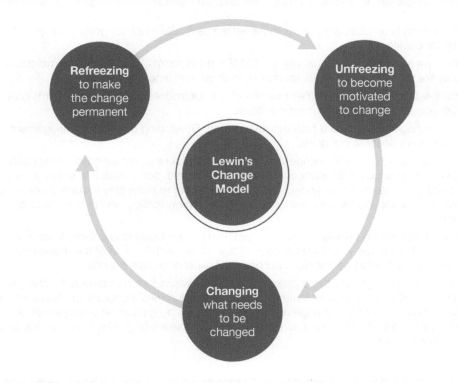

When we become comfortable with change, we are able to allow change into our professional lives. Often, people are too afraid to go after that promotion or a new job for various reasons.

 **WATCH THIS!**

Lewin's Change Model: This short video explains how Lewin's Change Model works. Willingness to change is necessary for career success!

View the video online at: http://www.youtube.com/embed/uHR8gw6derg?rel=0

Key Takeaways

- Goal setting is a necessary aspect to career success. We must set goals in order to have a map for our life.
- When we set goals, we should use the SMART goals format. This asks us to make sure our goals are specific, measurable, attainable, realistic, and time-oriented.
- When setting goals, we will also use objectives. Objectives are the shorter-term goals we must accomplish in order to meet our goals.
- Time management is also a factor in goal setting. Developing good time management skills can bring us closer to our goals.
- Learning how to deal with change is another way to ensure career success. Many people are adverse to change for a variety of reasons. For example, sometimes it is easier to maintain the status quo because we know what to expect. Other reasons may include concern about financial loss and job security, unclear leadership communication, and the existence of group norms.
- Besides attitude and behavior, career promotion means being uncomfortable with possible changes. People resist change because of fear of job security, fear of the unknown, fear of failure, their individual personality, and bad past experience with change.
- Lewin's model suggests three phases of change, which include unfreezing, change, and refreezing. These changes indicate that some motivation must occur for the change to happen (unfreeze). Once the change occurs, there can still be discomfort while people get used to the new reality. Finally, in the refreezing phase, people are beginning to accept the change as the new normal.

Exercises

1. Using the SMART model for setting goals, create at least three long-term goals along with objectives.
2. As you learned in this chapter, time management is an important part of meeting goals. Take this time management quiz to determine how well you currently manage your time: http://psychologytoday.tests.psychtests.com/take_test.php?idRegTest=3208. Do you feel the test results were accurate? Why or why not?

2.3 Continuous Learning

Learning Objective

1. Understand how continuous learning can help you achieve career and personal success.

continuous learning

Involves the process of constantly trying to update skills and learn new ones.

Continuous learning involves the process of constantly trying to update and learn new ones skills. This shows high emotional intelligence in the area of self-awareness and self-management ("I know I need to learn this new skill to be more valuable to my employer or to be more productive in my personal life"). Having self-awareness, or knowing our strengths and weaknesses, is the first step in improving our chances for career and personal success. Once we are aware (self-aware) of our weaknesses, we can better choose areas in which we would like to learn. For example, Anton knows he isn't very good at giving presentations, and being able to recognize this is self-awareness. Then, finding opportunities to work on this, such as joining a Toastmasters club, shows emotional intelligence in the area of self-management. Anton recognized his weakness and found ways to improve his abilities.

People who often learn new skills tend to be happier individuals and more valuable to their organizations. For example, Zappos, a shoe retailer based in Las Vegas, Nevada, maintains a "Wishez" program. Employees post things they are interested in learning, such as how to cook an ethnic dish, and they are connected with other members in the organization who have these skills. This focus on continuous learning makes for happier employees, which makes for more productive workers. In fact, happy workers are 20 percent more productive than unhappy ones.[17]

 WATCH THIS!

Zappos learning: Employees at Zappos can engage in continuous learning by participating in the Wishez program.

View the video online at: http://www.youtube.com/embed/oXhgee98fwQ?rel=0

Learning new skills, such as taking a pottery class or learning to ski or surf, can help people increase happiness, which in turn can build self-confidence. This confidence can result in a richer and more fulfilling life, since we learn new things that we enjoy doing. Don't limit yourself to in-person learning experiences, as much learning can be done online. During the COVID-19 pandemic, many companies have offered free online courses in a variety of topics, such as well-being, stress management, interview preparation, among many others.

Most people who find career success have a habit of being curious and interested in a variety of topics that can enhance their personal and professional lives. As management guru Brian Tracy points out, continuous learning is one of the "nine disciplines" to being successful.[18] But what does it mean to learn continuously? There are several ways we can learn, as depicted in Figure 2.4.

FIGURE 2.4 Some Suggestions for Continual Learning

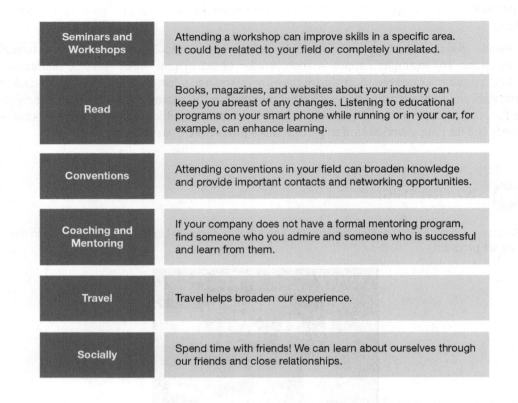

Seminars and Workshops	Attending a workshop can improve skills in a specific area. It could be related to your field or completely unrelated.
Read	Books, magazines, and websites about your industry can keep you abreast of any changes. Listening to educational programs on your smart phone while running or in your car, for example, can enhance learning.
Conventions	Attending conventions in your field can broaden knowledge and provide important contacts and networking opportunities.
Coaching and Mentoring	If your company does not have a formal mentoring program, find someone who you admire and someone who is successful and learn from them.
Travel	Travel helps broaden our experience.
Socially	Spend time with friends! We can learn about ourselves through our friends and close relationships.

From a career perspective, if we choose not to learn continuously, we end up becoming stale in both our skills and abilities. Since most industries change so quickly, it is likely our current skills will be outdated in five to ten years. This means we need to constantly update to understand the next set of skills we need to be successful. In addition, sometimes we have to "unlearn" skills as new and better ways to do things are introduced. For example, if you have golfed before, you may mimic the golf swings you see on television when you go out to play. Although this swing may work for you for some time, you may get to a point where you want to improve, so you take a lesson from a golf pro. The golf pro looks at your swing and offers advice on how to improve distance and accuracy. In this case, you may have to "unlearn" your old swing in order to improve your golf game. Unlearning can apply to all aspects of our life, not just sports. When things in an organization change, it can be challenging to unlearn the old way and be comfortable with the new way of doing things. Unlearning means you may have to let go of an old way of doing something that may have worked for a long period of time.[19] For example, when you are used to driving on the right side of the road but visit a country that drives on the left, the problem isn't learning how to drive on the left; it is unlearning how to drive on the right![20] This can happen in organizations, too. For example, an organization that had high sales prior to the 2007 recession had to unlearn their way of doing business before the recession in order to continue being successful. A company that needs to embrace technology to stay ahead of competitors may need to unlearn their own way of doing business. In society today, the ability to learn, unlearn, and then learn again can happen over a span of a few months rather than many years. Many organizations get "stuck" on a specific way of doing things, and when those things are unlearned, the company can begin to move forward and learn the new way of doing things.

Many organizations value people who can show their focus and dedication to continuous learning and unlearning. For example, the US Fish and Wildlife Service employs over 9,000[21] people. Because of their large staff, they have identified twenty-eight leadership competencies, one of which is continual learning. Continual learning is important because it makes us more valuable to our employers, which can result in promotions, higher salary, and more responsibility as we grow our career.

WATCH THIS!

Brian Tracy, management guru, discusses the importance of continuous learning in entrepreneurship.

WWW.BRIANTRACY.COM

View the video online at: http://www.youtube.com/embed/iGJ8oj7ymx8?rel=0

What's in it for me?

Learning new skills makes you smarter! Scientific research has shown that learning a new skill helps your brain create more "white matter,"[22] which can help improve performance not only on the new task you're learning but on other tasks as well! In addition to this benefit, learning makes you happier! To focus on learning something new is a core need for our psychological well being.[23] As an added benefit, learning something new can build confidence and a sense of self-efficacy (belief in yourself).

Everyone should consider creating a plan to help them develop their talents and create new skills. The plan might include the following:

- What skill(s) do I want to develop?
- What time frame will I give myself to develop them?
- How much time per week/month can I devote?
- What methods will I use? For example, seminars, classes, and so on.

As we learned in the earlier section on goal setting, being specific and writing down those new skills and abilities you want to develop can tend to make it more of a priority, which can result in more personal and career success.

Key Takeaways

- *Continuous learning* is the process of learning new things to enhance yourself professionally and personally.
- Continuous learning can help increase personal happiness and career success.

- One can engage in continuous learning by taking seminars, workshops, reading, working with a mentor, attending conventions, socializing, and traveling.
- Some organizations, such as the US Fish and Wildlife Service, make continuous learning a part of leadership career pathways.

Exercise

1. What new skills would you like to learn? Write down at least five new skills you would like to learn personally. Then write down five new skills you would like to learn for your career. Identify all of the options that can help you develop these new skills.

2.4 Chapter Summary and Case

Chapter Summary

- Emotional intelligence (EQ) is different from intelligence quotient (IQ) in that EQ can help predict career success and can be improved over time, whereas IQ is stable over time.
- Emotional intelligence consists of four main components. Self-awareness is the first and comprises the ability to understand one's own emotions and reactions to those emotions.
- Self-management refers to the ability to manage one's reactions and emotions.
- Social awareness refers to one's ability to read body language and social cues to develop positive relationships both professionally and personally.
- Relationship management skills require all of the three mentioned EQ skills. This skill allows us to handle conflict and get along with others.
- EQ is important because the majority of successful people have both the appropriate IQ levels for their job and also EQ skills.
- Goal setting is a necessary aspect to career success. We must set goals in order to have a map for our life.
- When we set goals, we should use the SMART goals format. This asks us to make sure our goals are specific, measurable, attainable, realistic, and have timelines associated with them.
- When setting goals, we will also use objectives. Objectives are the shorter-term goals we must accomplish in order to meet our larger goals. Time management is also a factor in goal setting. Developing good time management skills can bring us closer to our goals.
- Managing our time efficiently is a good way to help us achieve our goals. By looking at time management, we can make sure the time we spend on activities is geared toward meeting our end goals.
- Learning how to deal with change is another way to ensure career success. Many people are adverse to change for a variety of reasons. For example, sometimes it is easier to maintain the status quo because we know what to expect. Other reasons may include concern about financial loss and job security, unclear leadership communication, and the existence of group norms.
- Besides attitude and behavior, career promotion means being uncomfortable with possible change. People resist change because of fear of job security, fear of the unknown, fear of failure, their individual personality, and bad past experience with change.
- Lewin's model suggests three phases of change, which include unfreezing, change, and refreezing. These changes indicate that some motivation must occur for the change to happen (unfreeze). Once the change occurs, there can still be discomfort while people are

getting used to the new reality. Finally, in the refreezing part, people are beginning to accept the change as the new normal.

- Continual learning is an important part of personal phase as well as professional development.
- People who engage in continual learning tend to experience more personal happiness and career success.
- One can engage in continuous learning by taking seminars, workshops, reading, working with a mentor, attending conventions, socializing, and traveling.

Chapter Case

Overall, do you feel that you use your time wisely? Think about the ways you have spent your time over the last week. Write down the amount of time you spend doing the following things in an average week:

- Human needs activities (sleeping, cooking, and eating):
- School-related activities:
- Activities geared toward my specific long- and short-term goals:
- Transportation (commuting) activities:
- Continuous learning:
- Facebook, Twitter, other social media, or texting:
- Time-wasting activities:
- Activities for stress management:

1. When you look at how you spent your time, are there any areas where you could manage your time better?
2. Are there any areas that you feel you are spending the perfect amount of time?
3. What strategies do you need to implement to manage time better?
4. In our opening case, what emotional intelligence qualities is Reegan lacking? Does this have anything to do with her time management ability? What are some tips that could be used to improve emotional intelligence?

Endnotes

1. Institute for Health and Human Potential. (n.d.). What is emotional intelligence? Retrieved from https://www.ihhp.com/meaning-of-emotional-intelligence

2. Mayer, J.D., Salovey, P., & Caruso, D.R. (2000). Models of emotional intelligence. In R.J. Sternberg (Ed.). Handbook of intelligence (pp. 396–420). Cambridge, England: Cambridge University Press.

3. Goleman, D. (n.d.). Emotional intelligence. Retrieved from http://danielgoleman.info/topics/emotional-intelligence/

4. Bradberry, T., & Greaves, J. (2009). Emotional Intelligence 2.0 (p. 21) TalentSmart Publishing.

5. Bradberry, T., & Greaves, J. (2009). Emotional Intelligence 2.0 (p. 21) TalentSmart Publishing.

6. Bradberry, T., & Greaves, J. (2009). Emotional Intelligence 2.0 (p. 22) TalentSmart Publishing.

7. Bariso, J. (n.d.). How to increase your emotional intelligence. Retrieved from https://www.inc.com/justin-bariso/how-to-increase-your-emotional-intelligence.html

8. Virginia Tech. (5 October 2005). Emotional intelligence may be good predictor of success in computing studies. Retrieved from https://www.sciencedaily.com/releases/2005/10/051005072152.htm

9. Luthans, F. (2002). The need for and meaning of positive organizational behavior. Journal of Organizational Behavior, 23(6), 695–706.

10. Davis, B. (23 May 2013). There are 50,000 thoughts standing between you and your partner every day! Retrieved from https://www.huffpost.com/entry/healthy-relationships_n_3307916

11. Locke, E.A., Shaw, K,N., Saari, L.M., & Latham, G.P. (1981). Goal setting and task performance: 1969–1980. Psychological Bulletin, 90(1), 125–52.

12. Locke, E.A., & Latham, G.P. (1990). A theory of goal-setting and task performance. Englewood Cliffs, NJ: Prentice Hall.

13. Shalley, C.E. (April 1995). Effects of coaction, expected evaluation, and goal setting on creativity and productivity. Academy of Management Journal, 38(2), 483–503.

14. Knight, J. (2005). Exploring emotional intelligence and IQ: Comparing violent and non-violent criminal offenders. Dissertation. Retrieved from http://proquest.umi.com/pqdlink?did=913522881&Fmt=7&clientId=79356&RQT=309&VName=PQD

15. Sandberg, J. (10 September 2004). Though time-consuming, to-do lists are a way of life. The Wall Street Journal. Retrieved from http://www.careerjournal.com/columnists/cubicleculture/20040910-cubicle.html

16. Lewin, K. (n.d.). Frontiers of group dynamics. Human Relations, 1, 5–41.

17. Preston, C. (13 December 2017). Promoting employee happiness benefits everyone. Retrieved from https://www.forbes.com/sites/forbescoachescouncil/2017/12/13/promoting-employee-happiness-benefits-everyone/#45a42d12581a

18. Korn, M. (8 December 2011). Self-discipline: The art of continuous learning. Retrieved from http://marckornblog.com/discipline-of-continuous-learning/

19. Bonchek, M. (3 November 2016). Why the problem with learning is unlearning. Retrieved from https://hbr.org/2016/11/why-the-problem-with-learning-is-unlearning

20. Bonchek, M. (3 November 2016). Why the problem with learning is unlearning. Retrieved from https://hbr.org/2016/11/why-the-problem-with-learning-is-unlearning

21. US Fish and Wildlife homepage. (n.d.). Retrieved from http://www.fws.gov/help/about_us.html

22. Wong, B. (n.d.). How learning a new skill makes your mind grow stronger. Retrieved from https://www.inc.com/brian-wong/how-learning-a-new-skill-helps-your-mind-grow-stronger.html

23. Psychologies staff. (n.d.). Want to be happier? Learn something new. Retrieved from https://www.psychologies.co.uk/want-be-happier-learn-something-new

CHAPTER 3
Enhancing Your Self-Esteem

Low self-esteem is like driving through life with your hand-brake on.
—*Maxwell Maltz*

Creating a Positive Self Image

As you walk into work, you notice your colleague Susie has a new haircut. You point it out and tell her how nice it looks on her. She shuns your comment and answers, "unfortunately, now you can see more of my face with these bangs." You aren't sure how to answer, so you just take it as if she were joking and begin to look at your tasks for the day.

One of your tasks is to determine next quarter's budget, and this is something you'd like to work on with Susie, since she has incredible knowledge and abilities in this area. You send her an instant message and ask if she'd be willing to help. Her answer is, "I guess so, but I don't think I'll be much help." This is confusing to you, because you know she will, in fact, be a big help! As you sit down to work on the task, Susie is easily frustrated when it takes more than a few seconds to figure something out. She also makes suggestions, then needs extensive reassurance that you agree with her. Finally, she begins putting others in the company down, telling you she doesn't think they know what they are doing.

Susie's behavior is puzzling, because you look at her as one of the most knowledgeable people in your department. There is no reason for her to be unsure of herself, nor is there any reason for her to put others down. Since you just finished reading about self-esteem—you make the connection—Susie has low self-esteem!

You then consider ways you can help support Susie, and the benefits that would come to Susie if she were willing to work on her own self-esteem. Throughout this thought process, you realize there are some self-esteem areas you could work on too, and suggest to Susie you meet after work to discuss strategies for building self-esteem. She says yes, and admits, "I'm always too hard on myself. I need to get better at that." You look forward to the conversation, which will undoubtedly help you both.

3.1 What Is Self-Esteem, Self-Confidence, and Self-Image?

Learning Objectives

1. Be able to define and explain self-esteem and self-image.
2. Discuss the importance of self-esteem to your career.

Self-Esteem and Self-Confidence

self-esteem

The opinion you have of yourself and your value as a person.

Self-esteem is the opinion you have of yourself and your perception of your value as a person. Low (negative) self-esteem can cause people to be negative, lack motivation, and be moody. Those with higher (positive) self-esteem like themselves, so they expect others to like them, too. They don't harshly judge themselves and are comfortable with who they are.

self-confidence

Your belief in yourself and your abilities.

Self-confidence, on the other hand, is your belief in yourself and your abilities. Often, people with high self-esteem also have self-confidence, although this may not always be the case. Both self-esteem and self-confidence can translate to positive human relations, because if a person feels good about him- or herself, it is more likely he or she will be more comfortable communicating and working in teams—key components for success.

Where Does Self-Esteem Come From?

According to researchers George Hollenbeck and Douglas Hall[1], self-confidence can come from several sources:

1. **Actual experience.** When you have accomplished something and succeeded, it is likely you will have the self-confidence to be successful at the task again.
2. **Experiences of others.** If you watch another person perform a task, you may know you can do the same thing.
3. **Social comparison.** When we see others with similar abilities able to perform a task, we may feel more confident in our own abilities to perform the same task.
4. **Social persuasion.** A boost in self-confidence can come from the encouragement of someone we trust.
5. **Emotional arousal.** This refers to our inner feelings of being adequate or inadequate when it comes to accomplishing a certain task. This can come from negative or positive self-talk.

self-efficacy

The confidence you have to carry out a specific task.

Self-efficacy is the confidence you have to carry out a specific task. Someone may have generally lower self-confidence but have self-efficacy in certain areas of his or her life. For example, Michael may have low self-esteem in general, but he is a computer whiz so he has self-efficacy in his ability to rebuild a computer.

self-image

How an individual thinks others view him or her.

Self-image is a bit different than self-esteem in that it means how an individual thinks others view him or her. One's self-image may not always be in line with what people actually think, but you can imagine the impact this can have on human relations at work. If someone's self-image is that people think they are stupid, they may not try as hard since they believe this is what people think of them anyway. Obviously, this can be an unproductive and unhealthy way of working with others.

projection

Refers to how your self-esteem reflects in the way you treat others.

Projection refers to how your self-esteem reflects in the way you treat others. For example, if Cheng has low self-esteem, he may project this by putting down other people or belittling them. Likewise, if Cheng has high self-esteem, his projection onto others may be positive by giving them compliments and encouraging them.

Self-esteem can come in many forms, some more obvious than others, such as winning an award.

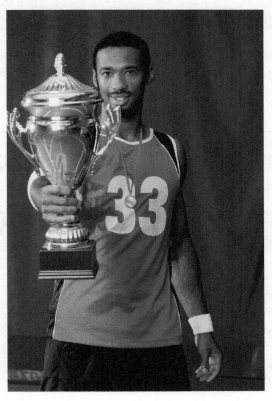

© Thinkstock

Self-esteem and self-image is important for career success are for many reasons:[2]

- People with self-esteem are more willing to try something new and put themselves "out there."
- People with higher self-esteem tend to make better decisions.
- People with high self-esteem tend to trust their own judgment, and aren't as afraid to voice their opinions.
- Confidence and self-esteem can help us overcome our fears.
- People with confidence tend to be driven and willing to try new things.
- Confidence can make us more willing to say "no" when needed, and also allow us to stand up for ourselves.

Key Takeaways

- Self-esteem is the opinion you have of yourself and your perception of your value as a person.
- Self-confidence is the belief in yourself and your abilities.
- Self-efficacy is confidence you have to carry out a specific task. Self-image refers to how you THINK people view you.
- Projection refers to how you treat others based on your self-esteem.
- Self-esteem and confidence can benefit us in our careers. For example, someone with high self-esteem is more willing to try new things.

Exercises

1. Reflect on the areas you find you have self-efficacy? What are those areas?
2. Reflect on your own self-esteem. What would you like to work on regarding self-esteem?

3.2 Causes of Low Self-Esteem

Learning Objective

1. Be able to explain some of the causes of low self-esteem.

As you already know, humans are complicated, which makes it hard to pinpoint specific causes for low self-esteem. However, researchers agree on some common causes of self-esteem issues, which we will address here. It is important to point out that although there may be deep rooted challenges from childhood and beyond that cause low self-esteem, there are ways to improve self-esteem, which we will address later in this chapter.

What's in it for me?

The following benefits can result from having a higher self-esteem:

- Have greater job satisfaction[3]
- Tend to earn higher salary[4]
- Higher self-esteem results in more favorable work conditions[5]

So, having a higher self-esteem not only helps you earn more and have good working conditions, but higher self-esteem will likely help you be happier at work! As you read throughout this chapter, reflect on your own self-esteem and take to heart the strategies that can help you improve self-esteem—your future self will appreciate it!

Social media can have a negative impact on our self-esteem.

© Shutterstock

Some causes of low self-esteem include:

- Disapproving authority figures while growing up.[6] In this case, a child may have never felt "good enough," resulting in low self-esteem now. If someone is constantly criticized as a child, no matter how hard they tried, this can create poor self-esteem later in life.
- Uninvolved caregivers while growing up. If your achievements were not recognized or noticed while growing up, this can result in low self-esteem later in life.
- Being bullied can harm self-esteem now and later in life.
- Trauma, such as physical, emotional, or sexual abuse, either in childhood or later in life, can cause low self-esteem.
- Society and social expectations can also cause low self-esteem. In fact, 60 percent of people using social media say it has a negative impact on self-esteem.[7] Reasons for this can include

only seeing others' "happy" posts (and never seeing their struggles), can create FOMO (fear of missing out), and comparing ourselves to others on social media can also create self-esteem issues.

- The media, along with airbrushed, photoshopped, and unrealistic images of people can also impact self-esteem.

 WATCH THIS!

Our past and its effects on self-esteem.

View the video online at: http://www.youtube.com/embed/wC9S_fFMnaU?rel=0

Key Takeaway

- There are many possible causes of low self-esteem, many of them occurring in childhood. A few possible causes of low self-esteem are social media, trauma, or bullying.

Exercise

1. Reflect on the possible causes of low self-esteem. Have you experienced any of those listed here? What are some ways you've overcome, or strategies you could use to overcome, some of the causes listed here?

3.3 Signs of Low Self-Esteem

Learning Objective

1. Be able to identify signs of low self-esteem.

As we addressed in the last section, there are many causes of low self-esteem. Recognizing the causes and signs of low self-esteem is key to determining how to overcome self-esteem issues.

Some of the signs of low self-esteem can be obvious, but some may not be as obvious. One of the first signs of someone with low self-esteem may be that they are extremely critical of themselves.[8] You may hear them say things like, "I'm so stupid," or "everyone is so much better than me when working on this task." A second sign of low self-esteem is negative self-talk. We are constantly talking to ourselves, and that self-talk can be positive or negative. Someone with low self-esteem tends to have a constant stream of negative self-talk. They may tell themselves, "you'll never get that job, you're not good enough," or "don't speak up in that meeting, no one cares what you have to say." This type of negative self-talk can occur within someones own mind, or they may say these things out loud—but usually both are occurring. People with low self-esteem are usually unable to take a compliment and they downplay their positive qualities. For example, suppose you tell someone their shirt really brings out their eyes (compliment), and instead of saying thank you, they may say something like, "this shirt makes me look fat." In this case, they are completely ignoring the compliment and downplaying a positive quality you've pointed out. Additionally, you may find someone with low self-esteem tending to use negative words to describe themselves; they may call themselves, ugly, unlovable, unworthy, and other negative words.

WATCH THIS!

Some warning signs of low self-esteem are shown in this video.

View the video online at: http://www.youtube.com/embed/45cvj-Nn5yA?rel=0

Besides these things, there may be other obvious outward signs of low self-esteem. Some of these outward signs might be:[9]

- Seeking constant reassurance
- Apologizing for things that don't need to be apologized for (such as saying "I'm sorry" when someone bumps into you)
- Putting others down
- Inability to make a decision about all things—big or small
- Not liking to be alone
- Easily frustrated

It is important to point out that everyone engages in some of the behaviors mentioned in this section. Someone with low self-esteem, however, will exhibit these behaviors the majority of the time. Now that we've addressed some of the causes and signs of low self-esteem, let's address how self-esteem can be improved in the next section.

Key Takeaways

- There are many signs to look for when determining self-esteem.
- People with low self-esteem tend to put others down, engage in negative self-talk, and have a hard time taking a compliment, to name a few.

Exercise

1. Keep track of your self-talk for one day. What do you find replaying most often in your mind? Is it positive or negative? What are some strategies you can implement when you find yourself saying negative things to yourself?

3.4 Ways to Build Self-Esteem

Learning Objectives

1. Implement effective tools for building self-esteem.
2. Define and use the Johari window as a tool for self-discovery.

Even if our self-esteem needs improvement, the good news is that there are many ways we can do that. The following are strategies we can use to improve our self-esteem:[10]

1. **Use positive self-talk and visual imagery.** Self-talk refers to the things we tell ourselves in quiet moments. It could be, "I did a really good job on that project" or "I am not good in math." We constantly have an internal dialogue and our subconscious does not know the difference between truth and reality. So when we use negative self-talk, our subconscious actually starts to believe whatever we are telling it! This is why it is important to use positive self-talk. Visual imagery is focusing on a positive outcome and imagining it. By focusing on a positive outcome, we begin to believe it, thereby making it more likely to happen. For example, before you swing a golf club, you may imagine yourself hitting it perfectly, with the ball going in just the right direction. This helps get us mentally ready to perform.

2. **Take risks.** Risk-taking is an important source of gaining self-confidence. Of course, not all risks work out the way we want them to, but until we take risks, we are unable to accomplish tasks.

3. **Accomplish.** Accomplishing something important, such as earning a degree or a promotion can help us gain self-confidence. Of course, as mentioned earlier, it often involves risk taking.

4. **Know your strengths and weaknesses.** Everyone has a set of things they are good at. Knowing what you are good at and focusing on those things can improve self-esteem. Also, knowing what you are not good at and working to improve those skills can build self-confidence, too.

5. **Choose to spend time with people who boost your self-esteem.** There are many negative people who do not want anyone to succeed because it makes them feel bad about themselves. Choose friends who boost your self-esteem and limit the time with people who harm your self-esteem.

6. **Avoid comparing yourselves to others.** Comparing ourselves to others can be a slippery slope! Everyone has different skills and abilities, and when you focus on someone else, you are not recognizing your own uniqueness. Limiting the use of social media can assist with this as well.

7. **Forgive yourself and others.** Sometimes this can be hard to do, but avoiding forgiveness can create that negative thinking loop. If your childhood was difficult, reflecting on what made it difficult and forgiving those who made it difficult can help you move past it.

8. **Focus only on those things you can change.** You can't change how your disagreeable colleague sees you—so why worry about it? Instead, focus on the improvements you want to make for yourself.

Everyone can continue working on their self-esteem and self-confidence throughout life. The **Johari Window** is tool that can help us determine how we see ourselves and how others see us. This can serve as a good starting point and self-assessment tool to help us become better at human relations and improve our self-esteem, since with low self-esteem, it can be challenging to see our own positive qualities.

The Johari window was created in 1955 by Joseph Luft and Harrington Ingham. When it was created, the researchers gave people fifty-six adjectives they could use to describe themselves. The subjects picked five or six adjectives and then had someone who knew them well pick six as well. Then, the adjectives were placed in the appropriate place in the grid, which consists of four windows. In the Johari window—The first window is the **open area** the area that the person knows about themselves and others know about them. The second window is the **blind area,** the area the person doesn't know about themselves but others know about them. The **hidden** area, is the area the person knows about themselves, but others do not know about them. In the **unknown area**, neither person knows what exists there. Through time, and as we change and grow, we may have more self-awareness and aspects of ourselves that were once in the unknown area may move into one of the other windows.

> **Johari Window**
>
> A technique that helps people better understand their relationship with themselves and others.

FIGURE 3.1 The Johari Window

	Known to self	Not known to self
Known to others	Arena	Blind spot
Not known to others	Façade	Unknown

 **WATCH THIS!**

Meet yourself: a users guide to building self-esteem.

View the video online at: http://www.youtube.com/embed/uOrzmFUJtrs?rel=0

Another tool you can use to improve self-esteem is journaling. The journal, though isn't a list of things that went wrong, it is a list of things that brought you happiness that day. For example, you can answer the following prompts:[11]

- My best quality today was . . .
- These four things went well today . . .
- I did a good job today at . . .
- I am going to continue working at . . . by doing . . . things.

There is no "right" way to improve your self-esteem. As you've already guessed, improving your self-esteem starts with YOU. Unfortunately there is no magical tool to increase self-esteem, as it takes extensive self-reflection and daily changes to improve, as we've noted in this section. Improving self-esteem can help us be successful at our jobs, and at our life!

The first step to improving our self-esteem is to really reflect on our own self-esteem, and implement strategies to improve it.

Key Takeaways

- There are many ways to improve self-esteem, all of which start with you and how you look at things. Use positive self-talk, reflection, and journaling as tools.
- The Johari window is a tool that can help you see the positive qualities others see about you, but you may not see about yourself.

Exercises

1. Ask someone who knows you well to write down adjectives to describe you. While they are doing that, you write down additional adjectives to describe yourself. Compare what both of you wrote, and place it in the appropriate Johari window area.
2. Based on the exercise above, what did you learn about yourself? How can you apply this to building self-esteem?

3.5 Chapter Summary and Exercises

Chapter Summary

- Self-esteem is the opinion you have of yourself and your perception of your value as a person.
- Self-confidence is the belief in yourself and your abilities.
- Self-efficacy is confidence you have to carry out a specific task.
- Self-image refers to how you THINK people view you.
- Projection refers to how you treat others based on your self-esteem.
- Self-esteem and confidence can benefit us in our careers. For example, someone with high self-esteem is more willing to try new things.
- There are many possible causes of low self-esteem, many of them occurring in childhood. A few possible causes of low self-esteem are social media, trauma, or bullying.
- People with low self-esteem tend to put others down, engage in negative self-talk, and have a hard time taking a compliment, to name a few.
- There are many ways to improve self-esteem, all of which start with you and how you look at things. Use positive self-talk, reflection, and journaling as tools.
- The Johari window is a tool that can help you see the positive qualities others see about you, but you may not see about yourself.

Chapter Exercises

1. Write down the five words that describe you the best. When you look at these words, are they positive? If they are not positive, what steps can you take to improve your self-esteem? How will the steps you take improve your human relations skills?
2. Reflect on your level of self-esteem by taking this quiz: https://testyourself.psychtests.com/testid/3102. Then discuss the results and strategies you'll implement to improve your self-esteem.

Endnotes

1. Hollenbeck, G.P., & Hall, D.T. (2004). Self-Confidence and Leader Performance. *Organizational Dynamics,* Vol. 33(3) 254-269. doi:10.1016/j.orgdyn.2004.06.003

2. Time Management Ninja. (n.d.). 10 Reasons why confidence leads to success. Retrieved from https://timemanagementninja.com/2012/07/10-reasons-why-confidence-leads-to-success/

3. Kuster, F., Orth, U., & Meier, L.L. (2013). High Self-Esteem Prospectively Predicts Better Work Conditions and Outcomes. *Social Psychological and Personality Science* 4(6) 668-675. doi: 10.1177/1948550613479806

4. Kuster, F., Orth, U., & Meier, L.L. (2013). High Self-Esteem Prospectively Predicts Better Work Conditions and Outcomes. *Social Psychological and Personality Science* 4(6) 668-675. doi: 10.1177/1948550613479806

5. Kuster, F., Orth, U., & Meier, L.L. (2013). High Self-Esteem Prospectively Predicts Better Work Conditions and Outcomes. *Social Psychological and Personality Science* 4(6) 668-675. doi: 10.1177/1948550613479806

6. Lachmann, S. (24 December 2013). 10 sources of low self esteem. Retrieved from https://www.psychologytoday.com/us/blog/me-we/201312/10-sources-low-self-esteem

7. Silva, C. (22 February 2017). Social media's impact on self-esteem. Retrieved from https://www.huffpost.com/entry/social-medias-impact-on-self-esteem_b_58ade038e4b0d818c4f0a4e4

8. Better Health. (n.d.). Self-esteem. Retrieved from https://www.betterhealth.vic.gov.au/health/HealthyLiving/self-esteem

9. Power of Positivity. (n.d.). 8 behaviors that reveal someone has low self-esteem. Retrieved from https://www.powerofpositivity.com/behaviors-low-self-esteem/

10. Abrams, A. (27 March 2017). 8 Steps to improving your self-esteem. Retrieved from https://www.psychologytoday.com/us/blog/nurturing-self-compassion/201703/8-steps-improving-your-self-esteem

11. Positive Psychology. (3 April 2019). 18 self-esteem worksheets and activities for teens and adults. Retrieved from https://positivepsychologyprogram.com/self-esteem-worksheets/#adults-self-esteem

CHAPTER 4

Managing Stress Levels

> *Some of the secret joys of living are not found by rushing from point A to point B, but by inventing some imaginary letters along the way.*
>
> —Douglas Pagels

> *When I look back on all these worries, I remember the story of the old man who said on his deathbed that he had had a lot of trouble in his life, most of which had never happened.*
>
> —Winston Churchill

Stressed Out

You are exhausted. When you get home, you drop your work bag and realize you forgot to send an e-mail to your supervisor about an upcoming project. You groan as you run downstairs to your computer. The clock says 7:03 p.m. and you feel like you haven't had a minute to yourself since you had your morning coffee! As you think about your day, you realize you haven't! It is your company's busy time, so the last few days have been booked with meetings and a huge project with a Friday deadline. You send the e-mail, make a quick sandwich for dinner, and sit back down at your computer. You are hoping to get a few more things done on the project before tomorrow morning. You take a quick break and check your Instagram account, and Snapchat with your friend for a few minutes. Realizing you got distracted, you get back to working on the project. Your status update meeting is at 9 a.m. and you want to be able to show the progress you've made, so you continue working. At 11:30 p.m., you shut down your computer, go to bed, and have a hard time falling asleep because you are thinking about everything you need to do before this project gets done. You also think about a few friends who you haven't talked with in a while, and put that on your to-do list also.

Does this sound like someone you know? Many people today are struggling with the ability to manage time, with so much work to do and personal/family lives to manage. Technology has certainly made working longer hours easier, as we are always in touch with the office. What we tend to forget is the importance of managing our stress levels so we can function more effectively. In this situation, having this much stress, with little personal time to yourself, can negatively affect your stress levels. This chapter will discuss some types of stress, the effects of stress, and what you can do to reduce stress.

4.1 Types of Stress

1. Be able to define stress and the types of stress that can impact how you relate to others.

Stress can be challenging to explain, because it means different things to different people. For example, going swimming might be stressful to some, but for others it might be enjoyable. Stress affects our ability to relate to others because too much stress causes us to be irritable, which affects our communication skills. We will discuss later on the effects of stress and human relations.

Hans Selye[1] defined **stress** as the nonspecific response of the body to a demand for a change. In 1936, Selye researched this topic and discovered something surprising. When subjecting lab animals to acute but noxious physical and emotional stimuli—such as blaring light, loud noises, extreme heat or cold, or frustration—they all experienced the same physical symptoms of stress, such as the enlargement of the adrenal glands. He saw that these intense stresses over long periods of time caused other issues such as heart attacks, strokes, and kidney disease. His conclusion was that stress actually caused these conditions,[2] not the stimuli themselves. Today, we usually define stress as the body's way of responding to a demand.

There are four types of stress. The first type of stress is called **acute stress** and tends to be short-term. This is the most common form of stress and normally comes from demands and pressures of the past and future.[3] For example, suppose you have a busy day. You have to drop your niece and nephew at school, stop by the post office, go to class, take a quiz, get an oil change, pick your niece and nephew up from school, drive home through traffic, and make dinner. A busy day such as this can create stress, but it is short-term, because perhaps tomorrow you are less busy or are looking forward to the weekend, where you don't have the same kinds of demands. Every person experiences this kind of stress. Acute stress is a laundry list of the things we must do or dealing with something that didn't go right. For example, your car breaking down on the way to the post office creates a certain amount of acute stress, but once the car is fixed there is no stress associated with it.

Episodic acute stress is a more serious form of acute stress. In this type of stress, the person feels stress on a daily basis and rarely gets relief.[4] Unlike acute stress, where there may be one or two busy, stressful days, episodic acute stress happens on a daily basis. The person who suffers from episodic acute stress feels stressed constantly, with little relief. People who suffer from episodic acute stress may constantly complain about how much work they have and may be constantly late, always in a rush, and may be anxious and irritable on a regular basis. Often, a person who suffers from this type of stress may have taken on too much and created self-imposed demands.

Chronic stress is the type of stress that happens month after month, year after year. This is long-term stress where people see little way out of a situation.[5] Sometimes, chronic stress begins with traumatic experiences such as Post Traumatic Stress Disorder (PTSD) or childhood experiences. In others, chronic stress can occur in response to everyday stressors that are ignored or not managed well.[6] For example, someone may have episodic acute stress, but over a long period of time, this can become chronic stress. With this type of stress, the person has given up looking for solutions to the stress and tends to just live with it. For example, consider a couple who is very unhappy in their relationship. While at one point in time in their relationship they may have experienced acute stress when arguing, this could have turned into episodic acute stress as the arguing occurred more frequently. Then, when that type of stress was unrelieved for a long time, it became chronic stress. It becomes chronic because the couple took no steps to repair their relationship.

stress

The nonspecific response of the body to a demand for a change.

acute stress

The most common form of stress and normally comes from demands and pressures of the past and future.

episodic acute stress

Can be a more serious form of acute stress; the person feels stress on a daily basis and rarely gets relief.

chronic stress

This is long-term stress where people see little way out of a situation.

We tend to think of all stress as negative, but as Seyle pointed out in his early research, some types of stress can actually cause us to challenge ourselves and work at a higher level.[7] For example, if you want to run a marathon, at some point you may have to physically challenge yourself to keep running even when you are exhausted. This type of stress—positive stress to help us achieve at a higher level—is called **eustress**, and it can motivate us to reach goals. For example, we may experience eustress before a job interview. That nervous feeling right before can help us achieve at a higher level and nail that interview! This eustress can be positive if it helps us achieve success in the interview. Some people may view positive stress as negative stress and vice versa. For some people, running a marathon may cause eustress, but for someone who doesn't like running, it could create one of the negative types of stress we mentioned above.

Sometimes life can make us feel as if we are burning a candle at both ends. The important thing to remember about stress is that it isn't always bad. Eustress can help us be ready for challenges.

© Thinkstock

eustress

Positive stress to help us achieve at a higher level and challenge us.

 WATCH THIS!

This video addresses the different types of stress.

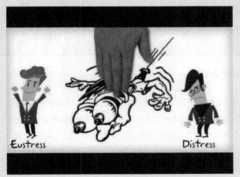

View the video online at: http://www.youtube.com/embed/ALiCToVg24g?rel=0

The Human Function Curve, originally developed by Peter Nixon, says there are different levels of stress that we may experience and our stress level affects our level of performance. He calls any state where we are awake and reacting to stimuli, such as being at work, an arousal state. If we compare the amount of stress to our performance, our performance actually improves when we experience eustress. However, according to this model, there is a point where chronic stress can impede our performance. Looking at Figure 4.1, you can see in the drone zone, for example, that our performance is low. We may be bored and not have enough positive stress for us to perform at a higher level. In the C zone, for example, we may experience eustress, which raises our performance. However, when we reach the fatigue zone, we could be experiencing chronic stress, which impedes our performance. Ideally, we would have the right balance of stress and challenge to continually improve our performance.

FIGURE 4.1 The Human Function Curve
As you can see, performance is actually improved with a certain amount of stress, but once that stress becomes episodic or chronic, our performance actually goes down.

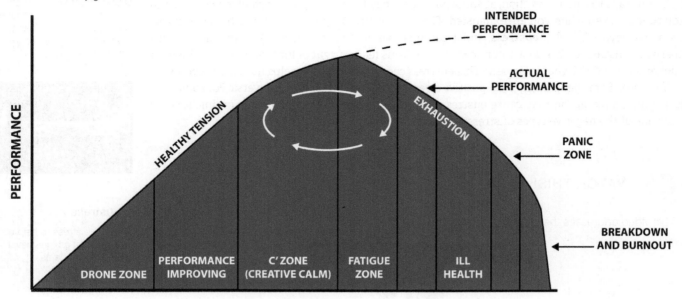

Another important thing to remember about stress is that it varies from one person to another. One person may feel intense acute stress when asked to give a speech in front of the class, while someone may feel eustress if asked to give the same speech. Likewise, it may take one person much longer—and more stress than another—to reach the C zone of performance. When dealing with stress, finding the ideal stress level—the one that creates eustress and gets you ready for challenges—is the goal.[8]

Key Takeaways

- *Stress* is the body's response to change. Stress means different things to different people and stress and the types of things that cause stress can vary from person to person. Today, we generally say that stress is the body's way of responding to a demand.

- *Acute stress* is the type of stress we experience on a day-to-day basis—for example, the stress of getting our to-do list finished or the stress of unplanned setbacks.

- When a person rarely gets relief from stress, this is called *episodic acute stress*. This type of stress usually goes on for longer periods of time with little relief.

- *Chronic stress* is characterized as long-term stress, where there is little hope for relief. These are long-term situations where the person has given up trying to find a solution.

- Not all stress is bad; some stress can actually help us to perform at a higher level and challenge us. This type of stress is called *eustress*.

Exercises

1. Take the quiz listed at http://www.stress.org.uk/individual-stress-test/

   and then answer the following questions:

   a. What was your score on the test? Do you feel this is accurate?

   b. What are some ways you handle stress in your life? Are these methods effective? Why or why not?

2. Discuss which types of stress these situations might be, and what zone on the Human Function Curve the person might be at:

   a. Michael has a project due on Monday.

   b. Tara just can't seem to like her job over the last few years.

   c. Mika puts a lot of pressure on herself to get everything done on her to-do list every day.

   d. Franc is nervous about his presentation in class tomorrow.

   e. Jacob has a long list of things that are due today.

   f. Karen has been struggling with financial issues her whole adult life.

4.2 Symptoms of Stress

Learning Objectives

1. Explain the physiological changes our body goes through when experiencing stress.
2. Identify the results when we have too much stress in our life.

Our bodies go through a number of changes when we are faced with a stressor. From prehistoric times, physical changes in our body had to occur in order to prepare us to handle the stress. For example, we needed to be able to run fast to get away from something that could hurt us. This is called the **fight or flight response**. This concept was developed by Walter Cannon in the 1920s, and he believed that these reactions in the body enabled us to mobilize to deal with a stressful situation.[9] More recent research has shown the addition of "freeze" to the response. This occurs when the fight or flight response didn't work—or couldn't work. For example, if you run into a bear in the woods, fighting is usually not an option. Running from the bear—given it is a faster runner—isn't an option either. So, we can choose to freeze (as in play dead) to try and survive. In our work life, we often freeze (or do nothing) when faced with stressful situations. For example, we can't just leave (flight), as we typically need the job to pay our bills; it also may not be worth it to fight, so we freeze in response to the situation. Although this is an oversimplification of the body's chemistry, it illustrates the point that the flight-fight-freeze response is actually a very prehistoric event. Today, even though our stresses may be different (we don't often run into bears in the woods!), our body still reacts the same way as it did in prehistoric times with the flight or fight or freeze response. To fully understand how stress impacts us, we need to understand how our bodies handles stress. When our brains initially perceive a threat, a few physiological effects occur within our bodies Figure 4.2.

fight or flight response

Physiological reactions in the body that enable us to mobilize to deal with a stressful situation.

FIGURE 4.2 Physiological Effects of Stress

Physically our bodies go through various changes to prepare us for a flight or fight response.

1 **Nervous System** Heart may beat faster and blood pressure may rise in order to help the body fight the perceived threat.

2 **Musculoskeletal System** Tension headaches may occur due to muscles tensing up.

3 **Respiratory System** Breathing becomes more rapid.

4 **Cardiovascular System** Heart rate quickens.

5 **Endocrine System** Glands send signals to the body that release cortisol to help the body fight the perceived threat.

6 **Gastrointestinal System** Eating habits change.

Courtesy of The American Institute of Stress, www.stress.org.

According to a survey of the American Psychological Association, 64 percent of adults are stressed by work-related issues and 64 percent are stressed by money issues.[10] Compare these numbers to Generation Z, who report 77 percent work stress and 81 percent money stress.[11] As we noted in the last section, some stress can be good—as it allows us to perform at a higher level. However, long-term chronic stress or episodic acute stress can cause a variety of problems, which are listed in Table 4.1.

TABLE 4.1 Common Effects of Stress on Our Bodies, Moods, and Behaviors

On Your Body	On Your Mood	On Your Behavior
Headache	Anxiety	Overeating or undereating
Muscle tension or pain	Restlessness	Angry outbursts
Chest pain	Lack of motivation or focus	Drug or alcohol abuse
Fatigue	Irritability or anger	Tobacco use
Disinterest in things we normally enjoy	Sadness or depression	Social withdrawal
Stomach upset		
Sleep problems		

Data from: Mayo Clinic Staff, "Stress Symptoms, Effects on Body, Feelings and Behavior," https://www.mayoclinic.org/healthy-lifestyle/stress-management/in-depth/stress-symptoms/art-20050987

© Shutterstock

In the 2018 American Psychological Association Stress survey,[12] in addition to work stress and money stress, Americans stress health-related concerns as well as concerns about the economy. In Section 3, we will look at some possible causes of stress and discuss some of the ways we can learn to better handle stress that occurs in our daily lives.

Why Human Relations?

Stress can shut down our ability to think rationally and feel emotions. As you know from Chapter 2, these two abilities are part of emotional intelligence (self-management and self-awareness). These abilities allow us to identify and then manage our emotions. When we identify our stressor and our emotion around that stressor, we can begin to make plans on how to handle it. Without the ability to identify this emotion, we are not as well equipped to handle the emotions that may come with stress. Without these stress-management skills, we can let our stress get out of control. **When stress occurs, the shutting down of our emotions doesn't allow us to make rational decisions, nor does it allow us to be emotionally available to others.** Because of this, stress can affect our ability to communicate and work effectively with people at work. People who are stressed often are impatient, poor listeners, and may lose their sense of humor. These temporary behaviors that occur when we are stressed can impact how others see us, and how well we interact with them. Also, consider the effect stress may have on our ability to manage conflict. If someone is stressed about day-to-day frustrations, such as traffic, bills, workload, and to-do lists, the stress does not allow him or her to manage conflict, as emotions are in a state of confusion. This can lead to poor decision making and thus result in the inability to interact effectively with others. Everyone has stress in both their personal and professional lives. **Learning how to manage this stress is one of the first steps in making sure we are mentally prepared to nurture our relationships at work and at home.**

 **WATCH THIS!**

This video illustrates how our flight or fight response is similar to that of prehistoric times.

View the video online at: http://www.youtube.com/embed/7S_BB7R8NMU?rel=0

Key Takeaways

- The *flight or fight response* is our body's physiological response to perceived threats. The basic physiological function is the same today as it was in prehistoric times.
- Having too much stress can cause many issues—like headaches, sleeplessness, and irritability—that can affect our human relations ability.

Exercise

1. Think of a time when you felt very stressed. What kinds of physiological effects occurred? How did you handle these situations?

4.3 Sources of Stress

Learning Objective

1. Explain the sources of stress people can experience, both personally and professionally.

Work Stress

As we have studied so far in this chapter, we can experience a number of possible stressors. We can divide these stressors into personal stresses and work stresses. Although we divide them to make it easier, it is intuitive that if someone is experiencing personal stress, he or she will also experience stress at work, which will result in lessened workplace performance. In fact, the American Institute of Stress estimates that for a larger company, the cost of stress can be $3.5 million. This is the result of lost productivity and absenteeism due to stress.[13]

According to the American Institute of Stress,[14] common causes of workplace stress include the following:

1. **Long hours and increased demands.** The average American works forty-four hours per week.[15] Much of this is due to increased technology and expectations that employees will be available to answer e-mail on weekends and evenings. As a result of this added work time, employees find less time to engage in leisure and household activities such as grocery shopping and cleaning.

2. **Being treated unfairly.** Workplace issues such as harassment and bullying (both discussed in Chapter 11) can cause people to feel stress at work. Additional issues, such as feeling overlooked for promotions, can also cause workplace stress. In extreme cases, perceived workplace unfairness and/or feelings of disrespect can erupt in violence. At a UPS warehouse in San Francisco, a worker shot and killed three co-workers and injured five.[16] Many organizations offer **Employee Assistance Programs** that can provide services such as counseling to help deal with workplace stress and other personal issues.

3. **Little or no acknowledgment or reward.** People can feel stress when they do not feel they are being recognized for the work they do. This kind of workplace stress can cause people to become withdrawn, unmotivated, or unfocused on being productive for the organization. This type of behavior can also materialize at home with people experiencing this stress being more irritable, cranky, and moody. At work, these feelings can negatively affect our ability to relate to our coworkers and managers.

4. **Lack of control. Micromanagement** refers to excessive control of work details by a supervisor. For example, a micromanager might direct an employee to work on specific tasks on a given day and give detailed instructions on how those tasks should be accomplished. This type of situation can create stress, as the employee feels he or she has little control of their own work.

5. **Office politics.** Dealing with difficult coworkers or supervisors and different personalities (Chapter 10) and communication styles (Chapter 5) can create stress at work. Conflicts, disagreements, and misunderstandings are common in today's workplace, especially with the use of technology. All of these factors—which we call office politics—can create stress, which results in lost sleep, productivity, and motivation, obviously affecting our ability to relate to others.

6. **Fear of Unknown.** During COVID-19, many workers feel stress due to fear of catching the virus, but also uncertainty about how the outbreak will affect them economically, for example, "Will I be laid off?" "Will my hours be cut?"

Employee Assistance Programs

Programs offered by companies that provide services such as counseling to help deal with workplace stress and other personal issues.

micromanagement

The excessive control of work details by a supervisor.

FIGURE 4.3 Some of the Reasons Cited for Workplace Stress

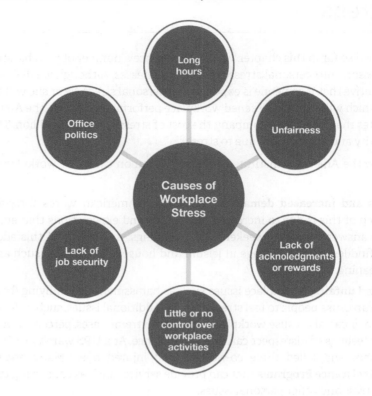

WATCH THIS!

Registered clinical psychologist Dr. Cheryl talks about some ways to manage stress at work.

View the video online at: http://www.youtube.com/embed/7oQWsjNNSR4?rel=0

FIGURE 4.4 Time Use on an Average Work Day for Employed Persons Ages Twenty-five to Fifty-four with Children
Since we spend more time at work than doing anything else, learning how to manage stress at work is an important part of our personal well-being and productivity. NOTE: Data include employed persons on days they worked, ages twenty-five to fifty-four, who lived in households with children under eighteen. Data include non-holiday weekdays and are annual averages for 2015. Data include related travel for each activity.

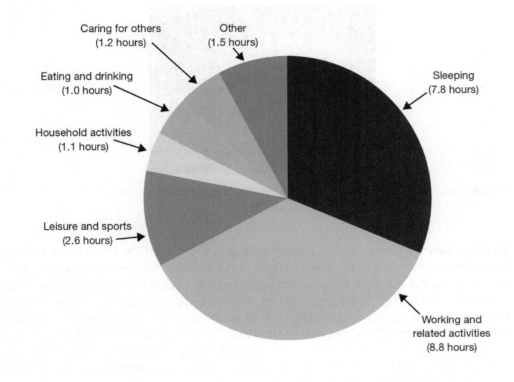

Source: Bureau of Labor Statistics, American Time Use Survey. https://www.bls.gov/tus/charts/chart1.pdf

Personal Stress

While job stress is important to consider, stresses in our personal life can cause issues in our work life. In this section, we will discuss some of the major personal stressors.

1. **Everyday challenges.** Getting caught in traffic or a leaky water heater would be examples of things that cause stress in our personal lives. Luckily, most of us have the abilities to cope with these daily stresses. However, too many of these types of stressors in one day can build up and cause major issues at work or in our personal life. Consider the COVID-19 crisis. The immense amount of stress created from the pandemic can increase over time and affect our work.

2. **Personality.** Our individual personalities (Chapter 1) can impact our ability to handle stress. Some people are born with character traits that predispose them to stress. Past experiences and our reaction to those experiences can also impact how we handle stress. Do you have a friend or colleague who you'd describe as "laid back?" Nothing seems to get to them, even in the most stressful of situations. This personality trait can impact one's reaction to stress, and how one deals with stress as well.

 **WATCH THIS!**

Examples of personality traits and stress are shown in this video.

View the video online at: http://www.youtube.com/embed/leZUJzRNe30?rel=0

3. **Work-life balance.** Everyone must manage multiple roles in their life. The roles of mother or father, boss, employee, spouse, sister, or brother have their own unique demands that can create stress at home and work. When we have challenges at work, it can affect our roles at home and vice versa. Although many organizations promote a work-life balance and create a culture that allows people to have a "home life," easy access to send that "one last e-mail" at 9 p.m. for work creates a blurred line between home and work. This creates an even greater need for our emotional intelligence skills (self-awareness and self-management) in that we must be aware of our emotions and handle them when they come—rather than just going about our day and plowing ahead.

4. **Life changes.** There are forty-three life changes that are characterized as creating stress. These life changes are measured on a scale called life change units, created by Thomas H. Holmes and Richard Rahe. The life changes are said to cause stress in one's personal life. However, personality type and situational factors may affect how much a particular event affects a person. For example, suppose a major life change, such as the death of a spouse occurs. This would cause an immense amount of stress, but assume the spouse was very ill for a long period of time. In this situation, the latter could have caused stress as well. So, while the scale has value in terms of determining what life changes cause the most stress, it is also important to consider the other factors around the life change, along with a person's personal coping ability.

5. **Financial issues.** Tough economic times, combined with increasing costs of fuel and other living expenses, create great stress on individuals and families. Not having enough money to buy basic needs, and lacking the ability to buy the wants we have, can lead to anxiety, tension, and depression. These emotions can carry over into our work life, resulting in lowered productivity and lowered human relations with our coworkers.

6. **Friends and family issues.** Challenges with family, in-laws, and friends create a great source of stress as well. While most of us depend on friends and family for support, tension and disagreements can cause stress.

TABLE 4.2 Life Changes
Thomas H. Holmes and Richard Rahe measured personal stress by Life Change Units. According to their research, the more "major changes" one experiences, the higher chance a person will end up with a stress-induced illness. Someone with a score of 300 or more is said to be at a high risk of illness. If you look at the events of your life over the last year, what is your score?

Life Event	Value	Life Event	Value
Death of a spouse	100	Foreclosure for mortgage or loan	30
Divorce	73	Change in responsibilities at work	29
Marital separation	65	Child leaving home	29
Jail term	63	Trouble with in-laws	29
Death of a close family member	63	Outstanding personal achievement	28
Personal injury or illness	53	Spouse begins or stops work	26
Marriage	40	Begin or end of school	26
Fired at work	47	Change in living conditions	25
Marital reconciliation	45	Revision of personal habits	24
Retirement	45	Trouble with boss	23
Change in health of family member	44	Change in work hours or conditions	20
Pregnancy	40	Change in residence	20
Sex difficulties	39	Change in schools	20
Gain of new family member	39	Change in recreation	19
Business readjustment	39	Change in church activities	19
Change in financial state	38	Change in social activities	18
Death of a close friend	37	Mortgage or loan less than $100,000	17
Change to a different line of work	36	Change in sleeping habits	16
Change in number of arguments with spouse	35	Change in number of family get-togethers	15
Home mortgage over $100,000	31	Change in eating habits	15

Holmes, T. H., & Rahe, R. H. (August 1967). "The Social Readjustment Rating Scale", *Journal of Psychosomatic Research* 11, no. 2, (August 1967): 213–18.

Now that we have discussed the things that cause stress, Section 4 will address some ways we can relieve stress in our lives.

Stress Quiz: How Stressed Are You?

Understanding your own stress level is an emotional intelligence skill (self-awareness). Take this quiz, and rate how you typically react in each of the situations listed below.

4 = Always

3 = Frequently

2 = Sometimes

1 = Never

Enter the appropriate number in the blank for each question below, and then add up your numbers to determine your stress level.

1. _____ Do you try to do as much as possible in the least amount of time?
2. _____ Do you become impatient with delays or interruptions?

3. _____ Do you always have to win at games to enjoy yourself?

4. _____ Do you find yourself speeding up the car to beat the red light?

5. _____ Are you unlikely to ask for or indicate you need help with a problem?

6. _____ Do you constantly seek the respect and admiration of others?

7. _____ Are you overly critical of the way others do their work?

8. _____ Do you have the habit of looking at your watch or clock often?

9. _____ Do you constantly strive to better your position and achievements?

10. _____ Do you spread yourself "too thin" in terms of your time?

11. _____ Do you have the habit of doing more than one thing at a time?

12. _____ Do you frequently get angry or irritable?

13. _____ Do you have little time for hobbies or time by yourself?

14. _____ Do you have a tendency to talk quickly or hasten conversations?

15. _____ Do you consider yourself hard-driving?

16. _____ Do your friends or relatives consider you hard-driving?

17. _____ Do you have a tendency to get involved in multiple projects?

18. _____ Do you have a lot of work deadlines?

19. _____ Do you feel vaguely guilty if you relax and do nothing during leisure?

20. _____ Do you take on too many responsibilities?

Total: _____

If your score is between 20 and 30, chances are you are nonproductive or your life lacks stimulation.

A score between 31 and 50 designates a good balance in your ability to handle and control stress.

If you tallied up a score ranging between 51 and 60, your stress level is marginal and you are bordering on being excessively tense.

If your total number of points exceeds 60, you may be a candidate for heart disease and need to immediately find ways to relieve your stress.

Source: http://www.arc.sbc.edu/stressquiz.html

Key Takeaways

- Workplace stress costs companies as much as $300 billion annually. Stress experienced at work can come from higher demands, layoffs, conflicts among coworkers, or office politics.
- Many people also can experience personal stresses, which affect workers' abilities to be productive. Personal stress can come from life changes, financial issues, family and friend issues, or our personality.

Exercises

1. Type A personalities tend to experience more stress than their type B personality counterpart. Take this quiz online at http://cl1.psychtests.com/take_test.php?idRegTest=2986 to see what type you fall into. How do you think your personality contributes (or not) to stress?

2. Do you agree or disagree with this statement? My personality contributes to the amount of stress I have in my life. Please explain in two to four paragraphs.

4.4 Reducing Stress

1. Explain techniques that can help us better cope with stress.

We all experience stress at one time or another. However, we can take action to assess and relieve the stress in our life. First, we do some self-analysis to determine the stressors in our life and how we handle it. This emotional intelligence skill (self-awareness) allows us to see what we need to improve upon. Then, we can apply self-management tools to help us manage the stress in our lives. The benefit of this identification and management is that it allows us to relate better to others both in our work and personal life.

What's in it for me?

There are many benefits to reducing stress in your life! Here are some of the benefits:

- Weight loss
- Greater happiness
- Better sleep
- Better relationships
- A longer life
- Greater productivity

What are some steps you can take now to reduce the stress you have in your life?

Look at your habits and emotions and really think about what is causing the stress. For example, Julie may be stressed about a project due on Friday, but the real stress may be because she procrastinated in starting the project, and now there isn't enough time to complete it. Or perhaps Gene is stressed because his personality type causes him to put too many things on his to-do list, and he isn't able to get them done. Accepting responsibility for the role we play in our own stresses can be the first step in maintaining a life with mostly positive stress!

Next, we can look at the way we currently deal with stress. For example, when you are stressed do you turn to alcohol and binge drink? Or do you turn to meditation and exercise? When you are stressed, do you lash out at the people you love, or do you become withdrawn? Understanding your current coping mechanisms for stress can help you determine what works to manage stress—and what doesn't.

FIGURE 4.5 The Four As for Dealing with Stress

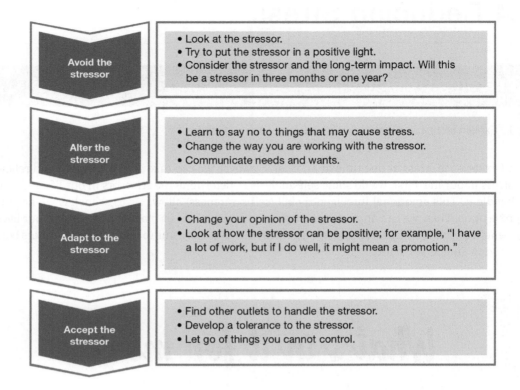

Avoid the stressor
- Look at the stressor.
- Try to put the stressor in a positive light.
- Consider the stressor and the long-term impact. Will this be a stressor in three months or one year?

Alter the stressor
- Learn to say no to things that may cause stress.
- Change the way you are working with the stressor.
- Communicate needs and wants.

Adapt to the stressor
- Change your opinion of the stressor.
- Look at how the stressor can be positive; for example, "I have a lot of work, but if I do well, it might mean a promotion."

Accept the stressor
- Find other outlets to handle the stressor.
- Develop a tolerance to the stressor.
- Let go of things you cannot control.

Once we do some self-analysis, we can use a method called the four As. The four As gives us four choices for dealing with a stressor:

1. **Avoid the stressor.** We can try to avoid situations that stress us out. If watching certain television programs causes stress, stop watching them! Spend time with people who help you relax. We can also try saying no more often if we do not have the time necessary to complete everything we are doing.

2. **Alter the stressor.** Another option in dealing with stress is to try to alter it, if you can't avoid it. When changing a situation, you can be more assertive, manage time better, and communicate your own needs and wants better. For example, Karen can look at the things causing her stress, such as her home and school commitments; while she can't change the workload, she can examine ways to avoid a heavy workload in the future. If Karen is stressed about the amount of homework she has and the fact that she needs to clean the house, asking for help from roommates, for example, can help alter the stressor. Often this involves the ability to communicate well.

3. **Adapt to the stressor.** If you are unable to avoid or change the stressor, getting comfortable with the stressor is a way to handle it. Creating your own coping mechanisms for the stress and learning to handle it can be an effective way to handle the stress. For example, we can try looking at stressful situations in a positive light, consider how important the stressor is in the long run, and adjust our standards of perfectionism. During the COVID-19 crisis, for example, many people have had no choice but to adapt to the challenges associated with the pandemic. Changing your attitude and coming up with ways to cope can be effective ways of dealing with those things we may not have a lot of control over.

4. **Accept the stressor.** Some stressors are unavoidable. We all have to go to work and manage our home life. So, learning to handle the things we cannot change by forgiving, developing tolerances, and letting go of those things we cannot control, is also a way to deal with a stressor. For example, if upcoming visits from your family cause you stress, you may not be able to prevent the visit from happening, but you can adapt to it and accept it. Since we cannot control another person, accepting the stressor and finding ways of dealing with it can help minimize

some negative effects of the stress. For example, in this case, maybe it is telling yourself (positive self-talk) that you will not let your family upset you, and maybe you can plan an hour day where you can have some alone time, such as by taking a walk or going to the gym.

When your roommate borrowed your car without asking, you need to pick up a friend from the airport, and you have friends coming over for dinner—all on the same night—finding a way to reduce stress is important. Reducing stress is going to be different for every person. Being able to recognize what helps you personally reduce stress is an important part to a healthy work and home life. For example, exercising may be a great stress reducer for Susie, but for Lisa finding time to exercise might cause more stress than the actual exercise helps!

Researchers have found the following activities cut stress significantly:[17]

- Meditating
- Listening to music
- Getting enough sleep
- Drinking black tea
- Spending time with a funny friend
- Pampering, such as a massage
- Doing something spiritual
- Chewing gum

Other ways to reduce stress might include the following:[18]

- Exercising
- Developing good time management skills
- Eating a healthy diet
- Organizing, such as keeping workspace organized
- Picturing yourself relaxed
- Breathing deeply
- Social interaction, such as spending time with family and friends
- Positive thinking

During times of crisis, such as the COVID-19 pandemic, doing specific things to reduce stress related to the virus might include:[19]

During a pandemic, handwashing can give you a sense of control and safety, which can reduce stress.

- Increase your own sense of safety, such as washing hands and taking measures to help make you feel safer.
- Stay connected with friends and family using video conferencing tools, such as Zoom.
- Recognize and allow yourself to feel anxious.
- Pinpoint those things making you feel anxious, such as watching too much news, and cutting down on those things that create greater anxiety during the crisis.

© Shutterstock

WATCH THIS!

Some additional stress reduction techniques to try.

View the video online at: http://www.youtube.com/embed/fAjdl7J4Gvo?rel=0

As this chapter has addressed, stress can be a positive motivator in our lives, but too much stress can create human relations, productivity, and other serious health issues. By practicing self-awareness and then self-management, we can begin to realize those things that cause us stress and deal with them in a healthier manner.

Key Takeaways

- The four As of stress reduction can help us reduce stress. They include: avoid, alter, adapt, and accept. By using the four As to determine the best approach to deal with a certain stressor, we can begin to have a more positive outlook on the stressor and learn to handle it better.
- There are a variety of things we can do to reduce stress. Exercise, a healthy diet, meditation, music, and social interaction can help reduce stress. Also, getting better at time management and organization can help reduce our stress.

Exercises

1. Of the ways to handle stress listed in this chapter, which ones do you already integrate in your life? Do you engage in other methods not listed here? Share your ideas for stress reduction in small groups.
2. Please review the self-assessments for stress on this website: https://www.stress.org/self-assessment. Please take the "stress" sensitivity test, as well as the stress 360 quiz. What were the results? Do you agree with them? Now, discuss specific strategies you might use to alleviate some of the stress.

4.5 Chapter Summary and Case

Chapter Summary

- *Stress* is defined as the body's response to change. Stress means different things to different people and stress and the types of things that cause stress can vary from person to person. Today, we generally say that stress is the body's way of responding to a demand.

- *Acute stress* is the type of stress we experience on a day-to-day basis—for example, the stress of finishing our to-do list or the stress of unplanned setbacks.

- When a person rarely gets relief from stress, this is called *episodic acute stress*. This type of stress usually goes on for longer periods of time with little relief.

- *Chronic stress* is characterized as long-term stress, where there is little hope for relief. These are long-term situations where the person has given up trying to find a solution.

- Not all stress is bad; some stress can actually help us to perform at a higher level and challenge us. This type of stress is called *eustress*.

- The *flight or fight response* is our body's physiological response to perceived threats. The basic physiological function is the same today as it was in prehistoric times.

- Having too much stress can cause many issues—such as headaches, sleeplessness, and irritability—that can affect our human relations ability.

- Workplace stress costs companies as much as $3.5 million per year. Stress experienced at work can come from higher demands, layoffs, conflicts among coworkers, or office politics.

- Many people also experience personal stresses, which affect their ability to be productive at work. Personal stress can come from life changes, financial issues, family and friend issues, or our personality.

- The four As of stress reduction can help us reduce stress. They include avoid, alter, adapt, and accept. By using the four As to determine the best approach to deal with a certain stressor, we can begin to have a more positive outlook on the stressor and learn to handle it better.

- There are a variety of things we can do to reduce stress. Exercise, a healthy diet, meditation, music, and social interaction can help reduce stress. Also, getting better at time management and organization can help reduce the stress we feel.

Chapter Case

Mandy feels like she can't deal with the stress anymore. First, her mother moved into her house for two months because of major home renovations. Mandy feels that her mother is always critical of the way she keeps her house and handles her life. While Mandy knows helping her mom for the next couple of months is the right thing to do, she can't help being annoyed. Mandy is also having trouble at her job. Her job in the medical lab is usually fun, but the organization laid off three workers recently, and as a result, the workload has increased significantly. It is the hospital's busy time, as well, so Mandy often works late to get the work done. On top of all that, Mandy had lent her best friend, Sylvia, $200 last month for rent, and Sylvia hasn't paid it back. Mandy not only needs the money but also feels that Sylvia was disrespectful when Mandy asked for the money back. Mandy is afraid this will affect their ten-year friendship.

1. Identify Mandy's stressors.
2. What type of stress is Mandy experiencing?
3. Using the four As model, how can Mandy go through the process to resolve her stress? Discuss in detail Mandy's options.

Endnotes

1. The American Institute of Stress. (n.d.). What is stress? Retrieved from http://www.stress.org/daily-life/

2. The American Institute of Stress. (n.d.). What is stress? Retrieved from http://www.stress.org/daily-life/

3. American Psychological Association. (n.d.). Stress: The Different Kinds. Retrieved from http://www.apa.org/helpcenter/stress-kinds.aspx

4. American Psychological Association. (n.d.). Stress: The Different Kinds. Retrieved from http://www.apa.org/helpcenter/stress-kinds.aspx

5. American Psychological Association. (n.d.). Stress: The Different Kinds. Retrieved from http://www.apa.org/helpcenter/stress-kinds.aspx

6. American Psychological Association. (n.d.). Stress: The Different Kinds. Retrieved from http://www.apa.org/helpcenter/stress-kinds.aspx

7. Chang, L.K. (n.d.). Eustress vs. Distress. Retrieved from https://www.mindfulnessmuse.com/stress-reduction/eustress-vs-distress

8. Selye, H. (n.d.). The Nature of Stress. Retrieved from http://www.icnr.com/articles/the-nature-of-stress.html

9. Psychologist World. (n.d). Stress: Fight or Flight Response. Retrieved from https://www.psychologistworld.com/stress/fight-or-flight-response

10. American Psychological Association. (October 2018). Stress in America: Generation Z. Retrieved from https://www.apa.org/news/press/releases/stress/2018/stress-gen-z.pdf

11. American Psychological Association. (October 2018). Stress in America: Generation Z. Retrieved from https://www.apa.org/news/press/releases/stress/2018/stress-gen-z.pdf

12. American Psychological Association. (October 2018). Stress in America: Generation Z. Retrieved from https://www.apa.org/news/press/releases/stress/2018/stress-gen-z.pdf

13. The American Institute of Stress. (n.d.). Workplace Stress. Retrieved from https://www.stress.org/workplace-stress

14. The American Institute of Stress. (n.d.). Stress in the Workplace. Retrieved from http://www.stress.org/workplace-stress/

15. Ward, M. (3 May 2017). A brief history of the 8-hour workday. Retrieved from https://www.cnbc.com/2017/05/03/how-the-8-hour-workday-changed-how-americans-work.html

16. Bryghtpath. (14 December 2017). 8 more notable workplace violence incidents in 2017. Retrieved from https://bryghtpath.com/8-more-notable-workplace-violence-incidents-in-2017/

17. Healthline. (n.d.). 16 simple ways to reduce stress and anxiety. Retrieved from https://www.healthline.com/nutrition/16-ways-relieve-stress-anxiety

18. Healthline. (n.d.). 16 simple ways to reduce stress and anxiety. Retrieved from https://www.healthline.com/nutrition/16-ways-relieve-stress-anxiety

19. U.S. Department of Veterans Affairs, (n.d.) managing stress associated with the covid-19 virus outbreak. Accessed from https://www.ptsd.va.gov/covid/COVID_managing_stress.asp.

CHAPTER 5

Building Communications Skills

The most important thing in communication is hearing what isn't said.

—Peter F. Drucker

Electric communication will never be a substitute for the face of someone who with their soul encourages another person to be brave and true.

—Charles Dickens

Improving Communication

When you walked into work this morning, you said your normal "good mornings" and everyone cheerfully said good morning back to you except one coworker. This is a coworker you have had problems with for quite some time.

The problems seem to stem from your two different styles of communication. You like to be quick and to the point, so you find yourself e-mailing a lot. Your coworker, Nanci, prefers to have every conversation in person. You feel that while talking in person is nice (and sometimes necessary and time-saving), it can also be difficult, since everyone has such a hectic schedule. Your work-style is focused on saving time and using time as wisely as possible. For example, Nanci asked you to give her a client's e-mail address. You copied and pasted it from an earlier e-mail and e-mailed it to Nanci. Nanci got very upset at this and commented about your need to always e-mail things instead of talking in person. You told her it was easier to do it that way, plus it prevented the chance that you would write the address down wrong. Nanci did not like this response.

In another example, Nanci stopped by your office to ask about your willingness to help set up for the company holiday party. Nanci starting talking with you about the decorations and you interrupted and told her you would be happy to do so and asked her what time you should be there. Nanci again got upset and told you she had no idea. Her body language showed frustration and you couldn't understand why, as you were only asking a reasonable question about timing.

Finally, you decide to talk with your supervisor about these issues. The supervisor gives you some information that was hard to take but also very valuable in the development of a good communication style. "Andree," she said, "while people in the office really like you, they don't find you very warm. People say that your facial expressions and the fact you don't smile very often makes you difficult to approach. To make matters worse, your one- and two-line e-mail responses are sometimes off-putting."

In your defense, you say that you are very busy and often don't have time to answer an e-mail with another line. You also say that you are there to work, not to make friends.

"Yes, this is true," says your supervisor, "but it is important to establish good relationships, which is something you have not seemed to make an effort to do. Good relationships happen with good communication."

As you leave, you understand that you will need to improve in this area. The first thing you do is stop by Nanci's office to hear about the decorations she wanted to tell you about for the company party. You feel this is a good start to creating better communication between her and your other coworkers.

5.1 Verbal and Written Communication Strategies

Learning Objectives

1. Describe the four types of communication in the workplace.
2. Explain the various communication styles and identify your own style.

Communication, as you see in our opening scenario, is key to any successful career. While communication is likely discussed in many of your other classes, it should also be addressed in a human relations book, since much of what we do at work is based on effective communication.

How many times do miscommunications happen on a daily basis, either in your personal life or at your job? The good news is that we can all get better at communication. The first thing we need to do is learn how we can better communicate with others. Then, we will want to look at our own communication style and compare that with other styles. Have you ever spoken with someone you just didn't "get"? It is probably because you have different communication styles. Body language is also a key contributor to communication; in fact, as was suggested in the late 1960s by researcher Albert Mehrabian, body language makes up 93 percent of our communication.[1]

One of the most important aspects of good communication is emotional intelligence (EQ). Emotional intelligence, as we discussed in Chapter 2 is the ability to know and manage our emotions, motivate ourselves, understand others' emotions, and manage relationships. Without EQ, it would be impossible to effectively communicate with people.

Communication Directions

As you probably already know, each of us has our own individual communication style. Many organizations give tests that may indicate their candidate's preferred style, providing the company with information about the best job fit.

Communication in companies is key to having a successful organization. Of course, learning how to communicate better, as a result, is the cornerstone of a successful career. Likewise, understanding how companies communicate with employees can result in employees who are more loyal and motivated. Those companies that don't communicate well, though, see increased turnover, absenteeism, dissatisfied customers, higher product defect rates, lack of focus on business objectives, and lack of innovation.[2]

Four main types of communications occur within a company: upward communication, downward communication, diagonal communication, and horizontal communication. Each type of communication can serve a different purpose in an organization, and many messages may be sent in a variety of ways.

Upward communication is when the lower levels of an organization communicate with the upper levels of an organization. Some examples might be an employee satisfaction survey. In such a survey, management in the organization learns about what's working (and not working) in the organization. Upward communication is important, because it gives employees a chance to give information about the organization to upper management. In another example, if your manager stops by your desk and asks you to take on a project, but you tell her you are too busy to do so, this is also upward communication.

Downward communication is the opposite of upward communication, in that the communication occurs from upper levels of management to employees. For example, a memo from Human Resources explaining the new health care plan, an email from the CEO explaining new procedures for dealing with the COVID-19 pandemic, or an e-mail from your boss telling you to set aside time to meet with a client on Friday would be examples of downward communication. As you can see, both upward and downward communication can occur in the larger group, or between individuals.

upward communication

When the lower levels of an organization communicate with the upper levels of an organization.

downward communication

The opposite of upward communication, in that the communication occurs from the upper levels of an organization down to the lower levels of the organization.

FIGURE 5.1 Types of Communication Flow in Organizations

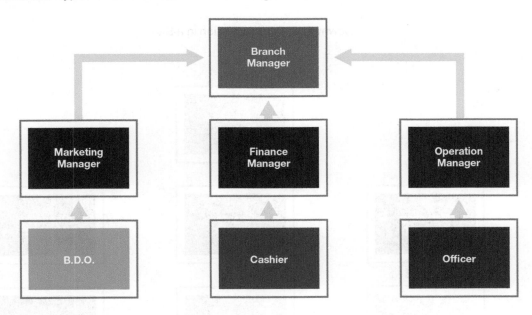

"Upward" Communication in a Bank

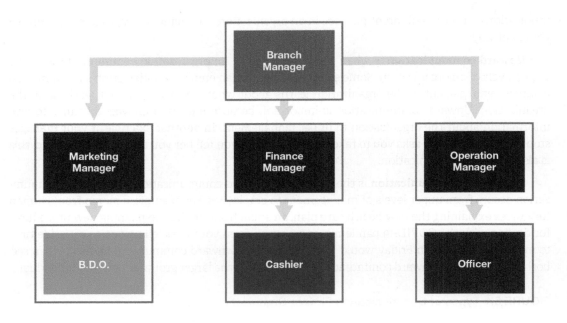

"Downward" Communication in a Bank

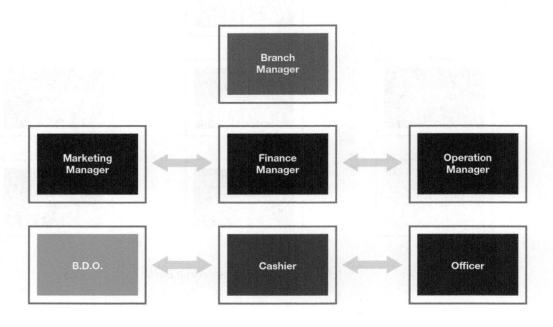

"Horizontal" Communication in a Bank

diagonal communication

Interdepartmental communication occurring at various levels of the organization.

A **diagonal communication** approach occurs when communication occurs between people within different departments of an organization. If the accounting department needs to ask the marketing department about a charge for a social media marketing campaign, this would be an example of diagonal communication.

Horizontal communication occurs when people of the same hierarchical level in an organization communicate with one another. For example, a manager in one department communicating with a manger in the same or different department. For example, if the VP of Sales of the Western Region communicates with the VP of sales in the Eastern region, this is an example of horizontal communication.

Within all the communication methods we discussed, there can be a variety of approaches to get your message across. Of course, the most obvious is informal communication. For example, an e-mail, a phone call, or instant message may be exchanged between individuals. Meetings are another way to communicate information.

Companies also use social networking sites to help them communicate internally. Nokia, for example, uses a social media site called Bloghub, Infopedia, and Videohub. This allows employees to communicate via social media to learn about new products, and also allows them to connect with each other based on their interests. This type of communication can create a strong employee community, resulting in greater engagement from employees.[3]

Companies also use intranets to communicate information to their employees. An **intranet** is an internal website, meaning that others generally cannot log in and see information there. The intranet may include information on pay and vacation time as well as recent happenings, awards, and achievements. Some intranets even have places to post items for sale or houses for rent. No matter how your company chooses to communicate with you, understanding the variety of methods can help make you a better employee. Now that we have discussed communication from the company perspective, we should discuss communication from the personal perspective.

horizontal communication
When people at the same level in the organization communicate.

intranet
An internal website, meaning that others generally cannot log in and see information there.

Communication Styles

In addition to the communication that occurs within organizations, each of us has our own individual communication style. Many organizations give tests that may indicate their candidate's preferred style, providing information on the best job fit.

 WATCH THIS!

Effective communication is necessary to be successful at work.

View the video online at: http://www.youtube.com/embed/aRE-uciREO4?rel=0

Our communication styles can determine how well we communicate with others, how well we are understood, and even how well we get along with others. As you can imagine, our personality types and our communication styles are very similar. Keep in mind, though, that no one person is "always" one style. We can change our style depending on the situation. The more we can understand our own dominant communication style and pinpoint the styles of others, the better we can communicate. The styles are expresser, driver, relater, and analytical. Let's discuss each of these styles next.

People with an **expresser communication style** tend to get excited. They like challenges and rely heavily on hunches and feelings. Depending on the type of business, this can be a downfall as sometimes hard data should be used for decision-making purposes. These people are easily recognized because they don't like long explanations and too many facts.

People with a **driver communication style** like to have their own way and tend to be decisive. They have strong viewpoints, which they are comfortable sharing with others. They like to take charge in their jobs but also in the way they communicate. Drivers usually get right to the point and do not waste time with small talk.

People with a **relater communication style** like positive attention and want to be regarded warmly. They want others to care about them and treat them well. Because relaters value friendships, a good way to communicate well with them is to create a communication environment where they can feel close to others.

People with an **analytical communication style** will ask a lot of questions and behave methodically. They prefer structure, and like time to think about potential decisions.

expresser communication style

A communication style that is easily excitable and relies heavily on hunches and feelings.

driver communication style

A communication style in which a person likes to have his or her own way and be decisive.

relater communication style

A communication style of someone who prefers to be warmly regarded and have positive attention.

analytical communication style

A communication style in which a person tends to ask a lot of questions and behave methodically.

TABLE 5.1 Which One of These Communication Styles Do You Tend to Use?

Factors	Expresser	Driver	Relater	Analytical
How to recognize	They get excited.	They like their own way; decisive and strong viewpoints.	They like positive attention, to be helpful, and to be regarded warmly.	They seek a lot of data, ask many questions, behave methodically and systematically.
Tends to ask	Who? (the personal dominant question)	What? (the results-oriented question)	Why? (the personal nongoal question)	How? (the technical analytical question)
Dislikes	Boring explanations/ wasting time with too many facts.	Someone wasting their time trying to decide for them.	Rejection, being treated impersonally, uncaring and unfeeling attitudes.	Making an error, being unprepared, spontaneity.
Reacts to pressure and tension by	"Selling" their ideas or becoming argumentative.	Taking charge, taking more control.	Becoming silent, withdrawn, introspective.	Seeking more data and information.
Best way to deal with	Get excited with them, show emotion.	Let them be in charge.	Be supportive; show you care.	Provide lots of data and information.
Likes to be measured by	Applause, feedback, recognition.	Results, meeting goals.	Friends, close relationships.	Activity and business that lead to results.
Must be allowed to	Get ahead quickly. Likes challenges.	Get into a competitive situation. Likes to win.	Relax, feel, care, know you care.	Make decisions at own pace, not feel cornered or pressured.
Will improve with	Recognition and some structure with which to reach the goal.	A position that requires cooperation with others.	A structure of goals and methods for achieving each goal.	Further development of interpersonal and communication skills.

Factors	Expresser	Driver	Relater	Analytical
Likes to save	Effort. They rely heavily on hunches, intuition, feelings.	Time. They like to be efficient, get things done now.	Relationships. Friendship means a lot to them.	Face. They hate to make an error, be wrong, or get caught without enough info.
For best results:	Inspire them to bigger and better accomplishments.	Allow them freedom to do things their own way.	Care and provide detail, specific plans, and activities to be accomplished.	Structure a framework or "track" to follow.

Let's discuss an example of how these communication styles might interact. Let's assume an analytical communicator and a relater are beginning a meeting where the purpose is to develop a project timeline. The analytical communicator will be focused on the timeline and not necessarily the rapport building that the relater would be focused on. The conversation might go something like this:

Relater: What are you doing this weekend? I am going to my son's baseball game. It is supposed to be hot—I am looking forward to it.

Analytical: That's great. OK, so I was thinking a start date of August 1st for this project. I can get Kristin started on a to-do list for the project.

Relater: That would be great. Kristin is a really hard worker, and I'm sure she won't miss any details.

Analytical: Yes, she's OK. So your team will need to start development now with a start day coming up. How are you going to go about this?

How do these two personality styles walk away from this conversation? First, the relater may feel ignored or rejected, because the analytical communicator didn't want to discuss weekend details. The analytical communicator may feel annoyed that the relater is wasting time talking about personal things when they have a goal to set a project timeline. These types of small miscommunications in business are what can create low morale, absenteeism, and other workplace issues. Understanding which style we tend to use can be the key in determining how we communicate with others. Here is another, personal example of these communication styles and how a conversation might go:

Expresser, to his partner:	*I am really excited about our hiking trip this weekend.*
Driver:	*I still think we should leave on Thursday night rather than Friday.*
Expresser:	*I told you, I don't think I can get all day Friday off. Besides, we won't have much time to explore anyway if we get there on Thursday; it will already be dark.*
Driver:	*It won't be dark; we will get there around seven, before anyone else, if we leave after work.*
Expresser:	*I planned the trip. I am the one who applied for the permit and the one putting together the food. I don't see why you have to change it.*
Driver:	*You didn't plan the trip; I am the one who applied for the permits.*

In this situation, you can see that the expresser is just excited about the trip and brings up the conversation as such. The driver has a tendency to be competitive and wants to win, hence his willingness to get there Thursday before everyone else. The expresser, on the other hand, tried to sell his ideas and didn't get the feedback he felt he deserved for planning the trip, which made the communication start to go south.

In addition to our communication personalities, people tend to communicate based on one of three styles. First, a **passive communicator** tends to put the rights of others before his or her own. Passive communicators tend to be apologetic or sound tentative when they speak. They do not speak up if they feel like they are being wronged.

An **aggressive communicator**, on the other hand, will come across as standing up for his or her rights while possibly violating the rights of others. This person tends to communicate in a way that tells others they don't matter or their feelings don't matter.

An **assertive communicator** respects his or her rights and the rights of others when communicating. This person tends to be direct but not insulting or offensive. The assertive communicator stands up for his or her own rights but makes sure the rights of others aren't affected.

passive communicator

A communication style in which a person puts the rights of others over his or her own.

aggressive communicator

The style of a person who stands up for his or her rights but possibly violates the rights of others.

assertive communicator

Respects the rights of his-or herself and others when communicating.

TABLE 5.2 Which One of These Communication Styles Do You Tend to Use?

	Passive	Assertive	Aggressive
Definition	Communication style in which you put the rights of others before your own, minimizing your own self-worth	Communication style in which you stand up for your rights while maintaining respect for the rights of others	Communication style in which you stand up for your rights but you violate the rights of others
Implications to others	My feelings are not important	We are both important	Your feelings are not important
	I don't matter	We both matter	You don't matter
	I think I'm inferior	I think we are equal	I think I'm superior
Verbal styles	Apologetic	I statements	You statements
	Overly soft or tentative voice	Firm voice	Loud voice
Nonverbal styles	Looking down or away	Looking direct	Staring, narrow eyes
	Stooped posture, excessive head nodding	Relaxed posture, smooth and relaxed movements	Tense, clenched fists, rigid posture, pointing fingers

	Passive	Assertive	Aggressive
Potential consequences	Lowered self-esteem	Higher self-esteem	Guilt
	Anger at self	Self-respect	Anger from others
	False feelings of inferiority	Respect from others	Lowered self-esteem
	Disrespect from others	Respect of others	Disrespect from others
	Pitied by others		Feared by others

Have you heard of a passive-aggressive communicator? This person tends to be passive but later aggressive by perhaps making negative comments about others or making snide or underhanded comments. This person might express his or her negative feelings in an indirect way instead of being direct. For example, you are trying to complete a project for a client and the deadline is three days away. You and your team are working frantically to finish. You ask one of your employees to work on it over the weekend, since it'll be presented to the client first thing on Monday. Your employee agrees, but when you show up on Monday, the project isn't ready to present. You find out that this person had plans to be out of town over the weekend but wasn't direct with you about this. So the project didn't get completed, and you had to change the appointment with the client. Later, you also find out that this employee was complaining to everyone else that you had asked her to come in on Saturday. As you can see from this example, passive-aggressive behavior doesn't benefit anyone. The employee should have been direct and simply said, "I'm not able to work on it this weekend, perhaps we can change the client meeting date?" Ideally, we want to be assertive communicators, as this shows our own self-esteem but at the same time respects others and isn't misleading to others, either.

When dealing with someone who exhibits passive-aggressive behavior, it is best to be direct with them. Tell that person you would rather she be direct than not show up. Often, passive-aggressive people try to play the martyr or the victim. Do not allow such people to press your buttons and get you to feel sorry for them. This gives them control and can allow them to take advantage.

Listening

competitive or combative listening

A type of listening that happens when we are focused on sharing our own point of view instead of listening to someone else.

passive listening

A type of listening in which we are interested in hearing the other person and assume we hear and understand what the person says correctly without verifying.

active listening

A type of listening in which we are interested in what the other person has to say and check our understanding with the speaker.

Listening is obviously an important part of communication. There are three main types of listening. **Competitive or combative listening** happens when we are focused on sharing our own point of view instead of listening to someone else. In **passive listening**, we are interested in hearing the other person and assume we hear and understand what the person says correctly without verifying. In **active listening**, we are interested in what the other person has to say and we are active in checking our understanding with the speaker. For example, we may restate what the person has said and then verify our understanding is correct. The feedback process is the main difference between passive listening and active listening.

FIGURE 5.2 Active Listening
Active listening involves four phases.

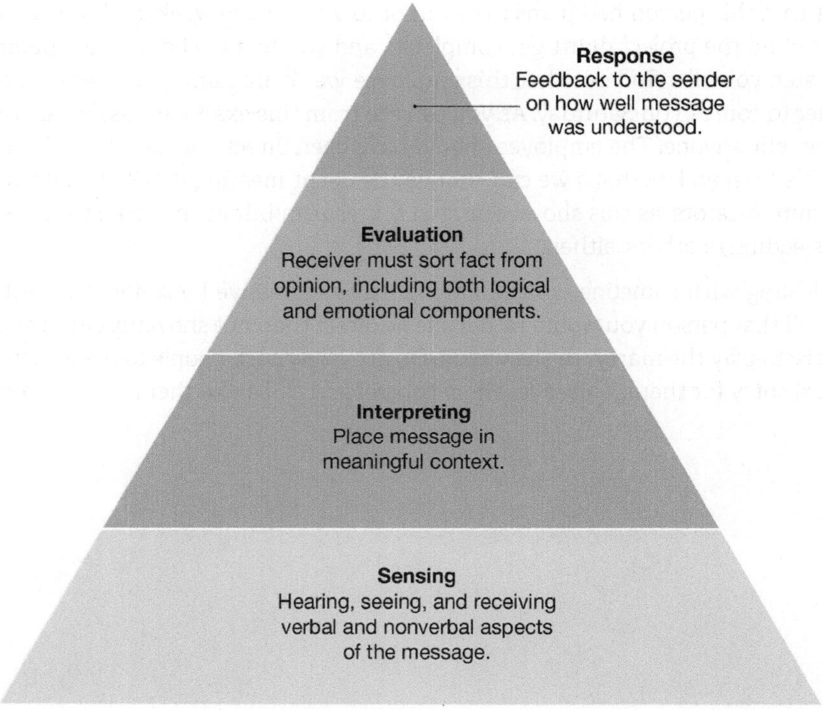

Response
Feedback to the sender on how well message was understood.

Evaluation
Receiver must sort fact from opinion, including both logical and emotional components.

Interpreting
Place message in meaningful context.

Sensing
Hearing, seeing, and receiving verbal and nonverbal aspects of the message.

Source: Steil, L., Barker, L., & Watson, K. (n.d.). SIER hierarchy of active listening. Provenmodels, http://www.provenmodels.com/554.

Written Communication

Besides verbal communication, much of our communication at work may happen in the written form, such as e-mail. When using e-mail as a communication tool, we should consider the four Cs:

- **Complete.** We want to make sure that all facts are included in the e-mail. When responding to an e-mail, also make sure all questions have been answered.

- **Concise.** Try to make e-mails as concise as possible. If your e-mail becomes long, it may be better to have a personal conversation rather than an e-mail to make sure the message gets across in the appropriate way.

- **Correct.** Be sure to check e-mail, grammar, and spelling. E-mails should always have a greeting, body, and closing.
- **Clear.** Is your writing easy to understand? Does it flow well?

When considering the four Cs, we also want to consider the following e-mail tips:

- Make sure the subject line is descriptive.
- Use upper and lower case letters, and avoid shortening words as you would with a text message.
- Do not use the "reply all" function if it isn't necessary. It clutters everyone's e-mail box, if the message doesn't directly pertain to them
- Make sure to sign your e-mail.
- Before sending, always reread your message to make sure you are conveying your message clearly.
- Do not send e-mails when you are angry or upset. Use a twenty-four-hour rule before replying to an e-mail that gave you this type of emotional response.
- Do not forward jokes, pictures, videos, and the like.

Following these e-mail tips will ensure your communication is clear and concise. It saves time in the long run to spend time writing a good e-mail rather than trying to e-mail back and forth with someone who did not understand your message the first time.

One of the challenges of written communication is the inability to see the receivers reaction to your e-mail. In other words, e-mail does not allow us to see the nonverbal responses from our receivers. The nonverbal aspects of communication will be the next topic in this chapter.

Key Takeaways

- There are four types of communication at work: *downward*, *upward*, *horizontal*, and *diagonal*. All types of communication can happen at once, between large or small groups, or individuals.
- Companies that use good communication tend to have less turnover and less absenteeism.
- There are four main types of communication styles: *expresser*, *driver*, *relater*, and *analytical*. The better we can understand our own style of communication and the communication styles of others, the easier it will be to communicate with them.
- Passive, aggressive, and passive-aggressive behaviors are not healthy ways of communicating. Assertive behavior, on the other hand, respects one's own rights and the rights of others.
- *Nonverbal communication* is one of the most important tools we can use to communicate how we feel. Watching others' body language can give us signals as to how they may really feel.
- Listening is also an important part of communication. *Active listening* occurs when we are interested in what the other person has to say, and we check with the speaker to make sure we understand what they have said. *Competitive or combative listening* is when we are focused on sharing our own point of view. *Passive listening* is when we listen to someone but do not verify that we understand what someone is saying.
- When sending e-mails, follow the four Cs: complete, concise, correct, and clear.

1. Which communication style—the expresser, driver, relater, or analytical—do you typically use? How can you get better at understanding other people's style and get comfortable communicating in their style?
2. Do you tend to be passive, assertive, or aggressive? Give an example of when you used each style and discuss the result.

5.2 Principles of Nonverbal Communication

Learning Objectives

1. Explain how your nonverbal communication can impact communication with others.
2. Explain how the principles of nonverbal communication should be considered when you communicate with others.

How do you know when your supervisor is happy with your performance on a project? Do they send congratulatory e-mails? Perhaps they also acknowledge you in a meeting with a smiling face? Maybe they schedule a meeting to talk about your future promotion? However your good performance is acknowledged (and hopefully it's done in a variety of ways to meet a variety of communication styles), chances are some of the communication is non-verbal, which lets you know you've done a good job. Nonverbal communication is an imperative part of communication, and understanding the effects of it can help us become better communicators.

Nonverbal Communication Is Fluid

FIGURE 5.3 Nonverbal Communication
What are each of these images telling us?

Chances are you've had an experience where there was a miscommunication. Perhaps you were talking with your partner about the upcoming trip you have planned, but you are distracted by thoughts of trying to finish a work e-mail before starting dinner. Your distraction (which could mean lack of eye contact or lack of enthusiastic response or smiling) could mean your partner believes you are not excited about the trip (when in fact, you are). These types of non-verbal cues are at times hard to decipher and create miscommunications. **Nonverbal communication** is the process of conveying a message without the use of words. It can include gestures and facial expressions, tone of voice, timing, posture, and where you stand as you communicate.

The challenge with non-verbal communication is that it is irreversible. Unlike a written message, where you can obtain clarification if something doesn't make sense, non-verbal communication is up to the interpretation of the person receiving the message. There are other characteristics of non-verbal communication, which make it challenging as well, and we will address those next.

nonverbal communication

The process of conveying a message without the use of words.

Nonverbal Communication Is Fast

Let's pretend you are at your computer at work. You see that an e-mail has arrived, but you are right in the middle of tallying a spreadsheet whose numbers just don't add up. You see that the e-mail is from a coworker and you click on it. The subject line reads "lay offs." Even though you are very busy (and maybe a bit frustrated), this message immediately gives you pause and worry.

Your emotional response is immediate. If the author of the e-mail could see your face, they would know that your response was one of disbelief and frustration, even anger, all via your nonverbal communication. In the same way, you express yourself via nonverbal communication all the time without much conscious thought.

Nonverbal communication gives our thoughts and feelings away before we are even aware of what we are thinking or how we feel. People may see and hear more than you ever anticipated. Your nonverbal communication includes both intentional and unintentional messages, but since it all happens so fast, the unintentional ones can contradict what you know you are supposed to say or how you are supposed to react.

Nonverbal Communication Can Add to or Replace Verbal Communication

People tend to pay more attention to how you say something than what you actually say. We use nonverbal gestures called **illustrators** to communicate our message effectively and reinforce our point. An illustrator is a body movement, such as spreading your arms wide when talking about something big. For example, you pass your girlfriend on campus and ask, "meet at the library after class?" and she gives you the thumbs-up sign in agreement. This is called an **emblem**, by signaling with the thumbs-up sign.

illustrators

Nonverbal expression that reinforces a verbal message.

emblem

Nonverbal gesture that carries a specific meaning and can replace or reinforce words.

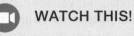 **WATCH THIS!**

Examples of how you can use illustrators to enhance nonverbal communication.

View the video online at: http://www.youtube.com/embed/ROKYP10Zcw4?rel=0

regulator

Nonverbal expression that controls, encourages, or discourages interaction.

In addition to illustrators or emblematic nonverbal communication, we also use regulators. "**Regulators** are nonverbal messages which control, maintain or discourage interaction."[4] For example, if someone is telling you a message that is confusing or upsetting, you may hold up your hand, a commonly-recognized regulator that asks the speaker to stop talking.

Let's say you are in a meeting presenting information that introduces your company's latest product. If your audience members nod their heads in agreement on important points and maintain good eye contact, it is a good sign. Nonverbally, they are using regulators encouraging you to continue with your presentation. In contrast, if they look away, tap their feet, and begin drawing in the margins of their notebook, these are regulators suggesting that you better think of a way to regain their interest or wrap up your presentation quickly.

affect display

An expression of emotion or mood.

Affect displays are nonverbal communication that express emotions or feelings."[5] An affect display that might accompany holding up your hand for silence would be to frown and shake your head from side to side. When you and your girlfriend are at the library and see your friends walk in, you might smile and wave at them, which is an example of affect display—you are expressing you are happy to see them.

Clicking your pen up and down is an example of an object-adaptor.

© Shutterstock

"**Adaptors** are displays of nonverbal communication that help you adapt to your environment and each context, helping you feel comfortable and secure."[6] A **self-adaptor** involves you meeting your need for security (e.g., playing with your hair) by adapting something about yourself in a way for which it was not designed or for no apparent purpose. Combing your hair would be an example of a purposeful action, unlike a self-adaptive behavior. An **object-adaptor** involves the use of an object in a way for which it was not designed. You may see audience members tapping, chewing, or playing with their pencils while ignoring you and your presentation. Or perhaps someone clicks their pen up and down, even though they are not using the pen; this would be an example of an object-adaptor.

Intentional nonverbal communication can complement, repeat, replace, mask, or contradict what we say. For example, we can give the thumbs-up sign and say yes at the same time (saying yes complements and repeats the thumbs up). Or, we can just give the thumbs-up sign (replaces a verbal yes). In addition, we can mask or contradict what we say with nonverbal communication. **Masking** or contradicting involves the substitution of appropriate nonverbal communication for nonverbal communication you may want to display.[7] For example, instead of a thumbs-up, you might make an unhappy face while displaying a thumbs-up sign moving up and down, nearing a thumbs-down sign. This doesn't give a certain cue of how you actually may feel about the situation. When Andrew invited you to Barney's, you said, "Yeah" and nodded, complementing and repeating the message. You could have simply nodded, effectively replacing the "yes" with a nonverbal response. You could also have decided to say no but did not want to hurt Andrew's feelings. Shaking your head "no" while pointing to your watch, communicating work and time issues, may mask your real thoughts or feelings. Finally, nonverbal messages that conflict with verbal communication can confuse the listener. Table 5.3 summarizes the concepts we've just addressed.

adaptor

Something that helps us feel comfortable or indicates emotions or moods.

self-adaptor

Adapting something about yourself in way for which it was not designed or for no apparent purpose.

object-adaptor

Use of an object for a purpose other than its intended design.

masking

Involves the substitution of appropriate nonverbal communication for nonverbal communication you may want to display.

TABLE 5.3 Some Nonverbal Expressions

Term	Definition
Adaptors	Help us feel comfortable or indicate emotions or moods
Affect displays	Express emotions or feelings
Complementing	Reinforcing verbal communication
Contradicting	Contradicting verbal communication
Emblems	Nonverbal gestures that carry a specific meaning and can replace or reinforce words
Illustrators	Reinforce a verbal message
Masking	Substituting more appropriate displays for less appropriate displays
Object-adaptors	Using an object for a purpose other than its intended design
Regulators	Control, encourage, or discourage interaction
Repeating	Repeating verbal communication
Replacing	Replacing verbal communication
Self-adaptors	Adapting something about yourself in a way for which it was not designed or for no apparent purpose

Nonverbal Communication Is Confusing and Contextual

Nonverbal communication can be confusing. We need contextual clues to help us understand, or begin to understand, what a movement, gesture, or lack of display means. Then we have to figure it all out based on our prior knowledge (or lack thereof) of the person, and hope to get it right. Consider a close friend who has a habit of touching the top of his head when he is thinking about how to respond. As a close friend, you know this nonverbal communication of his, but others may not. So, when he pauses before answering (and touches his head), people may interrupt because they don't understand that it's his nonverbal cue for considering what you've said. Talk about confusing! Now, consider the interactions we have with clients, customers, coworkers, along with others we may know very well. All interactions are within individual contexts and influenced by how well you know someone, what their mood is, what your mood is, and dependent upon the kind of day someone's had. Again, talk about confusing, because it is all within a specific context.

Nonverbal Communication Can Be Intentional or Unintentional

Assume you are at a job interview, and as the manager is telling you about the job, you nod your head. This nonverbal communication is intentional, with the intent to show the manager you understand. Now, suppose the manager asks you a question you can't think of an appropriate answer to. How might your unintentional nonverbal communication come across? Perhaps your eyes would widen for a second, or perhaps you'd stop making eye contact with the manager and look at the ground instead. This intentional nonverbal communication shows the manager you may be anxious about answering that particular question.

Can we tell when people are intentionally or unintentionally communicating nonverbally? Ask ten people this question and compare their responses. You may be surprised. It is clearly a challenge to understand nonverbal communication in action. We often assign intentional motives to nonverbal communication when, in fact, their display is unintentional and often hard to interpret.

Nonverbal Messages Communicate Feelings and Attitudes

Steven Beebe, Susan Beebe, and Mark Redmond offer us three additional principals of interpersonal nonverbal communication that serve our discussion. One is that you often react faster than you think. Your nonverbal responses communicate your initial reaction before you can process it through language or formulate an appropriate response. If your appropriate, spoken response doesn't match your nonverbal reaction, you may give away your true feelings and attitudes.[8]

Albert Mehrabian asserts that we rarely communicate emotional messages through the spoken word. According to Mehrabian, 93 percent of the time we communicate our emotions nonverbally, with at least 55 percent associated with facial gestures. Vocal cues, body position and movement, and normative space between speaker and receiver can also be clues to feelings and attitudes.[9]

 **WATCH THIS!**

A series of movie clips demonstrate the power of nonverbal communication.

View the video online at: http://www.youtube.com/embed/VfDWQG47pAQ?rel=0

Nonverbal Communication Is More Powerful than Verbal

According to William Seiler and Melissa Beall, most people tend to believe the nonverbal message over the verbal message. People will often answer that "actions speak louder than words" and place a disproportionate emphasis on the nonverbal response.[10] This is why it is important for us to be aware of our own nonverbal communication and ensure we are communicating what we mean.

- Reduction in eye contact while engaged in a conversation
- Awkward pauses in conversation
- Higher pitch in voice
- Deliberate pronunciation and articulation of words
- Increased delay in response time to a question
- Increased body movements like changes in posture
- Decreased smiling
- Decreased rate of speech

Key Takeaways

- Nonverbal communication is the process of conveying a message without the use of words; it relates to the dynamic process of communication, the perception process and listening, and verbal communication.
- Nonverbal communication is fluid and fast, universal, confusing, and contextual. It can add to, or replace, verbal communication and can be intentional or unintentional.
- Nonverbal communication communicates feelings and attitudes, and people tend to believe nonverbal messages more than verbal ones.

Exercises

1. Does it limit or enhance our understanding of communication to view nonverbal communication as that which is not verbal communication? Explain your answer and discuss with the class.
2. Choose a television or YouTube personality you admire. What do you like about this person? Watch several minutes of this person with the sound turned off, and make notes of the nonverbal expressions you observe. Turn the sound back on and make notes of their tone of voice, timing, and other audible expressions. Discuss your results with a classmate.
3. Create a survey that addresses the issue of which people trust more, nonverbal or verbal messages. Ask an equal number of men and women and compare your results with those of your classmates.

5.3 Nonverbal Communication Types

Learning Objective

1. Describe the similarities and differences among seven general types of nonverbal communication.

Now that we have discussed the general principles that apply to nonverbal communication, let's examine seven types of nonverbal communication to further understand this challenging aspect of communication:

1. Space
2. Time
3. Body movements
4. Touch
5. Paralanguage
6. Artifacts
7. Environment

Space

When we discuss space in a nonverbal context, we mean the space between objects and people. Space is often associated with social rank and is an important part of business communication. Who gets the corner office? Why is the head of the table important and who gets to sit there?

People from diverse cultures may have different normative space expectations. If you are from a large urban area, having people stand close to you may be normal. If you are from a rural area or a culture where people expect more space, someone may be standing "too close" for comfort and not know it.

Edward T. Hall, serving in the European and South Pacific regions in the Army Corps of Engineers during World War II, traveled around the globe. As he moved from one place to another, he noticed that people in different countries kept different distances from each other. In France, they stood closer to each other than they did in England. Hall wondered why that was and began to study what he called **proxemics**, or the study of the human use of space and distance in communication.[11]

proxemics

The study of the human use of space and distance in communication.

In *The Hidden Dimension*, he indicated there are two main aspects of space: territory and personal space. Hall drew on anthropology to address the concepts of dominance and submission and noted that the more powerful person often claims more space. This plays an important role in modern society, from who gets the corner office to how we negotiate space between vehicles. Road rage is increasingly common where overcrowding occurs, and as more vehicles occupy the same roads, tensions over space are predictable.

Territory is related to control. As a way of establishing control over your own room, maybe you painted it your favorite color or put up posters that represent your interests or things you consider unique about yourself. Families or households often mark their space by putting up fences or walls around their houses. This sense of a right to control your space is implicit in territory. **Territory** means the space you claim as your own, are responsible for, or are willing to defend.

territory

The space you claim as your own, are responsible for, or are willing to defend.

The second aspect Hall highlights is **personal space**, or the "bubble" of space surrounding each individual. As you walk down a flight of stairs, which side do you choose? We may choose the right side because we've learned that is what is expected, and people coming up the same stair choose their right. The right choice ensures that personal space is not compromised. But what happens when someone comes up the wrong side? They violate the understood rules of movement and often correct themselves. But what happens if they don't change lanes as people move up and down the stairs? They may get dirty looks or even get bumped as people in the crowd handle the invasion of "their" space. There are no lane markers, and bubbles of space around each person move with them, allowing for the possibility of collision.

personal space

The "bubble" of space surrounding each individual.

We recognize the basic need for personal space, but the normative expectations for space vary greatly by culture. You may perceive that in your home people sleep one to each bed, but in many cultures people sleep two or more to a bed and consider it normal. If you were to share that bed, you might feel uncomfortable, while someone raised with group sleeping norms might feel uncomfortable sleeping alone. From where you stand in a kick-boxing class in relation to others, to where you place your book bag in class, your personal expectations of space are often at variance with others.

FIGURE 5.4 Space: Four Main Categories of Distance

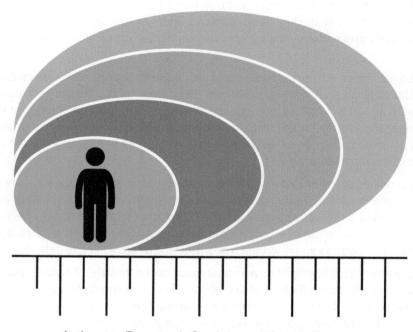

Intimate, Personal, Social, and Public Space

As the context of a staircase has norms for nonverbal behavior, so does the public speaking context. In North America, eye contact with the audience is expected. Big movements and gestures are not generally expected and can be distracting. The speaker occupies a space on the "stage," even if it's in front of the class. When you occupy that space, the audience will expect to behave in certain ways. If you talk to the screen behind you while displaying a PowerPoint presentation, the audience may perceive that you are not paying attention to them. Speakers are expected to pay attention to, and interact with, the audience, even if the feedback is primarily nonverbal. Your movements should coordinate with the tone, rhythm, and content of your speech. Pacing back and forth, keeping your hands in your pockets, or crossing your arms may communicate nervousness, or even defensiveness, and detract from your speech.

As a general rule, try to act naturally, as if you were telling a friend a story, so that your body will relax and your nonverbal gestures will come more naturally. Practice is key to your level of comfort; the more practice you get, the more comfortable and less intimidating it will seem to you.

Hall articulated four main categories of distance used in communication as shown in Figure 5.4.[12]

Time

Do you know what time it is? How aware you are of time varies by culture and normative expectations of adherence (or ignorance) of time. Some people, and the communities and cultures they represent, are very time-oriented. The Euro Railways trains in Germany are famous for departing and arriving according to the schedule. In contrast, if you take the train in Argentina, you'll find that the schedule is more of an approximation of when the train will leave or arrive.

"Time is money" is a common saying across many cultures and reveals a high value for time. In social contexts, it often reveals social status and power. Who are you willing to wait for? A doctor for an office visit when you are sick? A potential employer for a job interview? Your significant other or children? Sometimes we get impatient, and our impatience underscores our value for time.

Chronemics is the study of how we refer to and perceive time. Tom Bruneau at Radford University has spent a lifetime investigating how time interacts in communication and culture.[13],[14],[15] As he notes, across Western society, time is often considered the equivalent of money. The value of speed is highly prized in some societies.[16] In others, there is a great respect for slowing down and taking a long-term view of time.

chronemics

The study of how we refer to and perceive time.

When you order a meal at a fast food restaurant, what are your expectations for how long you will have to wait? When you order a pizza online for delivery, when do you expect it will arrive? If you order cable service for your home, when do you expect it might be installed? In the first case, you might measure the delivery of a hamburger in a matter of seconds or minutes, and perhaps thirty minutes for pizza delivery, but you may measure the time from your order to working cable in days or even weeks. You may even have to be at your home from 8 a.m. to noon, waiting for its installation. The expectations vary by context, and we often grow frustrated in a time-sensitive culture when the delivery does not match our expectations.

In the same way, how long should it take to respond to a customer's request for assistance or information? If they call on the phone, how long should they be on hold? How soon should they expect a response to an e-mail? As a skilled business communicator, you will know to anticipate normative expectations and do your best to meet those expectations more quickly than anticipated. Your prompt reply or offer of help in response to a request, even if you cannot solve the issue on the spot, is often regarded positively, contributing to the formation of positive communication interactions. It is important to note that technology has made our expectations of time much different than before. Have you ever texted someone and were irritated when you didn't get a response in a few minutes? Technology, and the quickness of communication has changed most people's view of how long it should take to respond to a text, e-mail, or social media post.

Across cultures the value of time may vary. Some Mexican American friends may invite you to a barbecue at 8 p.m., but when you arrive you are the first guest, because it is understood that the gathering actually doesn't start until after 9 p.m. Similarly, in France an 8 p.m. party invitation would be understood to indicate you should arrive around 8:30, but in Sweden 8 p.m. means 8 p.m., and latecomers may not be welcome. Some Native Americans, particularly elders, speak in well-measured phrases and take long pauses between phrases. They do not hurry their speech or compete for their turn, knowing no one will interrupt them.[17] Some Orthodox Jews observe religious days when they do not work, cook, drive, or use electricity. People around the world have different ways of expressing value for time.

Body Movements

The study of body movements, called **kinesics**, is key to understanding nonverbal communication. Since your actions will significantly contribute to the effectiveness of your business interactions, let's examine four distinct body movements that complement, repeat, regulate, or replace your verbal messages.

kinesics

The study of body movements.

Body movements can complement the verbal message by reinforcing the main idea. For example, you may be providing an orientation presentation to a customer about a software program. As you say, "Click on this tab," you may also initiate that action. Your verbal and nonverbal messages reinforce each other. You can also reinforce the message by repeating it. If you first say, "Click on the tab," and then motion with your hand to the right, indicating that the customer should move the cursor arrow with the mouse to the tab, your repetition can help the listener understand the message.

In addition to repeating your message, body movements can also regulate conversations. Nodding your head to indicate that you are listening may encourage the customer to continue asking questions. Holding your hand up, palm out, may signal them to stop and provide a pause where you can start to answer.

Body movements also substitute or replace verbal messages. Ekman and Friesen found that facial features communicate our feelings to others, but our body movements often reveal how intensely we experience those feelings.[18] For example, if the customer makes a face of frustration while trying to use the software program, they may need assistance. If they push away from the computer and separate themselves physically from interacting with it, they may be extremely frustrated. Learning to gauge feelings and their intensity as expressed by customers takes time and patience, and your attention to them will improve your ability to facilitate positive interactions.

Touch

haptics

Touch in communication interaction.

Touch in communication interaction is called **haptics**, and William Seiler and Melissa Beall[19] identify five distinct types of touch, from impersonal to intimate, as listed in Table 5.4.

TABLE 5.4 Types of Touch

Term	Definition
1. Functional-professional touch	Medical examination, physical therapy, sports coach, music teacher
2. Social-polite touch	Handshake
3. Friendship-warmth touch	Hug
4. Love-intimacy touch	Kiss between family members or romantic partners
5. Sexual-arousal touch	Sexual caressing and intercourse

Touch can show warmth, love, and caring for another. In a workplace setting, a social-polite touch, such as a handshake, shows you are friendly and open to doing business with the other person.

WATCH THIS!

Much of our nonverbal communication comes from those things that are not said. Learning how to read body language can help us become better communicators.

View the video online at: http://www.youtube.com/embed/0O3nPzuNIPo?rel=0

Paralanguage

Paralanguage is the exception to the definition of nonverbal communication. You may recall that we defined nonverbal communication as not involving words, but paralanguage exists when we are speaking, using words. **Paralanguage** involves verbal and nonverbal aspects of speech that influence meaning, including tone, intensity, pausing, and even silence.

Perhaps you've also heard of a **pregnant pause**, a silence between verbal messages that is full of meaning. The meaning itself may be hard to understand or decipher, but it is there nonetheless. For example, your coworker Jan comes back from a sales meeting speechless and with a ghost-white complexion. You may ask if the meeting went all right. "Well, ahh . . ." may be the only response you get. The pause speaks volumes. Something happened, though you may not know what. It could be personal if Jan's report was not well received, or it could be more systemic, like the news that sales figures are off by 40 percent and layoffs may not be far behind.

Silence or vocal pauses can communicate hesitation, indicate the need to gather thought, or serve as a sign of respect. Keith Basso quotes an anonymous source as stating, "It is not the case that a man who is silent says nothing."[20] Sometimes we learn just as much, or even more, from what a person does not say than what they do say. In addition, both Basso and Susan Philips found that traditional speech among Native Americans places a special emphasis on silence.[21]

paralanguage
Involves verbal and nonverbal aspects of speech that influence meaning, including tone, intensity, pausing, and silence.

pregnant pause
A silence between verbal messages that is full of meaning.

Artifacts

Artifacts are forms of decorative ornamentation that are chosen to represent self-concept. They can include rings and tattoos but may also include brand names and logos. From clothes to cars, watches, briefcases, purses, and even eyeglasses, what we choose to surround ourselves with communicates something about our sense of self. They may project gender, role or position, class or status, personality, and group membership or affiliation. For example, I have a tattoo on my forearm with a globe and plane flying around the globe. This communicates my interest in travel. Understanding the artifacts someone wears or beholds can help us understand more about them. In fact, it can be a great conversation starter when communicating with someone!

artifacts
Nonverbal representations of communication.

Why Human Relations?

How many times do we hear "we didn't communicate" or "it was a miscommunication"? Even though we are all aware of the importance communication plays in our work life, somehow these types of issues still happen. **Communication applies to human relations in that communication is really the only means we have of expressing ourselves to others.** In other words, every relationship you have built has relied on communication for it to be successful. Those relationships that may have been unsuccessful could have resulted from not understanding each other's communication style. **As you already know from this chapter, communication relates to relationship management skills as well as social awareness skills, which are part of emotional intelligence.** These are the skills that allow us to communicate with others and handle various personalities and work styles. For example, when your roommate or significant other comes home from work, it doesn't take but a second or two to see this person has had a bad day. Their facial expressions and the way they talk all point to a challenge at work. Social awareness skills help you understand this, empathize with that person, and bring up bad news—such as the fact rent is due—at a later time. These types of skills, or ability to handle social situations well, is what creates positive communication in our relationships.

The first step to applying communication skills is to understand your own style. Are you direct or indirect? Do you know how your facial expressions and other nonverbal language impact your verbal communication? When you write an e-mail, how does your communication style come across to others? Understanding (self-awareness emotional intelligence skill) our own style can help us understand our strengths and weaknesses and become better communicators. **Every successful relationship—work or personal—relies on good, open, and honest communication.**

Environment

environment

Involves the physical and psychological aspects of the communication context.

Environment involves the physical and psychological aspects of the communication context. More than the tables and chairs in an office, environment is an important part of the dynamic communication process. The perception of one's environment influences one's reaction to it. For example, Google is famous for its work environment, with spaces created for physical activity and even in-house food service around the clock. The expense is no doubt considerable, but Google's actions speak volumes. The results produced in the environment, designed to facilitate creativity, interaction, and collaboration, are worth the effort.

Key Takeaway

- Nonverbal communication can be categorized into seven types: space, time, body movements, touch, paralanguage, artifacts, and environment.

Exercises

1. Do a Google search on personal space and culture. Share your findings with your classmates.
2. To what degree is time a relevant factor in communication with technology? Give specific examples from your personal life on how you view time in context of technology.

5.4 Public Speaking as a Form of Communication

Learning Objective

1. Demonstrate how to use movement to increase the effectiveness of your presentation.

At some point in your career you will be called upon to give a presentation. It may be to a group of your colleagues about a project you are working on, or it could be in front of 100 people at a conference.

Customers and audiences respond well to speakers who are comfortable with themselves. Comfortable doesn't mean overconfident or cocky, and it doesn't mean shy or timid. It means that an audience is far more likely to forgive the occasional "umm" or "ahh," or the nonverbal equivalent of a misstep, if the speaker is comfortable with themselves and their message.

Let's start with behaviors to avoid. Who would you rather listen to, a speaker who moves confidently across the stage or one who hides behind the podium; one who expresses herself non-verbally with purpose and meaning or one who crosses his arms or clings to the lectern?

Audiences are most likely to respond positively to open, dynamic speakers who convey the feeling of being at ease with their bodies. The setting, combined with audience expectations, will give a range of movement. If you are speaking at a formal event, or if you are being covered by a stationary camera, you may be expected to stay in one spot. If the stage allows you to explore, closing the distance between yourself and your audience may prove effective. Rather than focusing on a list of behaviors and their relationship to environment and context, give emphasis to what your audience expects and what you yourself would find more engaging instead.

Novice speakers are often told to keep their arms at their sides or to restrict their movement to only that which is absolutely necessary. If you are in formal training for a military presentation or a forensics (speech and debate) competition, this may hold true. But in business and industry, "whatever works" rules the day. You can't say that expressive gestures—common among many cultural groups, like arm movement while speaking—are not appropriate when they are, in fact, expected.

The questions are, again, what does your audience consider appropriate and what do you feel comfortable doing during your presentation? Since the emphasis is always on meeting the needs of the customer, whether it is an audience of one on a sales floor or a large national gathering, you may need to stretch outside your comfort zone. On that same note, don't stretch too far and move yourself into the uncomfortable range. Finding balance is a challenge, but no one ever said giving a speech was easy.

Movement is an important aspect of your speech and requires planning, the same as the words you choose and the visual aids you design. Be natural, but do not naturally shuffle your feet, pace back and forth, or rock on your heels through your entire speech. These behaviors distract your audience from your message and can communicate nervousness, undermining your credibility.

Positions on the Stage

In a classical speech presentation, positions on the stage serve to guide both the speaker and the audience through transitions. The speaker's triangle (see Figure 5.5) indicates where the speaker starts in the introduction, moves to the second position for the first point, across for the second point, then returns to the original position to make the third point and conclusion. This movement technique can be quite effective to help you remember each of your main points. It allows you to break down your speech into manageable parts, and putting tape on the floor to indicate position is a common presentation trick. Your movement will demonstrate purpose and reinforce your credibility.

FIGURE 5.5 Speaker's Triangle

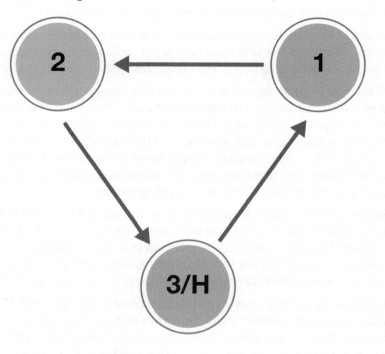

Gestures

Gestures involve using your arms and hands while communicating. Gestures provide a way to channel your nervous energy into a positive activity that benefits your speech and gives you something to do with your hands. For example, watch people in normal, everyday conversations. They frequently use their hands to express themselves. Do you think *they* think about how they use their hands? Most people do not. Their arm and hand gestures come naturally as part of their expression, often reflecting what they have learned within their community.

For professional speakers this is also true, but deliberate movement can reinforce, repeat, and even regulate an audience's response to their verbal and nonverbal messages. You want to come across as comfortable and natural, and your use of your arms and hands contributes to your presentation. We can easily recognize that a well-chosen gesture can help make a point memorable or lead the audience to the next point.

anticipation step

Raising the hand slightly to signal a nonverbal foreshadowing.

As professional speakers lead up to a main point, they raise their hand slightly, perhaps waist high, often called an **anticipation step**. The gesture clearly shows the audience your anticipation of an upcoming point, serving as a nonverbal form of foreshadowing.

implementation step

Holding one hand at waist level pointing outward and raising it up with your palm forward, as in the "stop" gesture.

The **implementation step**, which comes next, involves using your arms and hands above your waist. By holding one hand at waist level pointing outward and raising it up with your palm forward, as in the "stop" gesture, you signal the point. The nonverbal gesture complements the spoken word, and as students of speech have noted across time, audiences respond to this nonverbal reinforcement. You then slowly lower your hand down past your waistline and away from your body, letting go of the gesture and signaling your transition.

relaxation step

Lowering your hand past your waistline and away from your body.

The **relaxation step**, where the letting go motion complements your residual message, concludes the motion.

Facial Gestures

As you progress as a speaker from gestures and movement, you will need to turn your attention to facial gestures and expressions. **Facial gestures** involve using your face to display feelings and attitudes nonverbally. They may reinforce or contradict the spoken word, and their impact cannot be underestimated. As we have discussed, people often focus more on how we say something than what we actually say and place more importance on our nonverbal gestures.[22] As in other body movements, your facial gestures should come naturally, but giving them due thought and consideration can keep you aware of how you are communicating the nonverbal message.

Facial gestures should reflect the tone and emotion of your verbal communication. If you are using humor in your speech, you will likely smile and wink to complement the amusement expressed in your words. Smiling will be much less appropriate if your presentation involves a serious subject such as cancer or car accidents. Consider how you want your audience to feel in response to your message, and identify the facial gestures you can use to promote those feelings. Then practice in front of a mirror so that the gestures come naturally.

The single most important facial gesture (in mainstream US culture) is eye contact.[23] **Eye contact** refers to the speaker's gaze that engages the audience members. It can vary in degree and length and, in many cases, is culturally influenced. Both the speaker's expectations and the audience member's notion of what is appropriate will influence normative expectations for eye contact. In some cultures, there are understood behavioral expectations for male gaze directed toward females, and vice versa. In a similar way, children may have expectations of when to look their elders in the eye, and when to gaze down. Depending on the culture, both may be nonverbal signals of listening. Understanding your audience is critical when it comes to nonverbal expectations.

When giving a presentation, avoid looking over people's heads, staring at a point on the wall, or letting your eyes dart all over the place. The audience will find these mannerisms unnerving. They will not feel as connected, or receptive, to your message, and you will reduce your effectiveness. Move your eyes gradually and naturally across the audience, both close to you and toward the back of the room. Try to look for faces that look interested and engaged in your message. Do not focus on only one or two audience members, as audiences may respond negatively to perceived favoritism. Instead, try to give as much eye contact as possible across the audience. Keep it natural, but give it deliberate thought.

facial gestures

Using your face to display feelings and attitudes nonverbally.

eye contact

The speaker's gaze that engages the audience members.

Key Takeaway

- To use movement strategically in your presentation, keep it natural and consider using the speaker's triangle, the three-step sequence, facial gestures, and eye contact.

Exercises

1. Think of a message you want to convey to a listener. If you were to dance your message, what would the dance look like? Practice in front of a mirror.
2. Ask a friend to record you while you are having a typical conversation with another friend or family member. Watch the video and observe your movements and facial gestures. What would you do differently if you were making a presentation? Discuss your thoughts with a classmate.
3. Play "Lie to Me," a game in which each person creates three statements (one is a lie) and tells all three statements to a classmate or group. The listeners have to guess which statement is a lie.

5.5 Persuasion and Selling Yourself

Learning Objectives

1. Implement strategies to sell yourself.
2. Implement persuasion strategies.

Communication and Persuasion

All of us, at one time or another, will need to use communication to persuade another person. It could be persuading a client to use your services, or it may be persuading your roommate to do her share of the dishes! Persuasion is an important skill to have in our toolkit. First, let's look at the three types of persuasion, and address how we can use these techniques in our daily life.

There are three main types of persuasion, as Aristotle noted in his book, *Rhetoric*:[24]

- Ethos or credibility
- Pathos or appeal to emotion
- Logos or appeal to reason

Let's talk about each of these in turn. The first, ethos, refers to having credibility when you are communicating. For example, if you have been working in Human Resources for ten years and are persuading someone to use a set of interview questions, you can use ethos or credibility to persuade someone to do this. Consider the mother who says, "Because I'm the mom, that's why." This person is using credibility as a persuasion technique.

Appeal to emotion or pathos is another technique we can use to persuade. It can be any variety of emotion such as anger, fear, or shame. Consider how PETA (People for the Ethical Treatment of Animals) tries to persuade people to become vegetarian. Slogans like, "I'm not meat," or "your fur trim had a face" attempts to persuade people based on emotions of pity and kindness for animals. You've probably used pathos to persuade your best friend to go out by saying something like, "I really need some time with you because work is so stressful." This is persuading your friend to go out based on creating emotions within your friend which may consist of empathy.

The third form of persuasion is logos, or appeal to reason. In this type of persuasion, you might provide all of the reasons why, in logical order, they make sense. Say you are trying to get your roommate to do her share of the dishes. You might use logos to persuade her, which could sound something like, "Its hard when you make dinner and all of the dishes are dirty. If we did the dishes when we use them, we wouldn't have this problem. Also, it looks dirty and can attract bugs."

So, how can you apply each of these in your personal life in an attempt to persuade people? First, it is important to note that persuading effectively means to *never* be dishonest. This type of persuasion only lasts so long before people start to see through it. Approaching persuasion honestly and ethically is always the best policy. Here are some ideas on communication techniques[25] to persuade people, whether it be persuading your roommate to move his clothes out of the drier as soon as they are done, or something bigger, like persuading your boss to give you a high-profile project.

- **Get people to like you.** This one can take a bit of practice, but is worth doing to benefit all aspects of your work life. In his book, *How to Win Friends and Influence People*, Dale Carnegie[26] says there are several things (they are easy things!) you can do to get people to like you. First, smile. Be a good listener. Talk in terms of the other person's interest. For example, instead of saying, "I really want this project because it will be good for my career", say, "I'm a great choice for this project because I've never missed a deadline and I've proven this project is in my area of expertise." Treat people fairly, and when possible, use their name.

- **Use "I" rather than "you."** For example, rather than saying, "When you don't take clothes out of the drier, it makes me mad". Try to communicate with I, such as, "I feel stressed when I'm trying to do laundry and find clothes still in the drier." Or, in a workplace setting, "It makes me worried when deadlines are not met," instead of, "When you miss a deadline it makes it hard for me to finish my project." See how that works? Talking about how you feel, instead of telling someone else what they ought to do, can be a good communication technique to persuade people.

- **The communication channel.** We often want to persuade someone to do something—but communicate in the wrong way about it. For example, if you want that promotion, probably asking for it via e-mail isn't the best way. If you want your partner to get better about picking up their socks, talking to them in person is probably better than texting to them. Likewise, if you are negotiating a compensation package for a new job, e-mail may be the best way, so it is in writing, and it also allows time for you to think and consider counteroffers.

- **Timing.** Making sure we ask for what we want when the time is right is important. For example, asking your boss if you can take on that new project when she is not stressed is a good idea. Asking her when she is running late for a meeting would probably not be a good time. Likewise, trying to convince your partner to go to a concert he doesn't want to go to after a stressful day probably isn't the best timing. Waiting until the weekend, or after a good day might be the better option.

Source: a katz / Shutterstock.com

Selling Yourself

Whether you realize it or not, we are always selling ourselves. Selling ourselves, and learning how to persuade others go hand in hand to help predict our work success. The way we sell ourself and persuade others, is through communication—the focus of this chapter.

 WATCH THIS!

Steps to creating your elevator pitch.

View the video online at: http://www.youtube.com/embed/wVYyCUwDFhE?rel=0

- **Prepare a 30-second elevator pitch.** You walk into an elevator, and find the hiring manager of your dream job in the elevator. You have 30 seconds or less to tell him or her all about you, and leave a lasting impression. This is the purpose of the elevator pitch—a short version of you and what you bring to the table—while making a two-sided conversation.

- **Know your strengths**. It is hard to sell yourself if you can't identify what you are good at! Know what your strengths are, and more importantly, how those strengths will benefit someone else is key to selling yourself whether it be on a date or in a job interview.

- **Show, don't tell.**[27] Anyone can say they are ethical or, loves animals, to try and get what they want (a date, a job interview). Instead of telling someone, tell them a story about a time you were ethical. Or, tell them you have a dog you take for walks two times a day. These things illustrate what you are saying—making the communication more believable.

- **Be genuine.** People can tell if you say, "I love tennis too" but really you don't. Part of honesty in communications is being genuine, and should always be a priority.

- **Ask questions.** Asking questions shows interest in others, but there must be genuine interest, as we discussed above. Asking others about their kids, their likes and their dislikes, is a good way to build rapport and trust.

Understanding how your communication, including nonverbal communication, impacts others, understanding the message sent to others, and making an effort to understand and use persuasion and selling techniques can help launch your career!

 **WATCH THIS!**

Selling yourself: not used for used cars anymore!

View the video online at: http://www.youtube.com/embed/PWY4qMn12hQ?rel=0

Key Takeaways

- There are three forms of persuasion: Persuasion based on character, emotions, or logic. Use of each of these techniques will depend on individual situations.
- When trying to persuade someone, understand that likeability and timing, among others, are important factors.
- When selling yourself, have a 30-second elevator pitch ready to go.
- Knowing your own strengths can help sell yourself.

Exercises

1. Give an example of when you've used each of the three types of persuasion. Explain. Did it work? Why or why not?
2. Prepare an elevator pitch, and record it. Show it to at least two people for feedback, and make changes to your elevator pitch based on the feedback.

5.6 Chapter Summary and Case

Chapter Summary

- There are four types of communication at work: *downward*, *upward*, *horizontal*, and *diagonal*. All types of communication can happen at once, especially with the use of blogs and social networking sites.
- Companies that use good communication tend to have less turnover and less absenteeism.

- There are four main types of communication styles: *expresser*, *driver*, *relater*, and *analytical*. The better we can understand our own style of communication and the communication styles of others, the easier it will be to communicate with them.

- Passive, aggressive, and passive-aggressive behaviors are not healthy ways of communicating. Assertive behavior, on the other hand, respects one's own rights and the rights of others.

- Listening is also an important part of communication. *Active listening* occurs when we are interested in what the other person has to say, and we check with the speaker to make sure we understand what they have said. *Competitive* or *combative listening* is when we are focused on sharing our own point of view. *Passive listening* is when we listen to someone but do not verify that we understand what someone is saying.

- When sending e-mails, make sure to follow the four Cs: Complete, concise, correct, and clear.

- Nonverbal communication is the process of conveying a message without the use of words; it relates to the dynamic process of communication, the perception process and listening, and verbal communication.

- Nonverbal communication is fluid and fast, universal, confusing, and contextual. It can add to, or replace, verbal communication and can be intentional or unintentional.

- Nonverbal communication communicates feelings and attitudes, and people tend to believe nonverbal messages more than verbal ones.

- Nonverbal communication can be categorized into seven types: space, time, body movements, touch, paralanguage, artifacts, and environment.

Chapter Case

In each of the situations, identify the type of communication used (upward, downward, or horizontal). Then address the issues with the communication and strategies to improve the communication.

1. Joey is the branch manager and sends an e-mail to all of his employees, notifying them of a vacation time policy change. Employees are disappointed with this communication, as they felt they should have had some say in the way the policy has changed.

2. Mariette works on the factory floor and notified her supervisor verbally of some safety concerns. The supervisor is busy and forgets to follow up on the safety concerns.

3. Kashia works in the hospital's mental health unit and notifies her colleague via e-mail about the status of three patients. Her colleague doesn't see the e-mail until later in the day.

4. Amiee is the manager of an electronics store and leaves notes for her morning opening shift about what is expected for the day. The morning supervisor doesn't understand one of the notes, so the work does not get done.

5. At a car dealership, the parts manager and service manager need to work together to order parts needed for services scheduled the following week. This is done via a weekly meeting. However, last week's meeting was canceled, so all of the parts aren't in stock to complete the service jobs.

6. The chief executive officer used a survey to determine employee satisfaction. Only 10 percent of employees responded to the survey.

Endnotes

1. Mehrabian, A., & Ferris, S.R. (1967). Inference of attitudes from nonverbal communication in two channels, *Journal of Consulting Psychology* 31(3): 248–58.

2. Bosworth, P. (n.d.). The power of good communication in the workplace. Retrieved from https://leadershipchoice.com/power-good-communication-workplace/

3. Simply Communicate. (8 December 2015). Nokia's internal communication driven by social media. Retrieved from https://simply-communicate.com/nokias-internal-communication-driven-social-media/

4. McLean, S. (2003). *The basics of speech communication*. Boston, MA: Allyn & Bacon.

5. McLean, S. (2003). *The basics of speech communication* (p. 77). Boston, MA: Allyn & Bacon.

6. McLean, S. (2003). *The basics of speech communication* (p. 77). Boston, MA: Allyn & Bacon.

7. McLean, S. (2003). *The basics of speech communication* (p. 77). Boston, MA: Allyn & Bacon.

8. Beebe, S. [Steven], Beebe, S. [Susan], & Redmond, M. (2002). *Interpersonal communication relating to others* (3rd ed.). Boston, MA: Allyn & Bacon.

9. Mehrabian, A. (1972). *Nonverbal communication*. Chicago, IL: Aldine Atherton.

10. Seiler, W., & Beall, M. (2000). *Communication: Making connections* (4th ed.). Boston, MA: Allyn & Bacon.

11. Hall, E.T. (1963). Proxemics: The study of man's spacial relations and boundaries. In I. Galdston (Ed.), *Man's image in medicine and anthropology* (pp. 422–45). New York, NY: International Universities Press.

12. Hall, E. (1966). *The hidden dimension*. New York, NY: Doubleday.

13. Bruneau, T. (1974). Time and nonverbal communication. *Journal of Popular Culture, 8*, 658–66.

14. Bruneau, T. (1990). Chronemics: The study of time in human interaction. In J. DeVito & M. Hecht (Eds.), *The nonverbal reader* (pp. 301–11). Prospect Heights, IL: Waveland Press.

15. Bruneau, T., & Ishii, S. (1988). Communicative silence: East and west. *World Communication, 17*, 1–33.

16. Schwartz, T. (January/February 1989). Acceleration syndrome: Does everyone live in the fast lane? *Utne Reader, 31*, 36–43.

17. McLean, S. (1998). Turn-taking and the extended pause: A study of interpersonal communication styles across generations on the Warm Springs Indian reservation. In K.S. Sitaram & M. Prosser (Eds.), *Civic discourse: Multiculturalism, cultural diversity, and global communication* (pp. 213–27). Stamford, CT: Ablex Publishing Company.

18. Ekman, P., & Friesen, W. (1967). Head and body cues in the judgment of emotion: A reformulation. *Perceptual and Motor Skills, 24*, 711–24.

19. Seiler, W., & Beall, M. (2000). *Communication: Making connections* (4th ed.). Boston, MA: Allyn & Bacon.

20. Basso, K.A. (1970). To give up on words: Silence in western Apache culture. In D. Carbaugh (Ed.), *Cultural communication and intercultural contact* (pp. 301–18). Hillsdale, NJ: Laurence Erlbaum.

21. Philips, S. (1983). *The invisible culture: Communication in the classroom and community on the Warm Springs Indian Reservation*. Chicago, IL: Waveland Press.

22. Mehrabian, A. (1981). *Silent messages: Implicit communication of emotions and attitudes* (2nd ed.). Belmont, CA: Wadsworth.

23. Seiler, W., & Beall, M. (2000). *Communication: Making connections* (4th ed.). Boston, MA: Allyn & Bacon.

24. Bizzell, P. and Herzberg, B. (2000). The Rhetorical Tradition: Readings from Classical Times to the Present. NY: Bedford/St. Martin's. p. 3.

25. Cain, A. (13 November 2016). Tricks for getting people to do what you want. Retrieved from https://www.businessinsider.com/tricks-for-getting-people-to-do-what-you-want-2016-11

26. Carnegie, D. (1998). How to Win Friends and Influence People. New York: Gallery.

27. Smith, J. (15 May 2016). 5 ways to sell yourself in a job interview. Retrieved from https://www.businessinsider.com/how-to-sell-yourself-in-an-interview-2015-5

CHAPTER 6
Navigating Ethical Situations

You can fool some of the people all of the time, and all of the people some of the time, but you cannot fool all of the people all the time.

—Abraham Lincoln

Integrity is doing the right thing, even if nobody is watching.

—Unknown

Unethical, or "The Way We Do Business"?

As the assistant manager at an automotive parts chain, Jeremy has lots of experience with cars and the automotive parts business. Everyone has their own preference for car part brands, including him. When he works with customers, he might show them the other brand but tends to know more about his favorite brands and shows those brands more often. However, at the new product training seminar three weeks ago, all managers were told they would receive a bonus for every DevilsDeat brake pad they or their employees sold. Furthermore, it was recommended that managers train their employees only on the DevilsDeat products, so the managers and employees alike could earn a higher salary. Personally, Jeremy feels DevilsDeat brake pads are inferior and has had several products malfunction on him. But the company ordered this to be done, so Jeremy trained his employees on the products when he returned to the store.

Last week, a customer came in and said his seventeen-year-old daughter had been in an accident. The store had sold a defective DevilsDeat brake pad, and his daughter was almost killed. Jeremy apologized profusely and replaced the part for free. Three more times that week customers came in upset that their DevilsDeat products had malfunctioned. Jeremy replaced them each time but began to feel really uncomfortable selling an inferior product.

Jeremy called to discuss his discomfort with the district manager, who told him it was just a fluke, so Jeremy continued on as usual. Several months later, a lawsuit was filed against DevilsDeat and Jeremy's automotive parts chain because of three fatalities as a result of defective brake pads.

This story is a classic one of conflicting values between a company and an employee. This chapter will discuss some of the challenges associated with conflicting values, corporate social responsibility, and how to manage this in the workplace.

6.1 An Ethics Framework

What Are Ethics?

Before we begin our conversation on ethics, it is important to note that making ethical decisions is an emotional intelligence skill; specifically, self-management. We know that our emotional intelligence skills contribute to our career success, so learning how to make ethical decisions is imperative to development of this human relations skill.

ethics

A set of values that define right and wrong.

values

Principles or standards that a person finds desirable.

First, though, what exactly are ethics? **Ethics** is defined as a set of values that define right and wrong. Can you see the challenge with this ambiguous definition? What exactly is right and wrong? That obviously depends on the person and the individual situation, which is what makes ethics difficult to define more specifically. **Values** are defined as principles or standards that a person finds desirable. So, we can say that ethics are a set of principles that a person or society finds desirable and help define right and wrong. Often, people believe that the law defines this for us. To an extent it does, but there are many things that could be considered unethical that are not necessarily illegal, and vice versa. There are situations where something may be illegal, but also could be ethical at the same time. For example, until 2018 it was illegal for women to drive in Saudi Arabia.[1] So, if a women drove a car it would be illegal, but is it also unethical? Probably not. In fact, the unethical concern is why women weren't allowed to drive in the first place! In another example, one might consider it unethical to carry a concealed weapon into a children's play area; however, this may not be against the law.

Levels of Ethics: An Organizational Framework

While there may appear to be a difference in ethics between individuals and the organization, often individuals' ethics are shown through the ethics of an organization, since individuals are the ones who set the organization's ethics to begin with.[2] In other words, while we can discuss organizational ethics, remember that individuals are the ones who determine organizational ethics, which ties the conversation of organizational ethics into personal ethics as well. If an organization can create an ethically-oriented culture,[3] it is more likely to hire people who behave ethically. This behavior is part of human relations, in that having and maintaining good ethics is part of emotional intelligence. Of our four levels of ethics discussed next, the first two may not apply to us directly as individuals in the company. As possible leaders of an organization, however, we present all four in this section for context.

There are four main ethical levels within organizations.[4] The first level is societal issues. These are the top-level issues relating to the world as a whole, which deal with questions such as the morality of child labor worldwide. Deeper-level societal issues might include the role (if any) of capitalism on poverty, for example. Most companies do not operate at this level of ethics, although some companies, such as Tom's Shoes, feel it is their responsibility to ensure everyone has shoes to wear. As a result, their "one for one" program gives one pair of shoes to someone in need for every pair of shoes purchased. Concern for the environment, for example, would be another way a company can focus on societal-level issues. This level of ethics involves areas of emotional intelligence we have discussed; specifically, an individual's empathy and social awareness. Many companies take a stand on societal ethics in part for marketing but also because of the ethics the organization creates due to the care and concern for individuals.

Our second level of ethics is stakeholder's issues. A **stakeholder** is anyone affected by a company's actions. In this level, businesses must deal with policies that affect their customers, employees, suppliers, and people within the community. For example, this level might deal with fairness in employee wages or notification of the potential dangers of a company's product. Terranea Resort in California, for example, was sued by a class action lawsuit[5] of employees who claimed they were not paid, given rest breaks, nor provided the basic tools needed to do their jobs. This type of lawsuit would be considered a stakeholder issue, because it involves stakeholders of the company—the employees.

stakeholder

Anyone affected by a company's actions.

The third level of ethics is the internal policy issue level of ethics. In this level, the concern is internal relationships between a company and employees. Fairness in management, pay, and employee participation would all be considered ethical internal policy issues. If we work in management at some point in our careers, this is certainly an area we will have extensive control over. Creation of policies that relate to the treatment of employees relates to human relations—and retention of those employees through fair treatment. It is in the organization's best interests to create policies around internal policies that benefit the company, as well as the individuals working for them.

The last level of ethical issues is personal issues. These deal with how we treat others within our organization. For example, gossiping at work or taking credit for another's work would be considered personal issues. As an employee of an organization, we may not have as much control over societal and stakeholder issues, but we certainly have control over the personal issues level of ethics. This includes "doing the right thing." Doing the right thing affects our human relations in that if we are shown to be trustworthy when making ethical decisions, it is more likely we can be promoted, or at the very least, earn respect from our colleagues. Without this respect, our human relations with coworkers can be impacted negatively.

One of the biggest ethical challenges in the workplace is when our company's ethics do not meet our own personal ethics. For example, suppose you believe strongly that child labor should not be used to produce clothing. You find out, however, that your company uses child labor in China to produce 10 percent of your products. In this case, your personal values do not meet the societal and stakeholder values you find important. This kind of difference in values can create challenges working in a particular organization. When choosing the company or business we work for, it is important to make sure there is a match between our personal values and the values within the organization.

FIGURE 6.1 The Four Levels of Ethics in Organizations
How important is it for you to work for an organization that has values and ethics similar to yours?

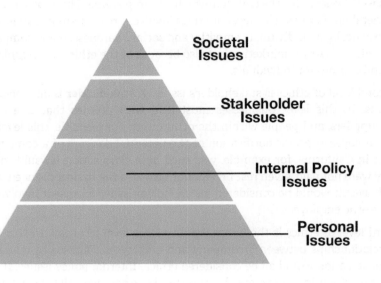

Sources of Personal Ethics

People are not born with a set of values—values develop during the aging process. We can gain our values by watching others, such as parents, friends, teachers, mentors, and siblings. The more we identify with someone, like our friend, for instance, the more likely we are to model that person's behavior. For example, if Jenny hears her best friend talk negatively about people, it is more likely she will engage in the same behavior. Besides models in life, other things that can influence our values are the following:

1. **Religion.** Religion has an influence on what is considered right and wrong. Religion can be the guiding force for many people when creating their ethical framework.

2. **Culture.** Every culture has a societal set of values. For example, in Costa Rica living a "pure life" (Pura Vita) is the country's slogan. As a result of this laid-back attitude, the culture focuses on a loose concept of time compared to the United States, for example. Similar to our models, our culture tells us what is good, right, and moral.

3. **Media.** Advertising shows us what our values "should" be. For example, if Latrice watches TV on a Thursday night, advertisements for skin creams and hair products might tell her that good skin and shiny hair are a societal value, so she may value those things, too.

4. **Models.** Our parents, siblings, mentors, coaches, and others can affect our ethics today and later in life. The way we see our models behave and the things they say affect our values.

5. **Attitudes.** Our attitudes, similar to values, start developing at a young age. As a result, our impression, likes, and dislikes affect ethics, too. For example, someone who spends a lot of time outdoors may feel a connection to the environment and try to purchase environmentally-friendly products.

6. **Experiences.** Our values can change over time depending on the experiences we have. For example, if we are bullied by our boss at work, our opinion of the right way to treat people might change when we become managers.

Our personality affects our values, as well. For example, consider your own values, such as work ethic, which is perhaps affected by the way you grew up.

Why Human Relations?

While companies may have codes of ethics and policies in place, there is no doubt that behaving ethically—with or without these codes—is a key ingredient to successful human relationships with others. As we have discussed so far throughout the book, emotional intelligence is a key component to career success. Aspects of emotional intelligence, which relate to ethics, include self-management, social awareness, and empathy. **Lacking social awareness and empathy when it comes to ethics can have disastrous effects.** For example, after the 2010 BP oil spill in the Gulf of Mexico, former CEO of BP Tony Hayward said, "I'd like my life back,"[6] but later watched yacht races, showing a lack of social awareness (how our actions affect others) and empathy. As he said this, thousands of gallons of oil were being leaked into the Gulf, affecting thousands of people living in the area. Even though Hayward apologized later, the damage had been done, as he showed his lack of social awareness and empathy for the situation. This can be taken for a sign of lack of ethics. Learning how to make ethical decisions makes us more trustworthy, honest, and caring about how our decisions affect others. When we make ethical decisions and are viewed as ethical individuals, our careers can begin to grow, and so can our relationships with others.

Sources of Company Ethics

Since we know that everyone's upbringing is different and may have had different models, religions, attitudes, and experiences, companies create policies and standards to ensure employees and managers understand the expected ethics. These sources of ethics can be based on the levels of ethics that we discussed earlier. Understanding our own and company ethics can apply to our emotional intelligence skills in the form of self-management and managing our relationships with others. Being ethical allows us to have a better relationship with our supervisors and organizations.

For example, companies create **values statements** to explain their values and which are tied to company ethics. Values statements are the organization's guiding principles, those things that the company finds important. Visit http://www.wholefoodsmarket.com/mission-values for Whole Foods' statement and view Banner Bank's core values at https://www.bannerbank.com/our-values/about-us/mission-vision.

When making decisions within our organizations, many companies have codes of conduct and ethical standards that must be abided by. This is to make sure everyone in the company follows the same ethics, since ethics can vary from person to person.

© Thinkstock

values statements

The guiding principles of the organization, those things that the organization finds important.

Examples of Ethical Situations

Have you found yourself having to make any of these ethical choices within the last few weeks?

- Cheating on exams
- Downloading music and movies from share sites
- Plagiarizing
- Breaking trust
- Exaggerating experience on a resume
- Using snapchat or other social media during company or class time
- Taking office supplies home
- Taking credit for another's work
- Gossiping
- Lying on time cards
- Conflicts of interest
- Knowingly accepting too much change
- Calling in sick when you aren't really sick
- Discriminating against people

- Taking care of personal business on company or class time
- Stretching the truth about a product's capabilities to make the sale
- Divulging private company information

What's in it for me?

Recognizing ethical situations is an important skill that is valued by organizations you work for. Consider this situation: During the COVID-19 pandemic, all employees are supposed to be working from home, and reporting actual hours worked. The company has no expectation for the number of hours worked and is paying everyone the same salary. When asked to report your hours for the week, you worked twenty-three hours at your normally forty-hour-per-week job, but got the job done. Many people might be tempted to report higher hours, just to make themselves look good. Recognizing this is an ethical situation and then consulting ethical decision-making tools can help you make the right decision on what hours to report.

▶ WATCH THIS!

A variety of ethical examples in a variety of industries.

View the video online at: http://www.youtube.com/embed/veXPk4Zeqtk?rel=0

code of conduct

A guideline for dealing with ethics in an organization.

A company publicizes its values statements but often an internal **code of conduct** is put into place in order to ensure employees follow company values set forth and advertised to the public. The code of conduct is a guideline for dealing with ethics in the organization, can outline many areas, and often companies offer training in one or more of these areas:

- Sexual harassment policy
- Workplace violence
- Employee privacy
- Misconduct off the job
- Conflicts of interest
- Insider trading

- Use of company equipment
- Company information nondisclosures
- Expectations for customer relationships and suppliers
- Policy on accepting or giving gifts to customers or clients
- Bribes
- Relationships with competition

Some companies have toll-free numbers run by outside vendors that allow employees to report ethics violations within the company anonymously. Someone who informs law enforcement of ethical or illegal violations is called a **whistleblower**. For example, after the Boeing 737 Max[7] was grounded due to a crash and other safety issues, there were reports of four former and current Boeing whistleblowers reporting on problems with the aircraft.

whistleblower
Someone who informs law enforcement of ethical or illegal violations.

FIGURE 6.2

Verizon, for example, has a forty-page code of conduct that outlines ethical expectations. This is an excerpt from that code of conduct. [8]

Maintaining Integrity and Fairness in the Workplace

Verizon's reputation depends heavily on the actions and integrity of its employees. It is imperative that you avoid any relationships or activity that might impair, or even appear to impair, your ability to make objective and fair decisions when performing your job. You owe a duty to Verizon to advance its legitimate interests when the opportunity to do so arises. You must never use Verizon property or information for personal gain or take personal advantage of any opportunity that arises in the course of your work for Verizon.

2.1   Avoiding Conflicts of Interest

You must disclose any potential or actual conflict to the VZ Ethics and EEO GuideLine. This chapter addresses some of the most common conflicts.

2.1.1   Personal Conflicts of Interest

You may not supervise someone with whom you share a close personal relationship, such as anyone in your family or household, someone with whom you have or had a romantic relationship or other close personal relationship. Nor may you participate in the selection process for, or supervise Verizon's relationship with, a company that does business with Verizon if it employs someone with whom you have such a close personal relationship.

If you supervise someone, even indirectly, with whom you have one of the relationships described above, or if you have such a relationship with an employee of a company that does business with Verizon, you must disclose the relationship promptly. In addition, you should not use your position at the company to advance your personal interests or those of a friend or relative at the expense of the company's interests.

2.1.2   Employment Outside Verizon

You may not - with or without compensation - be self-employed or employed by, consult with, own, perform services for or aid a company or organization (including a charitable organization) that is a vendor, supplier, contractor, subcontractor or competitor of Verizon, or that provides services that are provided by Verizon, or that Verizon is seeking to provide (examples of such services may include communications, cable, video, entertainment or information management, long-distance, Internet, network security, software or repair or service of computers, telephones or televisions). Outside work should not interfere with your work for Verizon. This limitation also applies to simultaneous employment by Verizon and its subsidiaries and affiliates.

Exceptions to the requirements of the previous paragraph may be granted only upon written approval by the Office of Ethics and Business Conduct.

Unless you receive the prior written approval of your supervisor and Human Resources, you may not engage in any outside employment or self-employment or perform any commercially-related services – with or without compensation – while absent from work on any company-approved leave of absence, absence due to sickness or disability, Family Medical Leave or comparable leave provided for by applicable law.

(https://www22.verizon.com/about/careers/pdfs/CodeOfConduct.pdf).

Like a person, a company can have ethics and values that should be the cornerstone of any successful business. Understanding where our ethics come from is an excellent introduction to how we can make sound personal and professional ethical decisions. Ethical decision making ties into human relations through emotional intelligence skills; specifically, self-management and relationship management. The ability to manage our ethical decision-making processes can help us make better decisions, and better decisions result in higher productivity and improved human relations. We will discuss ethical decision making and self-management in Section 2.

Key Takeaways

- *Ethics* is defined as a set of values that define right and wrong. *Values* are standards or principles that a person finds desirable.
- There are four levels of ethical issues. First, societal issues deal with bigger questions such as taking care of the environment, capitalism, or embargos. Sometimes companies get involved in societal-level ethics based on their company policies—for example, not using child labor in overseas factories.
- The second level of ethical issues is stakeholder issues. These are the things that a stakeholder might care about, such as product safety.
- Internal policy issues are the third level of ethical issues. This includes things like pay and how employees are treated.
- Personal-level ethical issues, our last level of ethical issues, refer to how we treat others within our organization.
- There are sources of personal and of company ethics. Our personal sources of ethics may come from the models we had in our childhood, such as parents, or from experiences, religion, or culture. Companies use values statements and *codes of ethics* to ensure everyone is following the same ethical codes, since ethics vary from person to person.

Exercises

1. Provide an example of each level of ethical issue and describe.
2. Create a personal values statement. This should include five to ten things you find important. Now assess your close relationships. Do they match? What can occur when your personal values do not match the values of another person?
3. Find a code of conduct online and write three paragraphs on some of the main areas of focus. Be prepared to present in small groups.
4. In our opening case, what do you think Jeremy should do and why?

6.2 Making Ethical Decisions

Learning Objective

1. Be able to explain the models you can use for ethical decision making.

Now that we have working knowledge of ethics, it is important to discuss some of the models we can use to make ethical decisions. Understanding these models can assist us in developing our self-management and relationship management skills. These models will give you the tools to make good decisions, which will likely result in better human relations within your organization.

Note that there are literally hundreds of models, but most are similar to the ones we will discuss. Most people use a combination of several models, which might be the best way to be thorough with ethical decision making. In addition, we often find ethical decisions to be quick. For example, if I am given too much change at the grocery store, I may have only a few seconds to correct the situation. In this case, our values and morals come into play to help us make this decision, since the decision making needs to happen fast.

 WATCH THIS!

Howard Gardner with the Massachusetts School of Law discusses ethics and youth.

View the video online at: http://www.youtube.com/embed/r-SE_wVoJWI?rel=0

The Twelve Questions Model

Laura Nash, an ethics researcher, created the Twelve Questions Model as a simple approach to ethical decision making.[9] In her model, she suggests asking yourself questions to determine if you are making the right ethical decision. This model asks people to reframe their perspective on ethical decision making, which can be helpful in looking at ethical choices from all angles. Her model consists of the following questions:[10]

1. Have you defined the problem accurately?
2. How would you define the problem if you stood on the other side of the fence?
3. How did this situation occur in the first place?
4. To whom and what do you give your loyalties as a person and as a member of the company?
5. What is your intention in making this decision?
6. How does this intention compare with the likely results?
7. Whom could your decision or action injure?
8. Can you engage the affected parties in a discussion of the problem before you make your decision?
9. Are you confident that your position will be as valid over a long period of time as it seems now?
10. Could you disclose without qualms your decision or action to your boss, your family, or society as a whole?
11. What is the symbolic potential of your action if understood? If misunderstood?
12. Under what conditions would you allow exceptions to your stand?

Consider the situation of Catha and her decision to take home a ream of printer paper from work, despite the company policy against taking any office supplies home. She might go through the following process, using the Twelve Questions Model:

1. My problem is that I cannot afford to buy paper. Since I do some work at home, it seems fair that I can take home the paper.

2. If I am allowed to take this paper home, others may feel the same, and that means the company is spending a lot of money on paper for people's home use.

3. It has occurred due to the fact I have so much work that I need to take some of it home, and often I need to use paper at home.

4. I am loyal to the company.

5. My intention is to use the paper for work purposes only.

6. If I take home this paper, my intention may show I am disloyal to the company and do not respect company policies.

7. The decision could injure my company and myself, in that if I get caught, I may get in trouble. This could result in loss of respect for me at work.

8. Yes, I could engage my boss and ask her to make an exception to the company policy, since I am doing so much work at home.

9. No, I am not confident of this. For example, if I am promoted at work, I may have to enforce this rule at some point. It would be difficult to enforce if I personally have broken the rule before.

10. I would not feel comfortable doing it and letting my company and boss know after the fact.

11. The symbolic action could be questionable loyalty to the company and respect for company policies.

12. An exception might be OK if I ask permission first. If I am not given permission, I can work with my supervisor to find a way to get my work done without having paper at home.

As you can see from the process, Catha came to her own conclusion by answering the questions involved in this model. The purpose of the model is to think through the situation from all sides to make sure the right decision is being made.

As you can see in this model, at first an analysis of the problem itself is important. Determining your true intention when making this decision is an important factor in making ethical decisions. In other words, what do you hope to accomplish and who can it hurt or harm? The ability to talk with affected parties upfront is telling. If you were unwilling to talk with the affected parties, there is a chance (because you want it kept secret) that it could be the wrong ethical decision. Also, looking at your actions from other people's perspectives is a core of this model.

FIGURE 6.3 Ethical Decision Making

Some of the possible approaches to ethical decision making. No one model is perfect, so understanding all of the possibilities and combining them is the best way to look at ethical decision making.

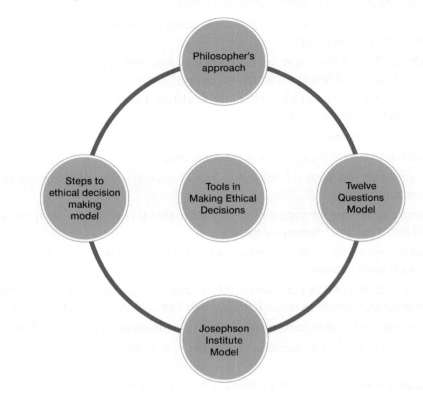

Josephson Institute of Ethics' Model

Josephson Institute of Ethics uses a model that focuses on six steps to ethical decision making. The steps consist of stop and think, clarify goals, determine facts, develop options, consider consequences, choose and monitor/modify.

As mentioned, the first step is to stop and think. When we stop to think, this avoids rash decisions and allows us to focus on the right decision-making process. It also allows us to determine if the situation we are facing is legal or ethical. When we clarify our goals, we allow ourselves to focus on expected and desired outcomes. Next, we need to determine the facts in the situation. Where are we getting our facts? Is the person who is providing the facts to us credible? Is there bias in the facts or assumptions that may not be correct? Next, create a list of options. This can be a brainstormed list with all possible solutions. In the next step, we can look at the possible consequences of our actions. For example, who will be helped and who might be hurt? Since all ethical decisions we make may not always be perfect, considering how you feel and the outcome of your decisions will help you to make better ethical decisions in the future. Figure 6.4 gives an example of the ethical decision-making process using Josephson's model.

FIGURE 6.4 An Example of Josephson's Model when Dealing with the Ethical Situation of Downloading Music from Share Websites.

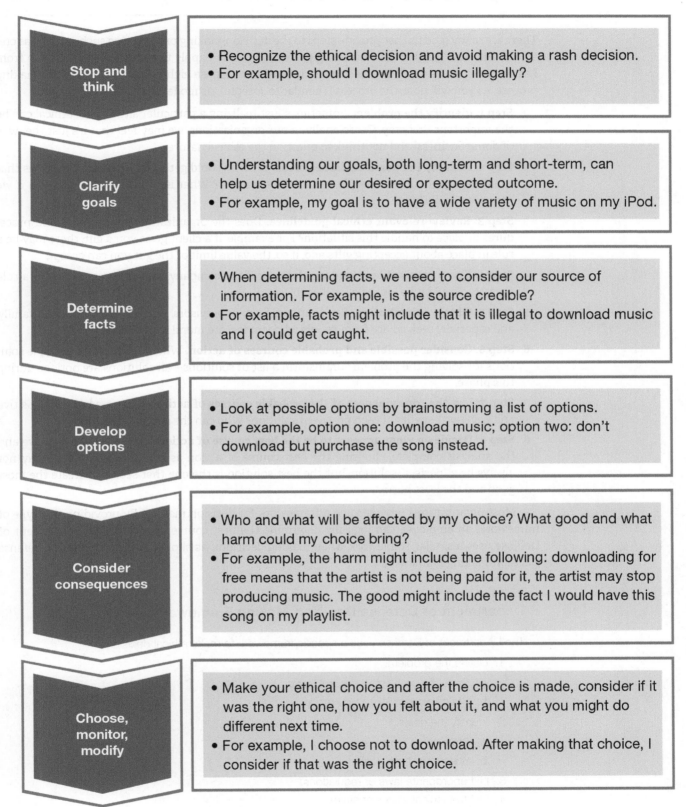

Stop and think
- Recognize the ethical decision and avoid making a rash decision.
- For example, should I download music illegally?

Clarify goals
- Understanding our goals, both long-term and short-term, can help us determine our desired or expected outcome.
- For example, my goal is to have a wide variety of music on my iPod.

Determine facts
- When determining facts, we need to consider our source of information. For example, is the source credible?
- For example, facts might include that it is illegal to download music and I could get caught.

Develop options
- Look at possible options by brainstorming a list of options.
- For example, option one: download music; option two: don't download but purchase the song instead.

Consider consequences
- Who and what will be affected by my choice? What good and what harm could my choice bring?
- For example, the harm might include the following: downloading for free means that the artist is not being paid for it, the artist may stop producing music. The good might include the fact I would have this song on my playlist.

Choose, monitor, modify
- Make your ethical choice and after the choice is made, consider if it was the right one, how you felt about it, and what you might do different next time.
- For example, I choose not to download. After making that choice, I consider if that was the right choice.

Steps to Ethical Decision Making

There are many models that provide steps to the decision-making process. One such model was created in the late 1990s for the counseling profession but can apply to nearly every profession from health care to business.[11] In this model, the authors propose eight steps to the decision-making process. As you will note, the process is similar to Josephson's model, with a few variations:

1. **Step 1: Identify the problem.** Sometimes just realizing a particular situation is ethical can be the important first step. Occasionally in our organizations, we may feel that it's just the "way of doing business" and not think to question the ethical nature.

2. **Step 2: Identify the potential issues involved.** Who could get hurt? What are the issues that could negatively impact people and/or the company? What is the worst-case scenario if we choose to do nothing?

3. **Step 3: Review relevant ethical guidelines.** Does the organization have policies and procedures in place to handle this situation? For example, if a client gives you a gift, there may be a rule in place about accepting gifts and, if so, the value limit of the gift you can accept.

4. **Step 4: Know relevant laws and regulations.** If the company doesn't necessarily have a rule against it, could it be looked at as illegal?

5. **Step 5: Obtain consultation.** Seek support from supervisors, coworkers, friends, and family, and especially seek advice from people who you feel are moral and ethical.

6. **Step 6: Consider possible and probable courses of action.** What are all of the possible solutions for solving the problem? Brainstorm a list of solutions—all solutions are options during this phase.

7. **Step 7: List the consequences of the probable courses of action.** What are both the positive and negative benefits of each proposed solution? Who can the decision affect?

8. **Step 8: Decide on what appears to be the best course of action.** With the facts we have and the analysis complete, choosing the best course of action as the final step. There may not always be a "perfect" solution, but the best solution is the one that seems to create the most good and the least harm.

Most organizations provide such a framework for decision making. By providing this type of framework, an employee can logically determine the best course of action. The Department of Defense uses a similar framework when making decisions, as shown in "Department of Defense Decision-Making Framework".

Department of Defense Decision-Making Framework

The Department of Defense uses a specific framework to make ethical decisions.[12]

1. Define the problem.
    a. State the problem in general terms.
    b. State the decisions to be made.
2. Identify the goals.
    a. State short-term goals.
    b. State long-term goals.
3. List appropriate laws or regulations.
4. List the ethical values at stake.
5. Name all the stakeholders.
    a. Identify persons who are likely to be affected by the decision.
    b. List what is at stake for each stakeholder.

6. Gather additional information.
    a. Take time to gather all necessary information.
    b. Ask questions.
    c. Demand proof when appropriate.
    d. Check your assumptions.
7. State all feasible solutions.
    a. List solutions that have already surfaced.
    b. Produce additional solutions by brainstorming with associates.
    c. Note how stakeholders can be affected (loss or gain) by each solution.
8. Eliminate unethical options.
    a. Eliminate solutions that are clearly unethical.
    b. Eliminate solutions with short-term advantages but long-term problems.
9. Rank the remaining options according to how close they bring you to your goal, and solve the problem.
10. Commit to, and implement, the best ethical solution.

Philosopher's Approach

Philosophers and ethicists believe in a few ethical standards, which can guide ethical decision making. First, the **utilitarian approach** says that when choosing one ethical action over another, we should select the one that does the most good and least harm. For example, if the cashier at the grocery store gives me too much change, I may ask myself, if I keep the change, what harm is caused? If I keep it, is any good created? Perhaps the good created is that I am not able to pay back my friend whom I owe money to, but the harm would be that the cashier could lose his or her job. In other words, the utilitarian approach recognizes that some good and some harm can come out of every situation and looks at balancing the two.

In the **rights approach**, we look at how our actions will affect the rights of those around us. So, rather than looking at good versus harm as in the utilitarian approach, we are looking at individuals and their rights to make our decision. For example, if I am given too much change at the grocery store, I might consider the rights of the corporation, the rights of the cashier to be paid for something I purchased, and the right of me personally to keep the change because it was their mistake.

The **common good approach** says that when making ethical decisions, we should try to benefit the community as a whole. For example, if we accepted the extra change in our last example but donated to a local park cleanup, this might be considered OK because we are focused on the good of the community, as opposed to the rights of just one or two people.

The **virtue approach** asks the question, "What kind of person will I be if I choose this action?" In other words, the virtue approach to ethics looks at desirable qualities and says we should act to obtain our highest potential. In our grocery store example, if given too much change, someone might think, "If I take this extra change, this might make me a dishonest person—which I don't want to be."

utilitarian approach

An ethical standard that says, when choosing one ethical action over another, we should select the one that does the most good and least harm.

rights approach

An ethical standard that says we look at how our actions will affect the rights of those around us.

common good approach

An ethical standard that says, when making ethical decisions, we should try to benefit the community as a whole.

virtue approach

An ethical standard that looks at desirable qualities and says we should act to obtain our highest potential.

The common good approach to ethics is similar to Robin Hood's approach. Steal from the rich to give to the poor, because that was better for the common good. What do you think are the challenges or downsides to this approach?

© Thinkstock

The imperfections in these approaches are threefold:[13]

- Not everyone will necessarily agree on what is harm versus good.
- Not everyone agrees on the same set of human rights.
- We may not agree on what a common good means.

Because of these imperfections, it is recommended to combine several approaches discussed in this section when making ethical decisions. If we consider all approaches and ways to make ethical decisions, it is more likely we will make better ethical decisions. By making better ethical decisions, we improve our ability to self-manage, which at work can improve our relationships with others.

Key Takeaways

- We can use a variety of models and frameworks to help us in ethical decision making. For example, one such model is the Twelve Questions Model. This model encourages us to ask questions, such as who this decision affects, to determine the best ethical choice.
- Josephson's model consists of six steps. They include stop and think, clarify goals, determine facts, develop options, consider consequences, choose and monitor/modify.
- Another model discussed has the following steps: identify the problem, identify the potential issues involved, review relevant ethical guidelines, know relevant laws and regulations, obtain consultation, consider possible and probable courses of action, list the consequences of the probable courses of action, and decide on what appears to be the best course of action.
- Philosophers look at ethical frameworks following a *utilitarian approach*, *common good approach*, *rights approach*, and the *virtue approach*. These approaches provide a framework for sound ethical decision making.

Exercises

1. Think of a recent ethical decision you have made. Using the model or framework of your choice, discuss how you went through the process of making a sound ethical decision.
2. What are the strengths and weaknesses of each model presented in this section? How can you combine them all to make ethical decisions?

6.3 Social Responsibility

Learning Objective

1. Explain and give examples of the levels of social responsibility in your professional and personal life.

No chapter on ethics would be complete without a discussion on social responsibility. People, not only companies, can engage in social responsibility. Being socially responsible shows both social awareness and self-management skills—that is, an awareness of how our decisions affect others. This section will first discuss social responsibility on the corporate level and then social responsibility on the individual level. As we discussed with ethical company standards, it is difficult to separate corporate ethics and corporate social responsibility from individual ethics and social responsibility, since people are the ones making the corporate policies. For purposes of this section, we will first discuss social responsibility on the corporate level and then on the individual level.

Since social responsibility was first mentioned in the 1960s, companies have felt pressure from society to behave in a more socially responsible manner. **Corporate social responsibility (CSR)** is the duty of business to do no harm to society. In other words, in their daily operations, businesses should be concerned about the welfare of society and mindful of how its actions could affect society as a whole. We know that social responsibility doesn't always happen, despite the seemingly best efforts of a company. For example, court papers accuse British Petroleum (BP) of gross negligence for safety violations and knowingly failing to maintain the oil rig, which caused the death of eleven workers and leaked oil into the Gulf of Mexico for eighty-seven days.[14] In this case, and others like it, people question the ability of companies to fulfill their duty to society. Ideally, companies should look at four main areas of social responsibility and act ethically in all four areas. In fact, even as individuals we should be aware of these areas of social responsibility, which we will discuss in this section. Those four areas are the following:[15]

> **corporate social responsibility (CSR)**
>
> The duty of business to do no harm to society.

1. **Economic aspects.** Companies need to maintain strong economic interests so they can stay in business. Being profitable and providing value to shareholders is part of a company being socially responsible.

2. **Legal aspects.** A company must follow the law and have a legal obligation to do so. For example, automobile companies are required to meet a certain level of emissions standards in car automobile production.

3. **Ethical aspects.** Acting ethically means going above and beyond the legal requirements and meeting the expectations of society. A notable example is Apple Inc., as their policies were questioned when it was discovered that workers producing iPhones in the Chinese Foxconn factory. As a result of the newfound awareness, Foxconn raised the salary for workers from 900 yuan ($143) to 1,800 yuan.[16] In other words, the ethical expectations (and outrage) of society can encourage companies to act ethically.

4. **Philanthropic aspects.** This is the expectation that companies should give back to society in the form of charitable donations of time, money, and goods. Some organizations such as REI, based in Seattle, Washington, donate 3 percent of profit and thousands of hours to nonprofit community groups each year.[17]

Based on these areas of social responsibility, many people believe business should go above and beyond the law to act ethically, meet expectations of society, and even go beyond by donating profit back to the communities in which the businesses operate. As we mentioned at the start of this section, businesses are not the only ones who engage in social responsibility. Since people run businesses, often we see business social responsibility initiatives that are directly related to individuals in the organization. For example, Ross Lohr, Project Repat co-founder,[18] started his company when doing non-profit educational work in Kenya, and saw people there wearing t-shirts that had been sent overseas. He saw an opportunity to help others and build a business, when he started a company that re-purposes people's t-shirts into quilts.

FIGURE 6.5 The Four Areas of Social Responsibility
Companies should strive to meet all areas of social responsibility.

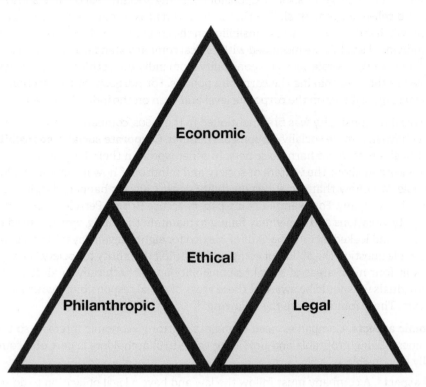

More recently, social responsibility has been looked at as going above and beyond even philanthropy. Past ideas on social responsibility implied that businesses must trade off social responsibility for profits—in other words, in order to make profit, businesses had to actually harm society. This way of thinking has changed with the idea of creating shared value. This concept, created by Michael E. Porter and Mark R. Kramer of Harvard University, attempts to dispel this myth by presenting a new view on social responsibility.[19] **Creating shared value (CSV)** is the premise that companies and the community are tied closely together, and if one benefits, they both benefit. For example, if companies donate money to schools, it actually benefits both the community and the company in that a better educated workforce can be profitable for the company in the long run. The idea that social responsibility is something that costs companies money is no longer in favor. In fact, behaving socially responsibly can help a company save money. Small things, such as turning off computers at night, result in cost savings in electricity and are the right thing to do from a social responsibility perspective, too. As Porter and Kramer have pointed out through their research, benefiting the community does not have to be at the cost of the company or of society; both can work in tandem.

> **◯ Watch This!**
>
> Erik Joule, senior vice president of merchandising and design for Levi Strauss, discusses social responsibility issues.
>
>
>
> View the video online at: http://www.youtube.com/embed/UYMBqVqEhss?rel=0

As we have already discussed, even though we say companies are socially responsible (or not), individuals in the organization are the ones who create policies surrounding social responsibility efforts. As individuals, our emotional intelligence skills, such as social awareness and empathy, can be shown through our use of social responsibility efforts within an organization but also through our personal social responsibility efforts. **Individual social responsibility (ISR)** is defined as an individual being aware of how personal actions have an effect on the community. ISR can include the following:

> **individual social responsibility (ISR)**
>
> An individual's awareness of how personal actions have an effect on the community.

1. Charitable acts, including donation of money.
2. Working for the community, such as volunteering, donating blood, and working at a food bank or animal shelter.
3. Supporting issues that affect society, such as advocating for political or social issues that can help others—for example, advocating for child labor laws, purchasing fair trade products, recycling.
4. Individual ethics, such as integrity and honesty. These individual ethics can also include the "golden rule": treat others how you wish to be treated; i.e., with empathy and a sense of fairness.

Based on this, many companies now focus on the triple bottom line,[20] which entails:

- Profit, the economic bottom line (traditional profit)
- Planet, the environmental bottom line (how well are we taking care of natural resources?)
- People, the social bottom line (how well we treat our people)

This new way of looking at organizations focuses companies on the social responsibility lens, instead of the profit-only lens that has been used extensively in the past. As employees, we can contribute to social responsibility personally and through our companies, as we've discussed in this section.

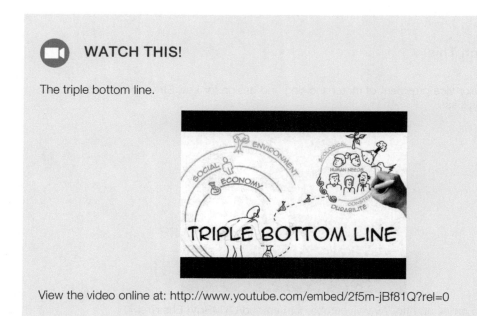

WATCH THIS!

The triple bottom line.

View the video online at: http://www.youtube.com/embed/2f5m-jBf81Q?rel=0

Engaging in ISR activities such as these can help us develop our emotional intelligence skills through the use of social awareness—that is, understanding how our actions can affect others and engaging in empathy for others. In addition, we can build our self-esteem and self-perception by helping others[21] and engaging in socially-responsible activities. As we have discussed throughout the chapter, to improve human relations skills, we must understand that ethics, social responsibility, and emotional intelligence skills are intertwined with each other. Those who continually develop their emotional intelligence skills will likely engage in ethical and socially responsible behavior, both personally and as leaders of their organizations.

FIGURE 6.6 Some Examples of Individual Social Responsibility

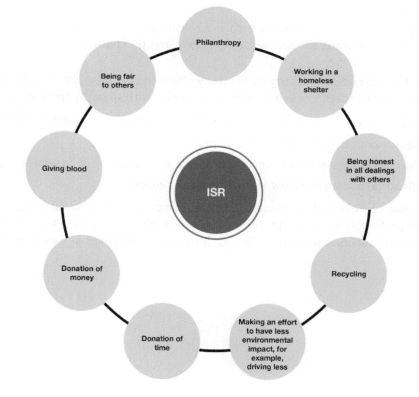

Key Takeaways

- *Social responsibility* is defined as the duty of business to do no harm to society.
- There are four levels of social responsibility: economics, or the responsibility of the business to be profitable; the responsibility to meet legal obligations—businesses must comply with the law and regulations; companies have a responsibility to act ethically and morally and to choose the action that causes the least, if any, harm; and finally, philanthropic responsibility is the idea that businesses should give back, either in time, money, or goods, to the community in which they serve.
- People used to believe that the relationship between social responsibility and the community was an inverse one, where if companies benefited society, it came at economic cost to them. Recent research has pointed out that, in fact, creating shared value (CSV) actually benefits both parties and not at a cost to one or the other.
- *ISR or individual social responsibility* refers to our awareness of how our actions affect the community as a whole. ISR can include volunteering time, giving money, and standing up for issues that affect the rights of others. The triple bottom line refers to people, profit, and planet and reminds organizations to consider other aspects besides only profit in its operations.

Exercises

1. Name and discuss at least two companies you believe to be socially responsible. Address each of the four areas of social responsibility in your discussion.
2. Is it possible for companies to be socially responsible in one area but not another? Provide an example and explain.

6.4 Chapter Summary and Case

Chapter Summary

- *Ethics* is defined as a set of values that define right and wrong. *Values* are standards or principles that a person finds desirable.
- There are four levels of ethical issues. First, societal issues deal with bigger questions such as taking care of the environment, capitalism, or embargos. Sometimes companies get involved in societal-level ethics based on their company policies—for example, not using child labor in overseas factories.
- The second level of ethical issues is stakeholder issues. These are the things that a stakeholder might care about, such as product safety.
- Internal policy issues are the third level of ethical issues. This includes things like pay and how employees are treated.
- Personal-level ethical issues refer to how we treat others within our organization.
- There are sources of personal and of company ethics. Our personal sources of ethics may come from models we had in our childhood, such as parents, or they could come from experiences, religion, or culture. Companies use values statements and *codes of ethics* to ensure everyone is following the same ethical codes, since ethics vary from person to person.

- We can use a variety of models and frameworks to help us in ethical decision making. For example, one such model is the Twelve Questions Model. This model encourages us to ask questions, such as who this decision affects, to determine the best ethical choice.

- Josephson's model consists of six steps. They include stop and think, clarify goals, determine facts, develop options, consider consequences, choose and monitor/modify.

- Another model discussed has the following steps: identify the problem, identify the potential issues involved, review relevant ethical guidelines, know relevant laws and regulations, obtain consultation, consider possible and probable courses of action, list the consequences of the probable courses of action, and decide on what appears to be the best course of action.

- Philosophers look at ethics in a framework following a *utilitarian approach*, *common good approach*, *rights approach*, and the *virtue approach*. These approaches provide a framework for sound ethical decision making.

- *Social responsibility* is defined as the duty of business to do no harm to society.

- There are four levels of social responsibility. First is economics, or the responsibility of the business to be profitable. Second is the responsibility to meet legal obligations. Businesses must comply with the law and regulations. Next, companies have a responsibility to act ethically and morally, and to choose the action that causes the least, if any, harm. Finally, philanthropic responsibility is the idea that businesses should give back—either in time, money, or goods—to the community in which they serve.

- People used to believe that the relationship between social responsibility and the community was an inverse one, where if companies benefited society, it came at economic cost to them. Recent research has pointed out that, in fact, creating shared value (CSV) actually benefits both parties and not at a cost to one or the other.

Chapter Case

Damon has just been promoted to program manager in his digital marketing agency. As program manager, he is responsible for working with vendors to provide services to his clients. One part of his job is to screen out potential vendors for clients and then make overall recommendations and provide project plans to the client based on his selected vendors. This relationship is important because the client places an immense amount of trust in the vendor choices made. Damon, with his straightforward communication style, is talented in picking and choosing the best vendors for the client, which was one reason he was hired. The nature of the job requires Damon to often meet with potential vendors and salespeople. One late afternoon, a vendor meeting with Valerie runs into dinnertime. Valerie asks Damon if he wants to have a drink and some appetizers while they continue discussing the services the vendor has to offer. They go next door to a pub and continue their discussion. When the check comes, Damon picks it up and then Valerie says, "No, you can't pay for this. I got it." Damon hands her the check and thanks her for dinner.

Later that week, after Damon has met with all possible vendors for the project, he decides to go with Valerie's company. They provide the highest-quality services at the best price. In fact, their pricing is about 10 percent less while the services they will provide get rave reviews from other clients. Damon is confident it is the right choice. When Damon goes to the project manager with this decision, the project manager, Janet, says she prefers not to work with that vendor, then asks, "Didn't Valerie take you to dinner the other night?"

Damon replies, "Yes, but that isn't why I choose them to be our vendor for this project." Janet doesn't respond and turns back to her computer and asks Damon to explain why Valerie's company is better.

1. What is the potential conflict of interest in this case?

2. How can outside perception impact our ethical choices? Should outside perception affect our choices at work?

3. Using one of the models discussed in the chapter, address how Damon should have gone about making this ethical choice.

Endnotes

1. Alexander, C. (18 January 2019). On women's rights, uneven progress in the Middle East. Retrieved from https://www.bloomberg.com/news/articles/2019-01-11/on-women-s-rights-uneven-progress-in-the-middle-east-quicktake

2. Brown, M. (2010). Ethics in organizations. Santa Clara University. http://www.scu.edu/ethics/publications/iie/v2n1/

3. Sims, R.R. (1991). *Journal of Business Ethics*, *10*(7), 493–506

4. Rao Rama, V.S. (17 April 2009). The levels of ethics. Citeman Network. Retrieved from http://www.citeman.com/5358-four-levels-of-ethical-questions-in-business.html

5. AP Wire. (30 April 2019). Terranea agrees to pay over $2m to settle workers wage lawsuit. Retrieved from https://www.apnews.com/BusinessWire/ccbcb4db6dd94276b6374247d969fea3

6. Durando, J. (1 June 2010). BP's Tony Hayward: I'd like my life back, *USA Today*. Retrieved from http://content.usatoday.com/communities/greenhouse/post/2010/06/bp-tony-hayward-apology/1

7. Van Cleave, K. (29 April 2019). At least four whistleblower calls made to FAA about Boeing 737 Max. Retrieved from https://www.cbsnews.com/news/boeing-737-max-8-at-least-4-potential-whistleblower-calls-made-to-faa-about-jetliner/

8. Verizon Code of Conduct. Accessed January 22, 2020.

9. Nash, L. (1981). Ethics without the sermon. *Howard Business Review*, *59*, 79–90, Retrieved from http://www.cs.bgsu.edu/maner/heuristics/1981Nash.htm

10. Nash, L. (1981). Ethics without the sermon. *Howard Business Review*, *59*, 79–90, Retrieved from http://www.cs.bgsu.edu/maner/heuristics/1981Nash.htm

11. Corey, G., Corey, M.S., & Callanan, P. (1998). *Issues and ethics in the helping professions.* Toronto: Brooks/Cole Publishing Company; Syracuse School of Education. (n.d.). An ethical decision making model, accessed February 24, 2012, http://soe.syr.edu/academic/counseling_and_human_services/modules/Common_Ethical_Issues/ethical_decision_making_model.aspx

12. United States Department of Defense. (1999). Joint Ethics Regulation DoD 5500.7-R.. Retrieved from http://csweb.cs.bgsu.edu/maner/heuristics/1999USDepartmentOfDefense.htm and http://ogc.hqda.pentagon.mil/EandF/Documentation/ethics_material.aspx

13. Santa Clara University. (n.d.). A framework for thinking ethically. Retrieved from http://www.scu.edu/ethics/practicing/decision/framework.html

14. United Press International. (24 February 2012). BP trial will push gross negligence claim. Retrieved from http://www.upi.com/Business_News/2012/02/24/BP-trial-will-push-gross-negligence-claim/UPI-22771330126860/

15. Carroll, A. (n.d.). The pyramid of corporate social responsibility. *Business Horizons.* Retrieved from http://cf.linnbenton.edu/bcs/bm/gusdorm/upload/Pyramid of Social Responsibility.pdf

16. Eaton, K. (24 February 2012). Apple and Foxconn's ethics hit your gadget prices. *Fast Company.* Retrieved from http://www.fastcompany.com/1819874/apple-and-foxconns-ethics-hit-your-gadget-prices?partner=gnews

17. REI Website. (n.d.). Retrieved from http://www.rei.com/jobs/environ.html

18. Lohr, R. (7 October 2018). Project Repat: $10MM Business Making Quilts From Old T-Shirts. https://www.starterstory.com/stories/project-repat

19. Porter, M.E., & Kramer, M.R. (January 2011). Creating shared value. *Harvard Business Review*, accessed February 24, 2012, http://hbr.org/2011/01/the-big-idea-creating-shared-value

20. Elkington, J. (2018). 25 Years Ago I Coined the Phrase "Triple Bottom Line." Here's Why It's Time to Rethink It. *Harvard Business Review*.

21. Bénabou, R. & Tirole, J. (2010). Individual and corporate social responsibility. *Economica, 77*, 1–19.

CHAPTER 7
Understanding Your Motivations

A champion needs a motivation above and beyond winning.

—Pat Riley

Ability is what you're capable of doing. Motivation determines what you do. Attitude determines how well you do it.

—Raymond Chandler

Prioritizing Your Motivations

Brenden decided to go to college with one goal in mind: to get a job where he could make lots of money. His hope was that the job would allow him to live in a large house, drive a nice car, and take two nice vacations per year. Once he graduated, he accepted a sales job that afforded him these things.

After five years on the job, Brenden realized he was working all the time, and didn't really enjoy his job anymore. Even though he was making lots of money, he still didn't feel satisfied. He barely had time to use the lake cabin he had purchased, and last summer only used his boat twice because he was always working. He also didn't enjoy working with clients, which was a major part of his job. Brenden then sat down and made a list of all the things important to him in life.

The more Brenden looked at his list, the more he realized what he wanted wasn't lots of money as he had thought. Other things, as he grew in his career, were far more important to him. For example, he realized he'd rather spend time with his wife and newborn son, and preferred not to travel for work as his job currently required him to do. He wanted more time to use his lake cabin, and good health insurance was important as his baby grows.

Brenden's situation is common. Often, people think they are motivated by money, but when they step back, they realize that money is just one part of a person's overall satisfaction at work. For years, managers have tried to motivate people based on money, but research has shown this can only be effective to an extent. Other things, such as flexible schedules or more vacation time, can motivate people more than a pay raise. Also, a good work–life balance is important as well. This is the topic of our chapter—human motivation and developing an understanding of what motivates you. Knowing what motivates you as you select a career path can help you be a successful, happy employee later on.

7.1 Human Motivation at Work

Learning Objectives

1. Be able to discuss why you or others may not be satisfied at work.
2. Be able to explain how the human motivation theories apply to you.

Theories on Job Dissatisfaction

There are a number of theories that attempt to describe what makes a satisfied employee versus an unsatisfied employee. Knowing what motivates us—and what doesn't—is the key to choosing the right career path. It may be surprising, but much of what makes us satisfied or unsatisfied at work has little to do with money. We will discuss theories of motivation next.

Progression of Job Withdrawal

Have you ever felt unhappy at a job? If you have, consider how you went through the process of being unhappy—because for most of us, we start out happy but then gradually become unhappy. One of the basic theories is the progression of job withdrawal theory, developed by Dan Farrell and James Petersen.[1] It says that people develop a set of behaviors in order to avoid their work situation. These behaviors include behavior change, physical withdrawal, and psychological withdrawal.

Within the behavior change area, an employee will first try to change the situation that is causing the dissatisfaction. For example, if the employee is unhappy with the management style, he or she might consider asking for a department move. In the physical withdrawal phase, the employee does one of the following:

*   Leaves the job;
*   Takes an internal transfer;
*   Begins to be absent or tardy.

If an employee is unable to leave the job situation, he or she will experience psychological withdrawal. They will become disengaged and may show less job involvement and commitment to the organization, which can lead to high costs to the organization in terms of dissatisfied customers and lost productivity.

Often, our process of job withdrawal has to do with our lack of motivation, which we will discuss in the next section.

FIGURE 7.1 Process of Job Withdrawal

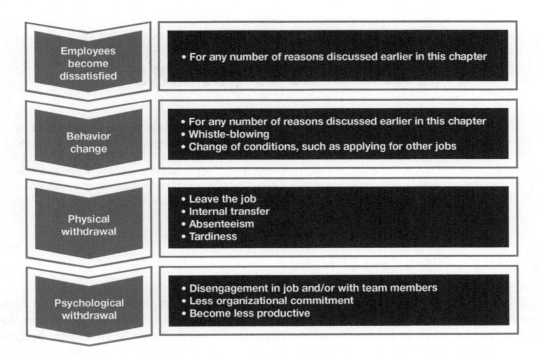

Theories on Human Motivation

Hawthorne Studies

Between 1927 and 1932, a series of experiments were conducted by Elton Mayo in the Western Electric Hawthorne Works in Illinois.[2] Mayo developed these experiments to see how physical and environmental factors of the workplace, such as lighting and break times, would affect employee motivation.

This was some of the first research that looked at human motivation at work. Mayo's results were surprising, as he found that no matter which experiments were performed, worker output improved. His conclusion and explanation for this was the simple fact that workers were happy to receive attention from researchers who expressed interest in them. As a result, these experiments, scheduled to last one year, extended to five years to increase the knowledge base about human motivation.

The implication of this research applies to us as employees, even today. It tells us that our supervisors and managers should try to do things that make us feel valued.

What's in it for me?

Did you know that work–life balance is one of the top predictors of happiness? Work–life balance refers to the ability to expend time in all areas of our life: work, friends, family, and hobbies. Work–life balance results in having a sense of purpose, belonging, and can help us achieve personal growth.[3] Do you have a work–life balance? If you don't, what are some ways you can achieve this to help your motivation at work? Determining this, and putting together a strategy to create work–life balance, can help you be a happier person in all aspects of your life.

Maslow's Hierarchy of Needs

In 1943, Abraham Maslow developed what was known as the theory of human motivation.[4] His theory was developed in an attempt to explain human motivation. According to Maslow, there is a hierarchy of five needs, and as one level of need is satisfied, it will no longer be a motivator. In other words, people start at the bottom of the hierarchy and work their way up. Maslow's hierarchy consists of the following:

- Self-actualization needs;
- Esteem needs;
- Social needs;
- Safety needs;
- Physiological needs.

Physiological needs are our most basic needs, and include food, water, and shelter. Safety needs at work might include feeling safe in the actual physical environment or job security. As humans, we have the basic need to spend time with others, which is a social need. Esteem needs refers to the need we have to feel good about ourselves. Finally, self-actualization needs are the needs we have to better ourselves.

The implications of his research tell us, for example, that as long as our physiological needs are met, increased pay may not be a motivator. Needs might include, for example, fair pay, safety standards at work, opportunities to socialize, compliments to help raise our esteem, and training opportunities to further develop ourselves.

 **WATCH THIS!**

This video explains Maslow's hierarchy in detail. After reviewing the video, which of Maslow's needs are you currently focused on?

View the video online at: http://www.youtube.com/embed/CF2c1q_OvdE?rel=0

Herzberg Two-Factor Theory

In 1959, Frederick Herzberg published *The Motivation to Work*,[5] which described his studies to determine which aspects in a work environment caused satisfaction or dissatisfaction. He performed interviews in which employees were asked what pleased and displeased them about their work. From his research, he developed the motivation-hygiene theory to explain these results.

The things that satisfied employees were motivators, while the dissatisfiers were the hygiene factors. He further said the hygiene factors were not necessarily motivators, but if not present in the work environment, they would actually cause demotivation. In other words, the hygiene factors are expected and assumed, while they may not necessarily motivate.

His research showed the following as the top six **motivation factors**:

1. Achievement;
2. Recognition;
3. The work itself;
4. Responsibility;
5. Advancement;
6. Growth.

The following were the top six **hygiene factors**:

1. Company policies;
2. Supervision;
3. Relationship with manager;
4. Work conditions;
5. Salary;
6. Relationship with peers.

The implication of this research is clear. Salary, for example, is on the hygiene factor list. Fair pay is expected, but it doesn't actually motivate us to do a better job. On the other hand, programs to further develop us as employees, such as management training programs, would be considered

motivation factor

Part of a theory developed by Herzberg that says some things will motivate an employee, such as being given responsibility.

hygiene factor

Part of a theory developed by Herzberg that says some things will not necessarily motivate employees but will cause dissatisfaction if not present.

a motivator. Therefore, the actual motivators tend to be the work and recognition surrounding the work performed.

McGregor's Theory

theory X manager

According to McGregor, a type of manager who has a negative approach to employee motivation.

Douglas McGregor proposed the X–Y theory in his 1960 book *The Human Side of Enterprise*.[6] McGregor's theory gives us a starting point to understanding how management style can impact the retention of employees. His theory suggests two fundamental approaches to managing people. **Theory X managers**, who have an authoritarian management style, have the following fundamental management beliefs:

- The average person dislikes work and will avoid it.
- Most people need to be threatened with punishment to work toward company goals.
- The average person needs to be directed.
- Most workers will avoid responsibility.

theory Y manager

According to McGregor, a type of manager who has a positive approach to employee motivation.

Theory Y managers, on the other hand, have the following beliefs:

- Most people want to make an effort at work.
- People will apply self-control and self-direction in pursuit of company objectives.
- Commitment to objectives is a function of expected rewards received.
- People usually accept and actually welcome responsibility.
- Most workers will use imagination and ingenuity in solving company problems.

As you can see, these two belief systems have a large variance, and managers who manage under the X theory may have a more difficult time retaining workers because of their management style.

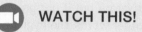 **WATCH THIS!**

Dan Pink talks about motivation in today's business world.

View the video online at: http://www.youtube.com/embed/rrkrvAUbU9Y?rel=0

Carrot and Stick

It is unknown for sure when this term was first used, although some believe it was coined in the 1700s during the Seven Years' War. In business today, the stick approach refers to "poking and prodding" to get employees to do something. The carrot approach refers to the offering of some reward or incentive to motivate employees. Many companies use the stick approach, as in the following examples:

- If you don't increase your sales by 10 percent, you will be fired.
- Everyone will have to take a pay cut if we don't produce 15 percent more than we are currently producing.
- If safety doesn't improve, everyone will have to retake the safety classes.

As you can imagine, the stick approach does little to motivate us in the long term! While it may work for some time, constant threats and prodding do not motivate.

The carrot approach might include the following:

- If you increase sales by 10 percent, you will receive a bonus.
- If production increases by 15 percent, the entire team will receive an extra day off next month.
- If safety improves, everyone will receive a bonus of $100.

The carrot approach normally means some incentive will occur if expectations are met. The expectations should be attainable and shouldn't be the only method used in retention planning and turnover reduction.

The carrot approach takes a much more positive approach to employee motivation but still may not be effective. For example, this approach can actually demotivate employees if they do not feel the goal is achievable. Has this ever happened to you at work? Some reward was offered, but you knew it wasn't really achievable? If so, you know how this can actually be demotivating! For example, what if your company said everyone would achieve a share of the profit if the profit is over 50 percent. This might not seem achievable, so even though this was meant to motivate, it could actually demotivate due to the fact it isn't achievable. If organizations use this as the only motivational technique, ignoring physiological rewards such as career growth, this could be a detriment as well.

All the employee satisfaction theories we have discussed have implications for our own understanding of what motivates us at work.

© Thinkstock

Why Human Relations?

Do you know why you do the things you do? **The emotional intelligence skill of self-awareness is the key to understanding your own motivations.** It isn't until we understand our own emotions that we can begin to understand what we need to do to motivate ourselves personally and professionally.

Of course, the more motivated we are, the more likely we are to experience career success. Most, if not all, managers want to hire and promote people who show extensive motivation in their job. This is impossible to do if we do not first identify what actually motivates us as individuals. If you are motivated by intrinsic rewards, such as feeling good about your job, you are more likely to be better at your job because you enjoy it! Not only will we be better at our job if we like it, but it is highly likely we will be happier. **When we are happier we tend to show better human relations skills**, and this happiness can come in part from understanding our own motivations and making sure we choose a career path that matches our motivations.

Why Does Motivation Matter?

This section gave you some ideas on the process people go through when they are not satisfied at work. In addition, we discussed motivation and the various motivational theories that can help us understand our own motivations. But why is this important? As you saw in the opening story, if we understand our own motivations, we can better choose a career path that will make us happy. Also, keep in mind that your motivations may change over time. For example, as a college student your motivation may lie in the ability to make money, but after working for a few years, your motivation may change to look at more flexibility in your job. It is important to keep your motivations, needs, and wants in check, because what you want today will change over time. Consider the recent twenty-two-year-old college graduate. What his priorities are today will change as his life changes; for example, meeting a significant other and maybe raising a family can make his priorities change when he is thirty-two. To continually understand our motivations, it is important to keep track, perhaps on a yearly basis, of what our priorities are. This can help us make the right career choices throughout our careers.

Key Takeaways

- The theory of job withdrawal explains the process someone goes through when they are not motivated, or happy, at work.
- There are many motivation theories that attempt to explain people's motivation or lack of motivation at work.
- The Hawthorne studies were a series of studies beginning in 1927 that initially looked at physical environments but found that people tended to be more motivated when they felt cared about. The implications to retention are clear, in that employees should feel cared about and developed within the organization.
- Maslow's theory on motivation says that if someone already has a need met, giving them something to meet more of that need will no longer motivate. Maslow divided the needs into physiological, safety, social, esteem, and self-actualization needs. Many companies only motivate based on the low-level needs, such as pay. Development of training opportunities, for example, can motivate employees on high-level self-actualization needs.
- Herzberg developed motivational theories based on actual motivation and hygiene factors. Hygiene factors are those things that are expected in the workplace and will demotivate employees when absent but will not actually motivate when present. If managers try to motivate only on the basis of hygiene factors, turnover can be high. Motivation on both of Herzberg's factors is key to a good retention plan.
- McGregor's theory on motivation looked at managers' attitudes toward employees. He found that theory X managers had more of a negative view of employees, while theory Y managers had a more positive view. Providing training to the managers in our organization can be a key retention strategy based on McGregor's theory.
- The carrot-and-stick approach means you can get someone to do something by prodding or by offering some incentive to motivate them to do the work. This theory implies these are the only two methods to motivate, which, of course, we know isn't true. The implication of this in our retention plan is such that we must utilize a variety of methods to retain employees.
- Finally, understanding our own motivations at work is an important step to making sure we choose the right career path.

Exercises

1. What types of things do you think will motivate you in your career? Name at least five things. Where would these fit on Maslow's hierarchy of needs and Herzberg's two-factor theory?
2. Have you ever been unhappy at a job? Or, if you haven't worked, have you ever felt unhappy in a specific team or group? Consider this experience and write about how you went through each phase of the job withdrawal progress.

7.2 Strategies Used to Increase Motivation

Learning Objective

1. Explain the strategies companies use to try to retain employees.

As we have addressed so far in this chapter, human motivation is an important aspect to understanding what makes us happy or unhappy at our jobs. Companies implement many strategies to keep us motivated at work. This section will discuss some of those specific strategies.

Salaries and Benefits

As we know from the earlier section, our paycheck can be a motivator to a certain extent. It is important to note that when we look at compensation, it is much more than the paycheck, but also things such as health benefits and paid time off.

Some of the considerations companies use surrounding pay can include the following:

1. **Instituting a standard process.** Many organizations do not have set pay plans or scales, which can result in unfairness when onboarding (the process of bringing someone "on board" with the company, including discussion and negotiation of compensation) or offering pay increases. Companies should make sure the process for receiving pay raises is fair and defensible, so as not to appear discriminatory.

2. **A pay communication strategy.** Many companies work hard to make sure the fair pay process is communicated to employees. Transparency in the process of how raises are given and then communicated can help companies retain good employees.[7]

3. **Paid time off (PTO).** Companies pay us not only with our salary but also from the time off we receive. Paid holidays and vacation time might be an example.

Training and Development

To meet our higher-level needs, we need to experience self-growth. As a result, many companies and managers offer training programs within the organization and pay for employees to attend career skill seminars and programs. It is a great idea to take advantage of these types of self-growth opportunities in your current or future organization. In addition, many companies offer tuition reimbursement programs to help you earn a degree. For example, Amazon offers leadership training for one month prior to hire, and they also pay 95 percent tuition for employees at fulfillment centers to take courses in high-demand fields.[8]

WATCH THIS!

Ideas for increasing your motivation at work.

View the video online at: http://www.youtube.com/embed/mCXmEmKwPrU?rel=0

Performance Appraisals

performance appraisal

A method by which job performance is measured.

The **performance appraisal** is a formalized process to assess how well an employee does his or her job. The effectiveness of this process can contribute to employee retention, in that we can gain constructive feedback on our job performance, and it can be an opportunity for the manager to work with us to set goals within the organization. This process can help ensure that our upper-level self-actualization needs are met, but it also can address some of the motivational factors discussed by Herzberg, such as achievement, recognition, and responsibility. Sometimes the challenge with performance appraisals is that they are not taken seriously by management, and treated as "another thing on the to-do list." If they are taken seriously, and really used as a tool to help improve performance, and set goals, they can be very valuable towards motivation.

Succession Planning

succession planning

A process for identifying and developing people in the organization who have the potential to fill positions.

Succession planning is a process of identifying and developing people in the organization who have the potential for filling positions. As we know, many people leave organizations because they do not see career growth or potential. Companies can combat this by having a clear career path for us to follow. For example, perhaps you start as a sales associate, become assistant manager, and then become manager. Proper succession planning shows what we must accomplish at each level in order to attain a higher-level position. This type of clear career path can help with our motivation at work. If your current or future organization does not have a succession plan, consider speaking with your manager about your own career path and potential. The performance appraisal process might be a good time to have this discussion with your manager.

Flextime, Telecommuting, and Sabbaticals

Remote working includes telecommuting and flextime. Two-thirds of managers say overall productivity is increased when their employees are allowed to work remotely.[9] However, this may not work for all types of jobs. For example, a retailer may not be able to implement this, since the sales associate must be in the store to assist customers. For many professions, it is a viable option, and can help motivate workers. During the COVID-19 pandemic, many workers began working from home, which slowed the spread of the virus, but also may have resulted in greater productivity.[10]

Some companies such as Recreational Equipment Incorporated (REI),[11] based in Seattle, offer twelve weeks of unpaid leave per year (beyond the time required under the Family and Medical Leave Act) for the employee to pursue volunteering or traveling opportunities. In addition, with fifteen years of service with the company, paid sabbaticals are offered, which include four weeks of leave plus already-earned vacation time.

Management Training

In a recent poll of employees, it was found that 92 percent of employees would be more likely to stay with their current companies if their manager showed more empathy.[12] Managers who bully, use the theory X approach, communicate poorly, or are incompetent may find it difficult to motivate employees to stay within the organization. While, as employees, we cannot control a manager's behavior, companies can provide training to create better management. Training of managers to be better communicators and motivators is a way to handle this retention issue.

Conflict Management and Fairness

Perceptions on fairness and how organizations handle conflict can be a contributing factor to our motivation at work. **Outcome fairness** refers to the judgment we make with respect to the outcomes we receive versus the outcomes received by others with whom we associate. When we are deciding if something is fair, we will likely look at **procedural justice**, or the process used to determine the outcomes received. There are six main areas we use to determine the outcome fairness of a conflict:

1. **Consistency.** We will determine if procedures are applied consistently to other persons and throughout periods of time.

2. **Bias suppression.** We perceive the person making the decision does not have bias or vested interest in the outcome.

3. **Information accuracy.** The decision made is based on correct information.

4. **Correctability.** The decision is able to be appealed and mistakes in the decision process can be corrected.

5. **Representativeness.** We feel the concerns of all stakeholders involved have been taken into account.

6. **Ethicality.** The decision is in line with moral societal standards.

For example, let's suppose JoAnn just received a bonus and recognition at the company party for her contributions to an important company project. However, you might compare your inputs and outputs and determine it was unfair that JoAnn was recognized because you had worked on bigger projects and not received the same recognition or bonus. As you know from the last section, this type of unfairness can result in being unmotivated at work. Excellent communication with your manager when dealing with these types of situations would be imperative.

Job Enrichment, Job Enlargement, and Empowerment

As we have discussed previously, one of the reasons for job dissatisfaction is the job itself. Ensuring our skills set and what we enjoy doing matches with the job is important. Some companies will use a change in job design, enlarge the job, or empower employees to motivate them.

Job enrichment means to enhance a job by giving employees more freedom to make their own work more rewarding. For example, if we as retail salespersons are good at creating eye-catching displays, allowing us to practice these skills and assignment of tasks around this could be considered job enrichment. Job enrichment can fulfill our higher level of human needs while creating job satisfaction at the same time. In fact, research in this area by Richard Hackman and Greg Oldham[13] found that we, as employees, need the following to achieve job satisfaction:

- Skill variety, or many different activities as part of the job;
- Task identity, or being able to complete one task from beginning to end;
- Task significance, or the degree to which the job has impact on others, internally or externally;
- Autonomy, or freedom to make decisions within the job;
- Feedback, or clear information about performance.

In addition, **job enlargement**, defined as the adding of new challenges or responsibilities to a current job (which are not in the job description), can create job satisfaction. Assigning us to a special project or task is an example of job enlargement.

Employee empowerment involves management allowing us to make decisions and act upon those decisions, with the support of the organization. When we are not micromanaged and have the power to determine the sequence of our own work day, we tend to be more satisfied than those employees who are not empowered. Empowerment can include the following:

- Encourage innovation or new ways of doing things.
- Make sure we, as employees, have the information we need to do our jobs; for example, we are not dependent on managers for information in decision making.
- Management styles that allow for participation, feedback, and ideas from employees.

job enlargement

Adding new challenges or responsibilities to a current job.

employee empowerment

A way to involve employees in their work by allowing them to make decisions and act upon those decisions, with the support of the organization.

Pay-for-Performance Strategies

Some organizations have a pay-for-performance strategy, which means that we are rewarded for meeting preset objectives within the organization. For example, in a merit-based pay system, we might be rewarded for meeting or exceeding performance during a given time period. Rather than a set pay increase every year, the increase is based on performance. Some organizations offer bonuses to employees for meeting objectives, while some organizations offer team incentive pay if a team achieves a specific, predetermined outcome. For example, each player on the winning team of the NFL Super Bowl earns a bonus of $118,000.[14] Players also earn money for each wild-card game and playoff game. Some organizations also offer profit sharing, which is tied to a company's overall performance. Gain sharing, different from profit sharing, focuses on improvement of productivity within the organization. For example, the city of Loveland, Colorado implemented a gain-sharing program that defined three criteria that needed to be met for employees to be given extra compensation. The city revenues had to exceed expenses, expenses had to be equal to or less than the previous year's expenses, and a citizen satisfaction survey had to meet minimum requirements.

As we have already addressed, pay isn't everything, but it certainly can be an important part of feeling motivated in our jobs.

🎥 WATCH THIS!

David Swinford, CEO of Pearl Meyer & Partners, discusses executive pay for performance.

View the video online at: http://www.youtube.com/embed/mMh8DjZwS5Q?rel=0

Other Ways to Motivate

Some companies offer unique benefits to reduce turnover. An on-site yoga class is an example of a unique, although expensive, benefit to consider including in a retention plan.

© Thinkstock

According to *Fortune's* "100 Best Companies to Work For,"[15] some things that companies do to motivate us may be more unusual. For example, the list includes the following:

- On-site daycare or daycare assistance;
- Gym memberships or on-site gyms;
- Concierge service to assist in party planning or dog grooming, for example;
- On-site dry cleaning drop-off and pickup;
- Car care, such as oil changes, on-site once a week;
- On-site doggie daycare;
- On-site yoga or other fitness classes;
- "Summer Fridays," when all employees work half days on Fridays during the summer;
- Various support groups for cancer survivors, weight loss, or support in caring for aging parents;
- On-site life coaches;
- Peer-to-peer employee recognition programs;
- Management recognition programs.

While some of these examples may not be options in the companies we work for, the important thing to remember is often our own motivation comes from us internally. As a result, we need to be aware of our changing motivations and ask for those things that could make us more motivated at work.

Key Takeaways

- Salary and benefits are a major component of what employers offer to motivate us. Consistent pay systems and transparent processes are important considerations.
- Many companies offer paid tuition programs, reimbursement programs, and in-house training to increase our skills and knowledge.
- *Performance appraisals* provide an avenue for feedback and goal setting. They also allow for us to be recognized for our contributions.
- *Succession plans* allow us, as employees, the ability to see how we can continue our career with the organization, and they clearly detail what we need to do to achieve career growth.
- Flextime and telecommuting are options some companies use as motivators. These types of plans give us flexibility when developing our schedule and some control of our work. Some companies also offer paid or unpaid sabbaticals to pursue personal interests after a certain number of years with the company.
- Since one of the reasons people are dissatisfied with their job is because of the relationship with their manager, many companies require management and communication training to ensure managers are able to establish good relationships with employees.
- Some companies may change the job through *empowerment* or *job enlargement* to help grow our skills.
- Other, more unique ways companies try to retain employees might include offering services to make the employee's life easier, such as dry cleaning, daycare services, or on-site yoga classes.

Exercise

1. Research two different companies you might be interested in working for. When reviewing their list of benefits, which ones are offered that might motivate you to stay with the organization?

7.3 Chapter Summary and Case

Chapter Summary

- The theory of job withdrawal explains the process someone goes through when they are not motivated or happy at work.
- There are many motivation theories that attempt to explain people's motivation or lack of motivation at work.
- The Hawthorne studies were a series of studies beginning in 1927 that initially looked at physical environments but found that people tended to be more motivated when they felt cared about. The implications to retention are clear, in that employees should feel cared about and developed within the organization.
- Maslow's theory on motivation says that if someone already has a need met, giving them something to meet more of that need will no longer motivate. Maslow divided the needs into physiological, safety, social, esteem, and self-actualization needs. Many companies only motivate based on the low-level needs, such as pay. Development of training opportunities, for example, can motivate employees on high-level self-actualization needs.
- Herzberg developed motivational theories based on actual motivation and hygiene factors. Hygiene factors are those things that are expected in the workplace and will demotivate employees when absent but will not actually motivate when present. If managers try to motivate only on the basis of hygiene factors, turnover can be high. Motivation on both of Herzberg's factors is key to a good retention plan.
- McGregor's theory on motivation looked at managers' attitudes toward employees. He found that theory X managers had more of a negative view of employees, while theory Y managers had a more positive view. Providing training to the managers in our organization can be a key retention strategy based on McGregor's theory.
- The carrot-and-stick approach means you can get someone to do something by prodding or by offering some incentive to motivate them to do the work. This theory implies these are the only two methods to motivate, which of course, we know isn't true. The implication of this in our retention plan is such that we must utilize a variety of methods to retain employees.
- Finally, understanding our own motivations at work is an important step to making sure we choose the right career path.
- Salary and benefits are a major component of what employers offer to motivate us. Consistent pay systems and transparent processes on pay raises should be clearly communicated.
- Training and development meets the higher-level needs of the individual. Many companies offer paid tuition programs, reimbursement programs, and in-house training to increase the skills and knowledge of the employee.
- *Performance appraisals* provide an avenue for feedback and goal setting. They also allow for employees to be recognized for their contributions.
- *Succession plans* allow us, as employees, the ability to see how we can continue our career with the organization, and they clearly detail what employees need to do to achieve career growth.

- Some companies use flextime and telecommuting options as motivators. These types of plans allow the employee flexibility when developing his or her schedule and some control of his or her work. Some companies also offer paid or unpaid sabbaticals after a certain number of years with the company to pursue personal interests.

- Since one of the reasons people are dissatisfied with their job is because of the relationship with their manager, many companies require management and communication training to ensure managers are able to establish good relationships with employees.

- Some companies may change the job through empowerment or job enlargement to help the growth of the employee.

- Other, more unique ways companies try to retain employees might include offering services to make the employee's life easier, such as dry cleaning, daycare services, or on-site yoga classes.

Chapter Case

1. The following is a list of some possible strategies companies use to motivate employees. Rank each one in order of importance to you (one being the most important). Then categorize where you think each would go in Maslow's Hierarchy and Hertzberg's theory.

   a. Salary

   b. Opportunity for bonuses, profit sharing

   c. Benefits

   d. Opportunity to grow professionally with the organization

   e. Team bonuses

   f. More paid time off

   g. Option to telecommute

   h. Flextime scheduling

   i. Sense of empowerment

   j. Tuition reimbursement

   k. Job satisfaction

Endnotes

1. Farrell, D., & Petersen, J.S. (August 1984). Commitment, Absenteeism and Turnover of New Employees: A Longitudinal Study. *Human Relations* 37(8), 681–92.

2. Mayo, E. (2007). *The Social Problems of an Industrial Civilization*. Arno Press: New York, NY.

3. Ferreira, S. (n.d.) The happiness value of work-life balance. Inc.com. Retrieved from https://www.inc.com/stacey-ferreira/the-happiness-value-of-work-life-balance.html

4. Maslow, A. (1998). *Toward a Psychology of Being*, Wiley: New York, NY.

5. Herzberg, F., Mausner, B., & Snyderman, B.B. (1993). *The Motivation to Work*. Transaction Publishers: New Brunswick, NJ.

6. McGregor, D. (1960). *The Human Side of Enterprise*. McGraw-Hill, New York, NY.

7. Anttila, A., & Kochanski, J. (February 2014). It pays to clearly communicate compensation. World at Work. Retrieved from https://www.worldatwork.org/docs/compensation-focus/2014/02-10-2014/it-pays-to-clearly-communicate-compensation.html

8. Thottam, I. (n.d.). Ten companies with awesome training and development programs. Monster.com. Retrieved from https://www.monster.com/career-advice/article/companies-with-awesome-training-development-programs

9. Remote.Co (2018). 17 stats about remote work in 2018. Retrieved from https://remote.co/10-stats-about-remote-work/

10. Caramela, S. (31 March 2020). Working from home increases productivity. Accessed from https://www.businessnewsdaily.com/15259-working-from-home-more-productive.html.

11. REI. (n.d.). Compensation policy. Retrieved from https://rei.jobs/portal/11/docs/rei-pay-and-benefits.pdf

12. Marvin, R. (8 August 2018). Why employees quite: 20 stats managers need to know. Medium Corporation. Retrieved from https://medium.com/@checkli/why-employees-quit-20-stats-employers-need-to-know-b921c253f767

13. Ford, N.R. (March-April 1969). *Motivation through the Work Itself*. American Management Association: New York, NY.

14. Tuttle, B. (3 February 2019). Here's How Much Money Tom Brady Has Made Playing in 9 Super Bowls — and It's Not as Much as You'd Think. Money.com. Retrieved from http://money.com/money/5633727/tom-brady-super-bowl-bonus-money-mvp/

15. Economy, P. (2019). Glassdoor just announced the best companies to work for. Inc.com. Retrieved from https://www.inc.com/peter-economy/glassdoor-just-announced-100-best-places-to-work-for-2019-is-your-company-on-list.html

CHAPTER 8
Working in Teams

Significant portions of this chapter were adapted from Scott McLean's *Business Communication for Success* textbook with permission of the author.[1]

> *Teamwork is the ability to work together toward a common vision. The ability to direct individual accomplishments toward organizational objectives. It is the fuel that allows common people to attain uncommon results.*
>
> —*Andrew Carnegie*

> *Never doubt that a small group of thoughtful, committed people can change the world. Indeed, it is the only thing that ever has.*
>
> —*Margaret Mead*

Teamwork at Quick-Lube

At Quick-Lube, the promise to customers is to change oil within ten minutes. There is no way that Quick-Lube could do this without teamwork. For example, in one shift, there is someone assigned as the customer interface, the below hood, and the above hood. The duties of the customer interface include checking people in, moving the car into the stall, and managing the oil change process. The below hood person is responsible for draining the oil and replacing it. The above hood person washes the windows, vacuums the floors, and also checks the above the hood items like the air filter. All of these people must communicate well to finish the job in ten minutes. Sometimes, on busy days such as Saturday afternoon, this can be stressful, but each team member knows their job, which creates a better and faster customer experience.

As humans, we are social beings. We naturally form relationships with others. Sometimes forming relationships is necessary to serve the customer best. In fact, relationships are often noted as one of the most important aspects of a person's life, and they exist in many forms. Interpersonal communication occurs between two people, while group communication may involve two or more individuals. Groups are a primary context for interaction within the business community. Groups may have heroes, enemies, and sages alongside new members. Groups overlap and may share common goals, but they may also engage in conflict. Groups can be supportive or coercive and can exert powerful influences over individuals.

Within a group, individuals may behave in distinct ways, use unique or specialized terms, or display symbols that have meaning to that group. Those same terms or symbols may be confusing, meaningless, or even unacceptable to another group. An individual may belong to both groups, adapting his or her communication patterns to meet group normative expectations. Groups are increasingly important across social media venues, and there are many examples of successful business ventures on the web that value and promote group interaction.

Groups use words to exchange meaning, establish territory, and identify who is a stranger versus who is a trusted member. Are you familiar with the term "internet troll?" It is often used to identify someone who is not a member of an online group or community; does not share the values and beliefs of the group; and posts a message in an online discussion board to initiate flame wars, cause disruption, or otherwise challenge the group members. Members often use words to respond to the challenge that are not otherwise common in the discussions, and the less-than-flattering descriptions of the internet troll can actually do harm to the group since the descriptions do not meet the group norms.

Groups have existed throughout human history and continue to follow familiar patterns across emerging venues as we adapt to technology, computer-mediated interaction, suburban sprawl, and modern life. We need groups, and groups need us. Our relationship and interdependence with groups warrant attention as we come to know our communities, our world, and ourselves; that will be the focus of this chapter.

8.1 What Is a Team?

Learning Objective

1. Be able to explain the meaning of a group and a team.

Our ability to work effectively in a team shows the emotional intelligence skills of social awareness, self-awareness, and also shows our ability to manage relationships. We cannot have relationships with others if we do not have a sense of ourselves and how we fit into a group or team. To maintain those relationships, we need to have social awareness and be able to manage relationships in a positive way.

Group communication is defined as the exchange of information with those who are alike culturally, linguistically, and/or geographically. Obviously, group communication is very important for success at work. A **team** is defined as a group that comes together as a team to achieve a common goal. We will first address types of teams, and then address how to communicate better in teams.

Formal and Informal Teams and Groups

A **formal team (group)** is one that is brought together to accomplish a certain task. It is created for some specific purpose, and is formed via authority. For example, a formal group might be a coffee stand manager and her employees. This group has a specific purpose, and is focused on a specific task or group of tasks.

An **informal team (group)** is one that does not have set goals, and usually forms independently of the organization. Usually, these types of groups form based on shared interests. For example, if there is a group of managers that meet for coffee on a monthly basis to discuss personal things and also talk about work, this would be considered an informal team. There is no real authority in this team; it is a network of relationships between individuals that have shared interests.

Consider this example: You are part of the sales department, and therefore, your formal team is made up of sales representatives, customer service agents, and the Director of Sales. This is your formal team. Assume you do yoga weekly with two of the people from this team, this would be the informal team. There are no set rules in structure—you get together due to common interests. This is unlike your formal team, where you have work to accomplish together in a more structured way.

It is important to understand both structures because the bonds of an informal team can create motivation and satisfaction at work. Likewise, the formal team is important as well, because it

---

group communication

The exchange of information with those who are culturally, linguistically, and/or geographically alike.

team

A group of people who come together as a team to achieve a common goal.

formal team (group)

A team is one that is brought together to accomplish a certain task.

informal team (group)

A type of team that does not have set goals, and usually forms independently of the organization.

has its own set structure and "rules." Now that we've discussed the two main types of teams and groups in the workplace, we can address the types of teams next.

Types of Teams in the Workplace

There are four main types of teams we can find in the workplace. The first is a **project team,**sometimes called a task force, or steering committee. This type of team is brought together for a specific purpose. For example, assume your organization has had five workplace accidents in the last month, which is way more than the normal three per year. A project team, or task force, might be formed to determine the cause and solution. The main difference between this type of team and others is the fact there is usually a start and end date. In other words, it is meant to identify and address specific issues.

A **functional team** is a group of people who work together in the same department, likely with different jobs within that department. For example, a functional team in a marketing department might include the marketing manager, the salespeople, the sales assistant, the marketing assistant, and the product development supervisor. Usually in this type of team, there is one person to whom everyone reports. In our example, all of the jobs listed would probably report to the marketing manager.

A **cross-functional team** is a group of people brought together from a variety of departments or different areas of the business. An example of a cross-functional team might be a team where all managers are brought together to discuss different aspects of the business. For example, the marketing manager, sales manager, accounting manager, and production manager. They all work in different areas of the business, which is what makes them cross functional.

A **self-directed work team** (or self-managed team) is one consisting of employees in a company that does not have the usual supervision of a manager. The self-directed work team combines a variety of skills and talents to get things done. Some companies have taken self-managed teams to the extreme; for example, Zappos. In 2013, Zappos[2] eliminated management and its operation now relies on self-managed teams to get things done.

 WATCH THIS!

This Ted Talk discusses the advantages and disadvantages of self-managed teams.

View the video online at: http://www.youtube.com/embed/tJxfJGo-vkl?rel=0

project team

This type of team is brought together for a specific purpose to solve a particular issue.

Groups and teams are an important part of any type of communication that happens at work.

© Thinkstock

functional team

Is a group of people who work together in the same department, likely with different jobs within that department, but all report to one manager.

cross-functional team

It is a group of people brought together from a variety of departments or different areas of the business.

self-directed work team

A team consisting of employees in a company that does not have the usual supervision of a manager. The self-directed work team combines a variety of skills and talents to get things done.

virtual team

A virtual team is one where teams form to get work done virtually.

A **virtual team** is one where teams form to get work done virtually. In fact, nearly 50 percent of global companies use virtual teams to achieve goals. Virtual teams have become increasingly more common due to technology, such as online video conference calls and instant messaging. Note that a virtual team could also be a functional or cross-functional team.

Now that we have addressed the types of teams, we will discuss the stages of the team development process, and some of the roles your team members can take.

Key Takeaways

- A team is a group that comes together to meet a common goal. There are informal teams, and formal teams, both of which have different structures.
- There are four main types of teams, which include functional teams, cross-functional teams, virtual teams, and self-directed (managed) teams.

Exercise

1. Give an example of teams you've been on for each of the four discussed in this section—functional, cross-functional, virtual, and self-directed. If you haven't had experience with all types of teams, discuss what that team might look like in your current or past organization. What were the advantages of each team? What were the downsides?

8.2 Team Life Cycles and Member Roles

Learning Objectives

1. Identify the stages in the team development process.
2. Describe different types of team member roles.

In this section, we will address team development stages and also the types of group members within any given group. As you'll read, the development stages are vital to understanding how teams form and work together. Also, understanding member roles is essential to know how to work with specific team members within your group. First, let's talk about the team development stages.

Team Development Stages

These stages were developed by Bruce Wayne Tuckman, and are the most widely-accepted description of team-development processes.[3] The first stage in the team development process is the **forming stage**, where the team is newly formed. This stage can also occur within an existing team which has added new members. There are a few things that normally happen during the forming stage.

- Positive feelings about the team;
- Some anxiousness as team members may not know their role in the team;
- Learning about other team members;
- Team is dependent on leader for guidance;
- Leader should be clear in this phase about goals and provide direction.

The next stage is the **storming stage**. In this stage, conflicts begin to occur as team members may have different working styles. Here are other characteristics of the storming phase:

- Conflict;
- Questioning team goals;
- Competition among team members for status;
- Team members compete for acceptance of ideas;
- Questioning authority;
- Can be a difficult stage for those who do not like conflict;
- The leader should focus on making sure team members listen to and respect one another.

It is important to note some teams never move beyond this stage. Power struggles and conflict can keep a team in this phase for an extended period of time, causing the team to never function well.

The next stage is the **norming stage**, where team members begin to accept one another and the strengths they bring to the team. This stage may move back and forth between the storming stage, as new tasks and responsibilities arise for the team. Some of the characteristics of this stage include:

- Respect for authority;
- Accepting differences in team member work styles (and appreciating them);
- Understanding of individual's strengths;
- Focused on developing procedures in terms of how the team will function;
- Team members begin to trust one another;
- The leader should step aside as much as possible to allow the team to make decisions.

The fourth stage in the process is the **performing stage**. In this stage, the team mostly works harmoniously together, and team goals are being met. Some characteristics of this stage include:

- Clear vision;
- Everyone working together to meet goals;
- Structures and processes set up and accepted by team members;
- No friction among team members;
- Team members are highly motivated;
- During this phase, the leader should step aside and let the team perform, celebrate milestones with the team, and only step in if there are issues within the team, or if they revert back to one of the earlier stages.

forming stage

The first step in the Tuckman team-development stage, where the group is newly formed.

storming stage

During this stage of Tuckman's group-development process, team members may experience conflict.

norming stage

The third stage in Tuckman's team-development process where team members begin to accept strengths each member brings to the team.

performing stage

In this stage of Tuckman's team-development process, the team members work harmoniously together.

The final stage is the **adjourning phase**, when the project or task may be over, and team members go their separate ways. This stage can be challenging and sadness may be experienced by team members at the end of their work together. Other aspects of this stage include:

- Recognition of team members;
- Goal accomplished and/or task completed;
- Sense of loss;
- In this phase, the leader should take time to celebrate contributions to the team and debrief anything that did not go well within the team.

It is important to note that each of these phases can revert to earlier phases if there are new team members added or removed. Also, as new goals for the team arise, they could enter the earlier stages again, even if they were in the performing stage at some point in the process.

FIGURE 8.1 Stages in the Team-Development Process

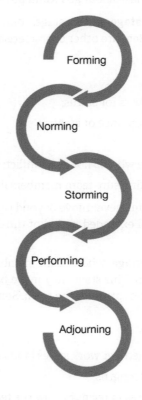

Have you ever been in a team that had difficulty making it past the storming phase? Or perhaps a team that went through all of the first stages quickly and spent most of the time in the performing stage? The next section will address some of the characteristics of a successful team, and how to spend more time working toward goals rather than handling conflict.

Characteristics of a Successful Team

As you've guessed, some qualities make up a successful team. Before we begin to discuss team member roles in the next section, we think it is important to address these now.

First and foremost, clear goals are a must for a successful team. Followed by this, clear communication among team members is imperative. In addition, here are some other things to consider to make your team successful:[4]

1. Clear communication among all members;
2. Regular brainstorming sessions with all members participating;

3. Consensus among team members;

4. Problem solving done by the group;

5. Commitment to the project and the other team members;

6. Regular team meetings are effective and inclusive;

7. Timely hand-off from team members to others to ensure the project keeps moving in the right direction;

8. Positive, supportive working relationships among all team members;

9. Effective conflict management.

Now that we have addressed some of the components of a successful team, let's address some of the roles individuals take on in a team.

🎥 **WATCH THIS!**

The stages of the team-development process.

View the video online at: http://www.youtube.com/embed/qtpY9zwuzFM?rel=0

Team Member Roles

There is extensive research on the type of roles within teams; however, the most generally accepted theory on team-member roles is that of Belbin,[5][6] who addressed nine major roles and behaviors within a team, and characteristics of each. Each falls into one of three categories—action oriented, people oriented, or thought oriented. Let's discuss each of them in turn.

FIGURE 8.2 Team Member Roles

Resource Investigator
This person is very optimistic and contributes to the enthusiasm of the team due their optimism. They are open to opportunities, and their strength is to explore options for the team.

Teamworker
This team member contributes to the team by assisting to alleviate friction among team members. They tend to cooperate well, but they also have the tendency to avoid confrontation.

Co-ordinator
This person focuses on meeting and clarifying goals and delegating. They need to be careful not to be seen as delegating too much of their own work.

Plant
The Plant focuses on creativity and generating ideas for the team. A downside to this team member role is they need to focus on details, and ensure they are communicating effectively.

Monitor Evaluator
This person takes a strategic approach in the team. They are able to see all possible avenues. They need to be sure they are open to others' ideas and focus on inspiring others.

Specialist
This is usually the person that has a specific expertise they can contribute to the group. Because of this, it is important for this person to take a broader view and avoid getting stuck on too many technicalities.

Shaper
The shaper is the person in the group who has the drive and willingness to overcome challenges that may occur in the group. However, because of their drive, they need to be careful not to offend others.

Implementer
The implementer is the reliable and efficient person in the group. They have the ability to take the ideas and turn them into action items. They need to be careful they are open to new possibilities and flexibility as new ideas are contributed.

Completer Finisher
This person perfects the final product the team has put together. They have great attention to detail, but may have trouble delegating, and worry needlessly about the final outcome.

Data from https://www.belbin.com/media/2307/belbin-team-role-summary-descriptions.pdf

action behaviors

Part of Belbin's research on team role behavior. Consists of the shaper, the implementer, and the completer/finisher.

people-oriented behaviors

Part of Belbin's research on team role behavior. Consists of the resource investigator, teamworker, and coordinator.

The first set of behaviors are **action behaviors**, and they consist of the shaper, the implementer, and the completer/finisher. First, the shaper has extensive drive and motivation. In doing so, they can sometimes offend other members of the team because of their laser focus. However, they have the drive and courage to get things done. The implementers are well organized, reliable, and efficient. They turn ideas into actions. However, they can have the tendency to be inflexible and slow to respond to new possibilities. Finally, the completer/finisher polishes and perfects, and is conscientious about looking for errors. They may be perfectionists, who are inclined to worry.

The second set of behaviors are the **people-oriented behaviors**, and they consist of the resource investigator, teamworker, and coordinator. The resource investigator is resourceful, outgoing, and likes to explore options. Their inquisitive nature allows them to explore and bring ideas back to the team. However, they can forget to follow up on leads, and while enthusiastic, can wane significantly once initial enthusiasm has passed. The teamworker averts friction among the group members and helps the team to gel. However, they do not like conflict or confrontation and may avoid healthy dissent in the group. The coordinator clarifies goals and is very good at delegating work. They are able to identify talent on the team and delegate work based on people's abilities. However, they sometimes have a tendency to overdelegate.

The third set of behaviors are the **thought-oriented behaviors**. They consist of the plant, the monitor evaluator, and the specialist. First, the plant is creative, free thinking, and are the problem solvers. They may tend to be introverts and lack the ability to communicate their ideas effectively. The monitor evaluator is strategic and looks at the big picture. They tend to be serious minded and cautious, which may create difficulty among team members. Finally, the specialist brings in-depth knowledge about a specific area, and can be an invaluable resource. They can overload team members with information and may, at times, be too-narrowly focused.

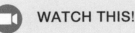 **WATCH THIS!**

Belbin's team roles explained in two minutes or less!

View the video online at: http://www.youtube.com/embed/hMesDq_rNOw?rel=0

Now that you know the roles that exist within a team, do you know what role you tend to take on when working in teams? Are you more of a creative thinker (plant) or more focused on people-oriented behaviors like averting friction among the team (teamworker)? Having the right set of talents within a team is important. Can you imagine a team where there were mostly specialists? This might leave out important aspects to a well-rounded team, such as the ability to drive the team or delegating work. As you can see, the ideal team has each of these. Also important to note is the fact that some people may take on a variety of roles on a team (not just one), depending on the type of project and the size of the group.

Now that we have addressed these roles, we will discuss team dynamics and strategies for dealing with difficult team members.

thought-oriented behaviors

Part of Belbin's research on team role behavior. Consists of the plant, monitor/evauator, and the specialist.

 **WATCH THIS!**

Belbin team roles explained.

View the video online at: http://www.youtube.com/embed/-efhOLVgEvM?rel=0

Key Takeaways

- The phases of the team development process consist of forming, storming, norming, performing, and adjourning.
- Everyone tends to take on a certain member role when working in teams. These can be divided into three main categories including action-oriented behaviors, people-oriented behaviors, and thought-oriented behaviors. This was based on research by Belbin and can be valuable when putting together and working within an effective team.

Exercises

1. As you know, an important part of self-awareness as an emotional intelligence skill is to know yourself. Given this, which of Belbin's team-member roles do you tend to be? When have you switched roles due to the needs of the team? Give a detailed example.
2. Discuss how you've experienced the stages of team development either in a team at school, or at your current or past job.

8.3 Team Dynamics and Difficult Team Members

Learning Objectives

1. Explain the concept of team dynamics.
2. Identify the five dysfunctions of a team, and how to overcome the dysfunctions.

What are Team Dynamics?

Understanding team dynamics can help us to better navigate groups and teams that we are part of. **Team dynamics** is defined as how each individual team member and their behaviors within a group affect other team members and the team as a whole. Team dynamics are unconscious[7] and can help determine if a team meets its goals or not. Have you ever had a grumpy colleague or team member? You might be in a great mood, but when this person comes to your regular Monday team meetings they complain and offer no solutions? This type of team dynamic can deflate the entire group. Likewise, have you ever had an upbeat teammate with a "can do" attitude? Often, their positive attitude will impact the group positively. Perhaps you've worked on a team where someone had a dominant personality and liked to share all of their opinions with the group—and talked twice as much as everyone else? This can influence the team dynamic because team members may not want to interrupt this person, and it gives less of a chance for everyone's ideas to be heard. Team dynamics can contribute significantly to the success of a team, but can also diminish the effectiveness of a team. Having positive team dynamics can boost creativity and productivity on your team.

As you can imagine, significant research has been done in this area to determine what makes positive team dynamics and what doesn't. In a book written by Patrick Lencioni,[8] he addresses what are considered the five main dysfunctions of a team—or team dynamics that make the team unsuccessful. The five dysfunctions are:

- Absence of trust;
- Fear of conflict;
- Lack of commitment;
- Avoidance of accountability;
- Inattention to results.

Absence of trust, the first dysfunction, occurs when team members do not trust one another to be vulnerable in the team, admit they need help or admit they've made a mistake. The next dysfunction, fear of conflict, may seem odd—since we often think about conflict as a negative thing—and refers to a team's inability to discuss important matters openly. Instead, comments are made outside of the group as a whole (backchanneling). Fear of conflict may mean the leader hasn't allowed for healthy discussion and opinions (even if they differ), and people are afraid to speak up. The third dysfunction, lack of commitment, if often a result of fear of conflict. Because teams can't openly discuss issues, there may be lack of direction and commitment to the team and team goals. Avoidance of accountability occurs when team members do not commit to clear plans of action to meet their goals and because of this people are not held accountable to the team as a whole. Finally, inattention to results usually occurs because people have no reason to focus on the team's goal.

team dynamics

Refers to how each individual team member and their behaviors within a group affect other team members and the team as a whole.

They put themselves and their own needs first, resulting in not focusing on the collective efforts and goals of the team.

Do you see how it would be difficult to have good team dynamics, resulting in a well functioning team, when these five dysfunctions are present? There are a few things we can do to try to create positive dynamics within a team:

- Have clear deadlines and goals for the team;
- Build trust;
- Allow for healthy conflict;
- Avoid blocking behaviors such as aggressiveness, inappropriate comments, and negativity;
- Address problems within the team quickly;
- Create a culture where people feel comfortable asking for help;
- Reward risk taking and avoid penalizing mistakes;
- Give open and honest feedback;
- Avoid letting people "free ride" by setting individual goals within the team.

These strategies, and understanding the different personalities that can exist within a team, are a good first step to analyzing your own team's dynamics. We will discuss how individual personalities on a team can help create good team dynamics in the next section.

WATCH THIS!

Ted Talk on improving team dynamics.

View the video online at: http://www.youtube.com/embed/4OBeysx55VE?rel=0

Dealing with Difficult Team Members

blocking personalities

A personality on a team that makes it difficult to accomplish team goals.

Every team has them—people that are difficult for any variety of reasons. In this section, we will discuss how team dynamics are affected by the variety of personalities on a team. Difficult team members have **blocking personalities**. These can come in a variety of forms, but their blocking behavior prevents the flow of information among team members. Blocking personalities include:[9]

What's in it for me?

Did you know that 75 percent of employers rate teamwork and the ability to collaborate as "very important?"[10] In addition, employees spend at least 14 percent of their workweek communicating and collaborating internally.[11] Given these statistics, it is likely you will work in a team, and team skills—especially those on how to deal with difficult team members—will benefit you in your future career!

1. **The aggressor:** the one who is very outspoken, so others do not have a chance to share.
2. **The negator:** this team member is often critical of others' ideas and is quick to put them down.
3. **The withdrawer:** Often this role will say nothing, and contribute very little to the group.
4. **The recognition seeker:** this role thinks about him or herself and tends to be dominant in their speaking and behaviors.
5. **The joker:** while humor can often be good to build teams, sometimes it can be distracting

Have you ever worked with these types of people before? What was the outcome of your team? Google performed research on the most productive teams and found the higher the overall emotional intelligence level and degree of communication between team members predicted better in a team success.[12] However, how do you deal with the types of personalities above, especially when you weren't able to choose your own team (as often happens in workplace situations)?

The first step is understanding what outside sources could be affecting the team member. This doesn't mean it is "ok," but having empathy for what someone else may be struggling with can go a long way in making things better on the team. Here are some possible factors for why that person is being so difficult:[13]

1. Does not enjoy their job;
2. Stress at home, such as childcare issues or challenges with significant other;
3. Lack of additional responsibilities bestowed on them;
4. Their skill sets don't match the evolving role, leaving them feeling like their current skills may not be valued;
5. No support from their supervisor;
6. Dislikes a member of the team;
7. Overly-optimistic view of themselves;
8. Non-responsive to feedback.

 **WATCH THIS!**

This video offers some practical tips on how to deal with a difficult team member if you are their supervisor.

View the video online at: http://www.youtube.com/embed/Dvm8StVpp54?rel=0

 **WATCH THIS!**

This video offers some practical tips on how to deal with a difficult team member when you are their colleague.

View the video online at: http://www.youtube.com/embed/iyUWeJy3LQI?rel=0

After you've tried to understand the issues outside of the team that could be affecting this person, the first step is to talk openly and honestly with them about what you are seeing (you do not have to be a manager to do this!). For example, if they are the withdrawer, you might consider asking them why they've been so quiet in meetings lately, and tell them how much you value their opinion. Have facts and examples available to share with that person.[14] Next, share the impact their behavior has on the team. Next, work with that person to come up with strategies to avoid the behavior that is disruptive to the team. Finally, make sure to follow up with the person.

The last bit of advice in this section is to become observant! You can understand a lot about team dynamics by watching others' body language and what they say. Does Sam always roll his eyes when David is talking? Does Susie suddenly look down at her notes when Sang begins to talk? Does Chris always seem to dislike and object to the ideas of Matt? Observing can go a long way in tracking and determining how dynamics are working on the team, and how you can improve them. This, by the way, is an emotional intelligence skill of social awareness.

Now that we have addressed teams at length, we will talk about one of the major methods of communication, the team meeting! These can be effective or ineffective, and our goal is for you to be able to run a very effective meeting after you've read the next section!

Key Takeaways

- Team dynamics refers to how people's personalities and behaviors affect a team.
- The five dysfunctions of a team include: absence of trust, fear of conflict, lack of commitment, avoidance of accountability, and inattention to results. When these dysfunctions occur in a team, the team dynamics are often poor and the result is lost productivity.
- There are several blocking personalities that can negatively affect team dynamics.
- Some of the strategies you can use to deal with challenging team members include first understanding what may be going on outside of the team that could be affecting them, having an honest conversation with them to discuss strategies on how to improve, then making sure to follow up.

Exercises

1. Choose one of the strategies on how to create better team dynamics. Put together a plan on how you could actually implement this within your team. Do this from two perspectives; first from the perspective of a team member, and second, from the perspective of being the team leader.
2. Remember all the way back to chapter 1 when we talked about the variety of personality tests, such as Meyers-Briggs? Please refer back to that chapter and your personality test results. Then do self-reflection on how your personality might positively and negatively impact team dynamics.

8.4 Effective Team Meetings

Learning Objective

1. Understand how you can prepare for and conduct effective meetings.

Whether you are a current manager or not, chances are you will have to run a meeting at some point. Running meetings can be tricky business, given all of the team dynamics that come into play! The key to preparing to run a meeting is just that—making sure you are prepared. Next, we will address the required steps to run a successful meeting.

Preparing for the Meeting

To prepare for your meeting, you need to figure out the following:

- What is the purpose of the meeting?
- What are the goals of the meeting?
- How long does the meeting need to be in order to accomplish the goals?
- What technology (Zoom or Skype) will you use to conduct the meeting, or will it be an in-person meeting? During the COVID-19 pandemic most meetings went virtual.
- What deliverables or "to-do" list do you hope to have at the end of the meeting?
- Is everyone available during the time and date you have decided to meet?
- Offer your meeting participants the option to test the planned meeting technology, such as Zoom, ahead of time, so at the start of the meeting you don't have to deal with technology issues. During COVID-19, for example, virtual meeting technologies were unfamiliar to many and resulted in some awkward experiences. Offering the option of testing allows for everyone's comfort level to be higher at the start of the meeting.

The next step, of course, is to create the meeting invitation (Google Calendar, Microsoft Outlook, and many others make it very easy to schedule and send meeting invitations!). Once you've done this, you'll want to create an agenda and attach it to your meeting request. The agenda should contain the following information:

- Time and date of the meeting;
- The meeting membership (who will attend the meeting);
- The meeting goal (what do you hope to accomplish by the end of the meeting?);
- Agenda items (topics) with times attached to them.

Meetings with an agenda containing these items are much more effective, because everyone knows what is expected. Meetings that do not have an agenda or if the agenda isn't followed can get unwieldy, and not a lot may get accomplished.

FIGURE 8.3 Sample Meeting Agenda

As you can see, this meeting agenda has all of the required components. The goal of the meeting is listed, and times have been assigned to each item. Having an agenda allows for a more focused meeting!

Safety Task Force Meeting Agenda

May 16, 2020

3:30-5:00

Members: Julie M (Committee Chair), Patrick L., Lavonne P., Naomi F., Akio C.

Meeting goals: Plan for safety celebration on June 5 and brainstorm ideas for future safety events.

1. Approval of minutes from meeting on May 1, 2020 (5 minutes)
2. Safety celebration (60 minutes)
   a. What is needed?
   b. Who will fill what role?
3. Discussion of statistics for 2nd quarter (10 minutes)
4. Potential future events to ensure safety (15 minutes)
   a. Brainstorming/ideas
   b. Will discuss ideas at next meeting
5. Next meeting: June 15, 2020
6. Adjourn

Conducting the Meeting

First, you want to make sure to start your meeting on time. If you start late, it will allow participants to think it is ok to run 5 or 10 minutes behind for every meeting. Here are some additional tips for making your meeting productive:

- Take minutes—these are notes you can share after the meeting to make sure everything was understood correctly.
- Make sure everyone gets a chance to talk. If some haven't spoken, ask them directly for their opinion.
- Don't allow people to interrupt one another.
- Set a good example—use your camera if in a virtual meeting, and avoid doing other things during the meeting, such as texting.
- Ensure the background in your camera is appropriate. For example, having baskets of laundry behind you or inappropriate artwork or posters can be distracting to participants.
- Make sure to mute your microphone and ask others to do the same if they aren't talking.
- Use the "parking lot" approach when the meeting gets off-topic. This allows a space for you to capture good ideas for later discussion—and also allows you to keep control of the meeting (and team dynamics!) by acknowledging good ideas, while still staying on track with the meeting goals.
- Take notes and write the next meeting agenda as you go along, based on shared ideas and goals that are addressed in your meeting.
- Make sure to stay on track and adhere to the timelines you have in your agenda.

Having an appropriate background during virtual meetings is necessary, and it shows your professionalism.

© Shutterstock

 **WATCH THIS!**

While this video may show some exaggerated bad meetings, it gives tips on how to make running a meeting most effective.

View the video online at: http://www.youtube.com/embed/tMrFLofQeSw?rel=0

As we've addressed in this section, planning for your meeting, then running it effectively will allow more to get done during your meeting.

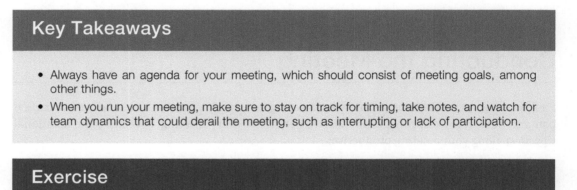

Key Takeaways

- Always have an agenda for your meeting, which should consist of meeting goals, among other things.
- When you run your meeting, make sure to stay on track for timing, take notes, and watch for team dynamics that could derail the meeting, such as interrupting or lack of participation.

Exercise

1. Create agendas for the following meetings, and feel free to make assumptions about the meeting details:
   a. A meeting to discuss recent tardiness among employees
   b. A meeting to address whether or not you should hire a new project manager
   c. A meeting to address how to cover shifts at a restaurant for an upcoming busy weekend

8.5 Chapter Summary and Case

Chapter Summary

- A team is a group that comes together to meet a common goal. There are informal teams, and formal teams, both of which have different structures.
- There are four main types of teams, which includes functional teams, cross-functional teams, virtual teams, and self-directed (managed) teams.
- The phases of the team development process consist of forming, storming, norming, performing, and adjourning.
- Everyone tends to take on a certain member role when working in teams. These can be divided into three main categories including action-oriented behaviors, people-oriented behaviors, and thought-oriented behaviors. This was based on research by Belbin and can be valuable when putting together and working within an effective team.
- Team dynamics refers to how people's personalities and behaviors affect a team.
- The five dysfunctions of a team include: absence of trust, fear of conflict, lack of commitment, avoidance of accountability, and inattention to results. When these dysfunctions occur in a team, the team dynamics are often poor and the result is lost productivity.
- There are several blocking personalities that can negatively affect team dynamics.
- Some of the strategies you can use to deal with challenging team members include first understanding what may be going on outside of the team that could be affecting them, having an honest conversation with them to discuss strategies on how to improve, then making sure to follow up.
- Always have an agenda for your meeting, which should consist of meeting goals, among other things.
- When you run your meeting, make sure to stay on track for timing, take notes, and watch for team dynamics that could derail the meeting, such as interrupting or lack of participation.

Chapter Case

Assume you have been put in charge of a new task force to determine the cause of lost sales in the Western region of your plastics manufacturing firm. As leader of the task force, it is your job to schedule and run effective meetings. The outcome of the meetings will be a report that includes research and possible reasons and solutions for the decline in sales. On your task force will be representatives from the marketing, accounting, and manufacturing departments. Traditionally, your marketing and manufacturing team have conflicting goals, and you are concerned about this as an issue in the meeting. Because you only have time to meet three times, you know the meetings need to be effective to complete the task at hand.

1. Write an agenda for your first meeting.
2. Discuss the phases of the group development process your team will likely go through.
3. As the team leader, you are concerned about personality conflicts that may occur during the storming phase. What are some strategies you can use to reduce or eliminate any issues?

Endnotes

1. McLean, S. (2010). *Business Communication for Success* (Version 1.0). Irvington, NY: FlatWorld Knowledge.

2. Guzman, Z. (13 September 2013). Zappos CEO Tony Hsieh on getting rid of managers: What I wish I'd done differently. *CNBC*. Retrieved from https://www.cnbc.com/2016/09/13/zappos-ceo-tony-hsieh-the-thing-i-regret-about-getting-rid-of-managers.html

3. Tuckman, B.W. (n.d.). Bruce Tuckman forming, storming, norming and performing in groups. Retrieved from http://infed.org/mobi/bruce-w-tuckman-forming-storming-norming-and-performing-in-groups/

4. Abdui, G. (9 May 2010). The five stages of team development: a case study. Project Smart. Retrieved from https://www.projectsmart.co.uk/the-five-stages-of-team-development-a-case-study.php

5. Merchant, P. (4 February 2019). What are the nine types of team roles? *Business Chron*. Retrieved from https://smallbusiness.chron.com/nine-types-team-roles-15566.html

6. Belbin, M. (n.d.). About team roles. Retrieved from https://www.belbin.com/about/belbin-team-roles/

7. DeakinCo. (8 December 2017). 6 strategies for managing and improving team performance. Retrieved from https://www.deakinco.com/media-centre/news/6-strategies-for-managing-and-improving-team-dynamics

8. Lencioni, P. (11 April 2002). The five dysfunctions of a team. Jossey-Bass. Retrieved from https://www.tablegroup.com/books/dysfunctions

9. Mindtools. (n.d.). Improving group dynamics. Retrieved from https://www.mindtools.com/pages/article/improving-group-dynamics.htm

10. Collaboration Statistics. (n.d.). 21 Collaboration Statistics that show the power of teamwork. Retrieved from https://blog.bit.ai/collaboration-statistics/

11. Collaboration Statistics. (n.d.). 21 Collaboration Statistics that show the power of teamwork. Retrieved from https://blog.bit.ai/collaboration-statistics/

12. Winsborough, D., & Chamorro-Premuzic, T. (25 January 2017). Great teams are about personalities not just skills. *Harvard Business Review*. Retrieved from https://hbr.org/2017/01/great-teams-are-about-personalities-not-just-skills

13. EDUCBA. (n.d). Dealing with difficult team members. Retrieved from https://www.educba.com/deal-with-difficult-team-members/

14. Zwillling, M. (n.d.). How to manage a difficult team. *INC*. Retrieved from https://www.inc.com/martin-zwilling/how-to-manage-a-difficult-team-7-ways-to-talk-business-not-emotion.html

CHAPTER 9
How to Make Great Decisions

A peacefulness follows any decision, even the wrong one.
—Rita Mae Brown

The hardest thing to learn in life is which bridge to cross and which to burn.
—David Russell

Too Many Choices

Andi graduated from Spokane Community College two weeks ago with her degree in Business Management. She is anxious to put her knowledge to good use at a job she enjoys.

Andi has an idea of her perfect job and begins work to apply to those organizations that meet her criteria. Using social media and traditional approaches to job searching, Andi gets three interviews at well-known companies in the Spokane area.

After what seems like a week interviewing, Andi receives two job offers! She is thrilled but isn't sure which one to choose. One of the offers is for a higher salary than she expected but requires one week of travel per month. The other job is a lower salary and position, but the possibilities to grow with the company seem better. Andi isn't sure which job to choose.

Big decisions, such as career choices, take a lot of thought and planning to make sure we make the right decision for our needs. This chapter will discuss the ways we can learn to make good personal decisions and also good decisions for the organizations we work for.

9.1 What is Decision Making?

Learning Objective

1. Define and give examples of the types of decisions.

Decision making involves the selection of a course of action from among two or more possible alternatives with the goal of arriving at a solution. We make decisions everyday—from small decisions, such as what to wear and whether to RSVP for that party next weekend, to big decisions such as which job offer to take or whether to move to a new state.

Decision making can occur in groups or at an individual level. As you have probably guessed, the key to positive human relations in these situations is communication and application of emo-

decision making

Involves the selection of a course of action from among two or more possible alternatives with the goal of arriving at a solution.

tional intelligence skills such as self-awareness when making decisions. Emotional intelligence is required in the form of relationship management when making decisions in groups. But what types of decisions need to be made? We will address this next.

"What was the decision making process that led to hiring a cat?"

© Shutterstock

Types of Decisions

programmed decision

A decision where there is a habit, a rule, or a procedure already in place to help you make the decision.

There are two main types of decisions: programmed decisions and non-programmed decisions. A **programmed decision** is one where there is a habit, a rule, or a procedure already in place to help you make the decision. Personally speaking, if you always buy the same type of bread, this would be a programmed decision. You don't need to look at all of the options and consider the best option—because you already know which one you are going to buy. In business, a programmed decision may be deciding the salary for a new hire because your company already has a set pay scale. Or, suppose you are a server at a restaurant and a customer complains about their food. Your company may have a procedure for how to handle this, such as offering a free dessert. This means you do not need to make a decision on how to handle the customer arises as there is already a set procedure in place.

non-programmed decision

When an unusual or unique situation arises where there is not a rule or policy in place to handle it.

A **non-programmed decision** is when an unusual or unique situation arises, where there is not a rule or policy in place to handle it. For example, if you are trying a new recipe and need to buy sage, you might not already have a particular brand or type in mind, so making this decision at the grocery store could take a bit more time. In a business setting, allocating a budget or handling a difficult employee would likely be examples of non-programmed decisions.

In organizations, there are three main types of decisions to be made: operational, tactical, and strategic. **Strategic decisions** are those that guide the direction of the business, and have long-term impacts. For example, a strategic decision might include whether or not to offer a new product line or relocate a factory. As you can tell, these decisions are long term in nature, and often they affect the other two types of decisions—tactical and operational. **Tactical decisions** are those that help implement the strategic decisions that have been made. For example, if a company decides to offer a new product line (strategic), then a practical decision might be a decision relating to packaging and where the products will be sold. A tactical decision can't be made effectively until a strategic decision has been made. **Operational decisions**, on the other hand, refer to the day-to-day running of the business. They might include decisions on how many people to staff in marketing in order to develop the new product line.

Usually, upper management will make strategic decisions, while middle managers make tactical decisions, and "leads" or supervisors often make the operational decisions. Let's look at an example. Suppose the organization has decided to relocate a factory. This is a strategic decision, and management has decided the new factory will be located in Birmingham, Alabama. Then, tactical decisions are made to implement this factory relocation, such as decisions on purchasing the land and construction of the building. Finally, operational decisions are made once the factory is ready, pertaining to how many hours it will need to be staffed, and what shifts people will work. As you've already guessed, this type of decision is an example of a non-programmed decision.

Now that we've looked at the types of decisions, let's address some of the models we can use to make decisions.

strategic decisions

Decisions that guide the direction of the business, and have long-term impacts.

tactical decisions

A type of decision that helps implement the strategic decisions that have been made.

operational decisions

A type of decision based on the day-to-day running of a business.

Key Takeaways

- Decision making involves selecting a course of action among several alternatives.
- Programmed decisions are those where there are habits, rules, or policies in place to help you make the decision, while non-programmed decisions are decisions made when there isn't a rule or policy to dictate what action should be taken.
- Upper level managers tend to make strategic decisions, while middle managers tend to make tactical decisions. Finally, supervisors or "leads" tend to make operational decisions.

Exercise

1. Give two examples of a non-programmed decision you've made recently, and two examples of a programmed decision you've made recently, and discuss how you made the decisions.

9.2 Rational Decision-Making Model and Pitfalls to Avoid

Learning Objectives

1. Be able to apply the rational decision-making model.
2. Discuss and give examples of decision-making pitfalls.

The Rational Decision-Making Model

Now that we've addressed the types of decisions made in our personal and professional lives, it is important to identify a commonly-accepted model for decision making. This model is called the Rational Decision-Making Model, and consists of the steps needed to make a sound decision. These steps include:

1. Identify the problem (or opportunity);
2. Identify the criteria for making the decision;
3. Weight the established criteria;
4. Identify alternatives;
5. Analyze the alteratives;
6. Make the decision;
7. Evaluate the decision.

FIGURE 9.1 The Rational Decision-Making Model
The steps in the rational decision-making model.

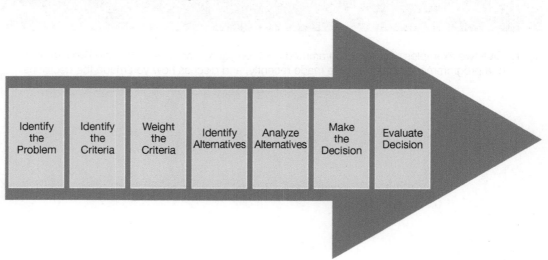

| Identify the Problem | Identify the Criteria | Weight the Criteria | Identify Alternatives | Analyze Alternatives | Make the Decision | Evaluate Decision |

The first step, identify the problem, might be one of the most important steps in the process! Identifying there is a problem and determining exactly what the problem is can be challenging. Suppose sales are down in your department. On the surface, this could appear to be the problem.

But suppose, as you dig deeper, you notice ten sales staff were laid off about a year ago, when sales started to decline. Is the real problem the sales decline, or perhaps it is actually the fact that sales staff were laid off? Identifying the actual problem is a very important first step. From the personal approach, let's say you find you are often late to work. Is this the problem, or is the actual problem the fact you might need to wake up earlier? As you can see, identifying the wrong problem could cause your decision-making process to go in a completely different direction!

The next step, identifying the decision criteria, is important. This is the step that actually allows us to compare those things important to us to figure out the best solution. In this step, you are going to later compare each of your alternatives to this criteria. In our example above, let's say you've identified the problem as lack of sales staff. You might consider key decision criteria to be things like cost and timing. If you are making a personal decision about whether you should accept job A or B, your key decision criteria might be commute time, salary, and benefits, as well as long-term career opportunities. In other words, key decision criteria are those things that are important to you, which you will compare to each alternative.

The problem with coming up with general key decision criteria is that some may be more important to others when making a decision. This is where the next step comes in—allowing you to weigh each of the criteria. Suppose as you are deciding which job to take, you determine salary as most important, and development opportunities as second most important. The other key criteria are important too, but not as important to you as these two. Then, you can create a weighted score to illustrate this importance to you. For example:

- Salary: weight; 50 percent;
- Development opportunities: weight; 30 percent;
- Commute time: weight; 10 percent;
- Benefits: weight; 10 percent.

See how this works? It allows you to determine the most important criteria before you even begin to analyze the alternatives!

The next step is to identify the alternatives. In this case, you are comparing job A to job B. Once these are listed, you can move to the next step, which consists of two parts. The first part is to compare each of the criteria to your alternatives, then come up with a list of pros and cons. This step is analysis of your alternatives. Please see the figure as an example of how to score each of your key decision criteria.

FIGURE 9.2 Identifying Alternatives

Steps to using weighted key decision criteria

STEP ONE: We used a scale of 1-5, with 5 being the best. As you can see, this position scored high on salary and benefits, low on commute and medium on development opportunities.

STEP TWO: Remember how we weighted each of the key decision criteria based on importance to us? We do simple math here to assign each criteria with a score.

Key Decision Criteria	Job A	Weight	Total
Salary	5	50%	5 * .5 = 2.5
Benefits	5	10%	5 * .10 = .5
Commute Time	1	10%	1 * .10 = .1
Development opportunities	1	30%	3 * .30 = .6
			3.7
Pros	• High salary • Great benefits • Ok development opportunities • Excellent manager • Opportunities to move to other locations		
Cons	• Long commute		

STEP THREE: Add up the numbers to determine a final score.

Key Decision Criteria	Job B	Weight	Total
Salary	3	50%	3 * .5 = 1.5
Benefits	1	10%	1 * .10 = .1
Commute Time	5	10%	5 * .10 = .5
Development opportunities	1	30%	1 * .30 = .3
			2.4
Pros	• Ok salary • Close to my house		
Cons	• Not a lot of opportunities for growth • Poor benefits		

STEP FOUR: Follow steps 1-3 above for all your alternatives.

STEP FIVE: Note that job A earned 3.7 points, while job B earned 2.4 points. Based on your weighted key decision criteria, you should choose job A.

As you can see from the chart, the decision should be to choose job A.

The last step is to evaluate the decision. This is an important step, because it allows you to revisit your logic in making the decision, and learn from any mistakes you may have made. For example, let's say you went ahead and picked job A, but there were a few things you didn't consider, such as how awful the commute would be. After reconsidering, you might have weighted the commute higher as a key decision criteria, since it affects your work–life balance. The goal always in this last step is to learn more about yourself!

Obviously, for certain decisions you may not want to go through such a lengthy process. But as you can see, considering all alternatives with a method that tries to leave out bias can be an important part in the decision-making process. But what about some of the mistakes we can make when determining the best course of action? We will address those next!

Pitfalls in Decision Making

As we make decisions, even if we use the rational decision-making model, there are some pitfalls to be aware of either personally or professionally. The first pitfall to avoid is anchoring. **Anchoring** refers to our judgment being clouded by information already presented. It "anchors" us to information that may or may not be true.[1] Say, for example, you have been offered a job and you wish to negotiate for a higher salary. However, when you looked at the Indeed.com posting, it listed the pay was between $45,000 and $50,000 per year. This is anchoring—you already have a baseline of what the salary should be and can be difficult to avoid this pitfall. However, awareness that anchoring could be clouding a decision can help us understand these factors and make better decisions.

The next pitfall is called a **sunk decision**. A sunk decision bias is one where you feel "trapped" in a decision you have made previously. This pitfall often occurs due to ego, as it can be hard to admit we made a wrong decision.[2] Consider a situation where you are in a relationship with another person. You know the relationship isn't going well, so rather than decide to end the relationship, you stay with the person because you've already been with them for three years. Likewise, suppose you've been in your job for three years. You may not want to change jobs because you've already spent so much time with this company. This pitfall is important to recognize, as it can prevent us from moving forward in a way (both professionally and personally) that allows us to make the right decision. The important thing to remember when you try to overcome a sunk decision is sometimes it is better to look toward the future, regardless of what decisions have been made in the past.

Another pitfall can be the status quo pitfall. **Status quo** bias refers to the fact that change can be difficult, therefore it may seem easier to stick with what has already been done or stick with the current decision. In other words, it is easier to stay with the status quo than it is to make a change or a decision. Fear of the unknown with our new decision can be scary. People often stay in the same town or the same job because of status quo—it is easier to know what to expect than make a decision to change, bringing about unknown consequences. Consider Kodak, who created the first digital camera in 1975,[3] but decided not to move forward with it because they were afraid it would cannibalize their existing business. Obviously, sticking with the status quo for Kodak was comfortable, but probably not the right decision in the long run, since few people use film in cameras today.

anchoring

Refers to a pitfall in decision making which occurs when our judgement is already clouded based on information presented already. It "anchors" us to information that may or may not be true.

sunk decision

A sunk decision is one where you feel "trapped" in a decision you have made previously. This pitfall often occurs due to ego, as it can be hard to admit we made a wrong decision.

status quo

Status quo refers to the fact that change can be difficult, therefore it may seem easier to stick with what has already been done or stick with the current decision.

 **WATCH THIS!**

This video addresses the rational decision-making model in the context of a common business decision.

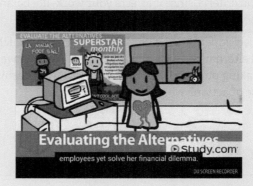

View the video online at: http://www.youtube.com/embed/pOqi9NPTVoY?rel=0

overconfidence bias

Overconfidence bias is one that occurs when we believe our abilities, or our companies' abilities to be better than they are, resulting in misleading of our own abilities or skills.

Overconfidence bias is one that occurs when we believe our abilities, or our companies' abilities to be better than they are, resulting in misleading of our own abilities or skills. Have you ever texted while driving? If so, that may be as a result of overconfidence bias, or the overconfident thought of, "I am an excellent driver even if I am distracted." One of the prime examples of overconfidence bias is the Deepwater Horizon oil spill. BP chose casing for the oil rig based on expected value, rather than safety. They were overconfident in their ability to control the gas "kicks" that resulted from choosing this cheaper casing.[4] As it turned out, they were not able to effectively control the gas "kicks," resulting in the death of eleven people, a major environmental disaster in the Gulf of Mexico, and socioeconomic loss for the southern United States.

Having an awareness of these pitfalls when making decisions can assist us in making better decisions, because understanding them allows us to question ourselves as we make decisions. For example, you can ask yourself:

- What information am I using to make this decision (Anchoring bias)?
- Am I making a decision (or not making a decision) based on time or money already spent (Sunk decision bias)?
- Is fear of the unknown causing me to avoid making a decision (Status Quo bias)?
- Am I being realistic with my own abilities or those of my company (Overcondience bias)?

Now that we have addressed the decision-making process, and pitfalls to avoid, let's talk about the types of decisions managers can make

Management Options in Decision Making

Managers make all kinds of decisions every day. There are some decisions, such as salary, that must be made only by managers, while there are others which can benefit from other options. Let's look at each of those now:[5]

- Make a decision and announce it. This might be appropriate for some situations, such as policy changes on safety or paid time off. However, managers should be careful using this approach, as being "told" what the decision is, depending on the type of decision, may make employees feel unappreciated.

- Present the decision and invite comment. This option, more participative than the last, allows people time to understand the reasoning and rationale for the decision. However, with this option, employees are still not involved in the decision-making process. Depending on the type of decision, there may be more benefit from choosing another approach.

- Present the situation and invite discussion for a joint decision. This highly-participative method gives your employees a chance to speak their mind and allows you to look at the problem and decision from the perspective of the employees. This participative approach should be used in management decision making wherever possible, because it allows for "buy in" from employees. Plus, they may have ideas on the decision-making process you haven't thought of!

- Explain the situation and ask the team to make the decision. This approach can be effective, depending on the development level and trust you have in the employees. It allows the employees to understand the situation—you just have to make sure they have all of the needed data to make the decision. A pitfall with this option is if you decide to go against the team decision. For example, assume you form a hiring committee to hire a new person, and you give your employees free rein to make this decision. They choose a candidate, then you decide to go with someone completely different. This can negatively affect morale, so you need to be prepared to go with whatever decision the team makes.

- Have the team determine the problem along with possible solutions. If the problem is unclear, or your employees have data input to help determine the problem, this is a great option for decision making. However, the same pitfall exists as with the prior option we mentioned—you must be prepared to go with what the team decides.

Although we will address group decision making in the next section, we feel it is important to mention this here, as the way we go about making decisions as a manager can assist us in making rational decisions using the model discussed earlier in this section. But what about personal decision making? Besides using the rational decision-making model, there are some things to consider.

Personal Decision-Making Considerations

When making personal decisions, considering your values—or what is important to you, must be part of the decision-making process.[6] For example, if you are determining whether to take job A or B, and you know your value is time with friends and family, this can help you determine which job is the best option. If flexibility of your time is a value, then choosing a job that allows flex time might be important. In other words, knowing what is important to you as you make decisions is key to making decisions you'll be happy with.

Next, make sure you know not only your values, but your goals (both long and short term) before making a decision.[7] Suppose your goal is becoming a regional sales manager in five years. You are offered a district sales manager position (one level below your goal) and a Digital Marketing manager position (a lateral move from your current position). The question becomes: Which option will help you meet your goal of regional sales manager? Most likely, the best option would be the district sales manager position, since your goal is in direct line with that job. If you take the digital marketing manager position, it may not set you up on the right career path. If you know your goals before making decisions, it can be easier to apply the rational decision-making model, because then you know what weight your key decision criteria should be.

Now that we have addressed decision making as a manager and personal decision making, let's talk about decision making in groups. Group decision making follows a similar process as we've discussed in this section, with a few differences. We will address those in the next section.

Key Takeaways

- The rational decision-making model consists of multiple steps, and allows you to make decisions by way of an organized process.
- There are several pitfalls to avoid when making decisions, including anchoring, sunk decisions, status quo, and overconfidence bias.
- There are a variety of ways you can make management decisions. Some involve little or no input from employees; others allow to identify the problem and make the final decision.
- When making personal decisions, considering values and goals is an important part of the process.

Exercises

1. Address a recent decision you've made, and discuss how you went through each step of the rational decision-making model.
2. Discuss the types of bias when decision making. How can you alleviate these biases?

9.3 Decision Making in Groups

Learning Objectives

1. Understand the concept of groupthink and how to avoid it.
2. Implement strategies for good group decision making.

Group Decision Making

At times, we make decisions on our own, but fairly frequently in business situations, we will make decisions as a group. The advantage to group decision making is the variety of opinions and experiences each member brings to the group. This can assist us in making good decisions because we have more perspectives to make those decisions. In fact, when we make decisions in diverse groups, allowing for discussion of issues can be better for the company—because of the variety of perspectives.[8]

However, there are some possible pitfalls to consider when making group decisions, and also a variety of processes that can help groups make better decisions. Let's address those next.

Groupthink

groupthink

Groupthink occurs when a group of people make a decision that isn't optimal and which is spawned by the urge to conform to what the person believes the group wants.

Have you ever been with a group of friends on a Friday night, and you are deciding what to order for dinner? The group decides on pizza, and they all seem enthusiastic about it. Even though you had pizza last night, you don't say anything because you think it is what the rest of the group wants? This is an example of groupthink. **Groupthink** occurs when a group of people make a decision that isn't optimal and which is spawned by the urge to conform to what the person believes the group wants. As a result, no one speaks up because they do not want to go against the wishes of the group, and the wrong decision is made. Groupthink is characterized by several factors, according to research performed by Irving Janis in the 1970s.[9]

1. **Illusion of invulnerability**. People in the group feel they can't be "wrong" and therefore may not think thoroughly about the courses of action.
2. **Unquestioned beliefs.** This can lead people to ignore possible outcomes and moral problems in the decision they are making.
3. **Stereotyping.** Can cause "in-group" members to ignore "out-group" members who may challenge the ideas of the group.
4. **Self-censorship.** Can cause people to avoid speaking out against what they believe to be the wishes of the group.
5. **Illusions of unanimity.** Can lead members to believing everyone is in agreement.
6. **Direct pressure to conform.** This can be placed on members who pose questions and question the group. It can give a feeling that these individuals are unloyal to the group, which often leads to self-censorship.

There are some things the team can do to avoid groupthink. First, the team should ensure there is a culture of being able to speak up and openly discuss matters without fear. Second, check yourself and make sure you don't self-censor your real feelings when making group decisions. Next, avoid an out-group and in-group mentality. Know that all members are important contributing members and do not shun those that may not agree. Avoid being fearful of questioning assumptions and beliefs. Challenge the groups' assumptions!

There are some ways to help us avoid groupthink, and we will address those next.

What's in it for me?

Do you know we make approximately 35,000 decisions a day?[10] Sure, these decisions may not be big decisions about whether to take job A or B, or whether to take that dream trip to Italy or go to Spain instead, but they are choices still the same. It may be as simple as whether to look at that notification on your phone or whether to wear the brown or black shoes. It may be whether to have a breakfast bar or yogurt for breakfast. No matter the decision—big or small—understanding how many decisions we make per day (and it is a staggering number!) can actually help us make better decisions. By being aware of the decisions and choices we make every day, we can become more self-aware (an emotional intelligence skill!). Remember in the last section we talked about goals and values being an important part of personal decision making? Recognizing all of the decisions we make can assist us in seeing patterns in ourselves, which allows us to determine our possible biases more readily. Which, of course, results in more sound big decisions.

© 2019 https://go.roberts.edu/leadingedge/the-great-choices-of-strategic-leaders

 **WATCH THIS!**

This video shows how groupthink can affect our decisions.

View the video online at: http://www.youtube.com/embed/KwFUkm-p404?rel=0

Tools and Techniques for Making Better Decisions

Nominal Group Technique (NGT)

A technique designed to help with group decision making by ensuring that all members participate fully.

To avoid groupthink, using the rational decision-making model and being aware of the factors that influence groupthink are important.

© Jupiterimages

Nominal Group Technique (NGT) was developed to help with group decision making by ensuring that all members participate fully. NGT is not a technique to be used routinely at all meetings. Rather, it is used to structure group meetings when members are grappling with problem solving or idea generation. It follows four steps. First, each member of the group begins by independently and silently writing down ideas. Second, the group goes in order around the room to gather all the ideas that were generated. This process continues until all the ideas are shared. Third, a discussion takes place around each idea, and members ask for and give clarification and make evaluative statements. Finally, group members vote for their favorite ideas by using ranking or rating techniques. Following the four-step NGT helps to ensure that all members participate fully, and it avoids group decision-making problems such as groupthink.

The Delphi Technique is unique because it is a group process using written responses to a series of questionnaires instead of physically bringing individuals together to make a decision. This allows everyone to give their own opinion first, before hearing the opinions of others, and can help generate new ideas. The first questionnaire asks individuals to respond to a broad question such as stating the problem, outlining objectives, or proposing solutions. Each subsequent questionnaire is built from the information gathered in the previous one. The process ends when the group reaches a consensus. Facilitators can decide whether to keep responses anonymous or not, and responses are sometimes discussed (after questionnaires are filled out) in meetings once all ideas are generated.

Majority rule refers to a decision-making rule in which each member of the group is given a single vote and the option receiving the greatest number of votes is selected. This technique has remained popular, perhaps due to its simplicity, speed, ease of use, and representational fairness. Research also supports majority rule as an effective decision-making technique.[11] However, those who did not vote in favor of the decision will be less likely to support it. This can be a disadvantage, since often we need all team members to have "buy in" in order for the decision to be implemented.

Consensus is another decision-making rule that groups may use when the goal is to gain support for an idea or plan of action. The main downside to consensus is time—as it takes much longer than the other methods mentioned so far. The process works by discussing the issues at hand, generating a proposal, calling for consensus, and discussing any concerns. If concerns still exist, the proposal is modified to accommodate them. These steps are repeated until consensus is reached. Thus, this decision-making rule is inclusive, participatory, cooperative, and democratic. This method may not work for decisions that need to be made quickly. Research shows that consensus can lead to better accuracy,[12] and it helps members feel greater satisfaction with decisions.[13] However, groups take longer with this approach, and if consensus cannot be reached, members tend to become frustrated.[14]

Do you feel ready to make good group decisions? Understanding the pitfalls of groupthink, and also understanding methods that can be used in group decision making will assist us in making better decisions!

The Delphi Technique

A group process that utilizes written responses to a series of questionnaires instead of physically bringing individuals together to make a decision.

majority rule

A decision-making rule in which each member of the group is given a single vote, and the option receiving the greatest number of votes is selected.

consensus

A decision-making rule that groups may use when the goal is to gain support for an idea or plan of action. This decision-making rule is inclusive, participatory, cooperative, and democratic.

Key Takeaways

- Groupthink occurs when a group of people make a decision that isn't optimal and which is spawned by the urge to conform to what the person believes the group wants.
- Groupthink can be minimized by awareness of the factors that contribute to groupthink.
- There are several tools to help make decisions in groups, including the nominal group technique and consensus, to name several.

Exercises

1. Have you ever been part of a group that used one of the group decision-making techniques listed here? How did you feel about the final outcome? If you haven't used these techniques before, please list which one you think is best and explain why.
2. Give an example of a groupthink situation you have personally experienced (at work or in your personal life), and the causes.

9.4 Chapter Summary and Case

Chapter Summary

- Decision making involves selecting a course of action among several alternatives.
- Programmed decisions are those where there are habits, rules, or policies in place to help you make the decision while, non-programmed decisions are decisions made when there isn't a rule or policy to dictate what action should be taken.
- Upper level managers tend to make strategic decisions, while middle managers tend to make tactical decisions. Finally, supervisors or "leads" tend to make operational decisions.
- The rational decision-making model consists of multiple steps, and allows you to make decisions by way of an organized process.
- There are several pitfalls to avoid when making decisions, including anchoring, sunk decisions, status quo, and overconfidence bias.
- There are a variety of ways you can make management decisions. Some involve little or no input from employees; others allow them to identify the problem and make the final decision.
- When making personal decisions, considering values and goals is an important part of the process.
- Even when specific models are followed, groups and individuals can often fall into potential decision-making pitfalls. If too little information is available, decisions might be made based on a feeling. On the other hand, if too much information is presented, people can suffer from analysis paralysis, in which no decision is reached because of the overwhelming number of alternatives.
- Groupthink occurs when a group of people make a decision that isn't optimal and which is spawned by the urge to conform to what the person believes the group wants.
- Groupthink can be minimized by awareness of the factors that contribute to groupthink.
- There are several tools to help make decisions in groups, including the nominal group technique and consensus, to name several.

Chapter Case

Moon Walk and Talk[15]

Warning: *Do not discuss this exercise with other members of your class until instructed to do so.*

You are a member of the moon space crew originally scheduled to rendezvous with a mother ship on the lighted surface of the moon. Due to mechanical difficulties, however, your ship was forced to land at a spot some 200 miles (320 km) from the rendezvous point. During reentry and landing, much of the equipment aboard was damaged, and because survival depends on reaching the mother ship, the most critical items available must be chosen for the 200-mile (320 km) trip. Please see the list of the fifteen items left intact and undamaged after landing. Your task is to rank the items in terms of their importance for your crew to reach the rendezvous point. Place the number 1 by the most important, 2 by the next most important, and so on, with 15 being the least important. This goes in the "my ranking" column.

Once you've ranked each item, you will be put in a team which will agree on a group ranking for each item. Once this is complete, we will discuss the actual NASA ranking and reasoning behind each item.

Once this is complete, please answer the questions that follow.

Undamaged items	My ranking	Group ranking	NASA ranking	My difference	Group difference
Box of matches					
Food concentrates					
50 feet of nylon					
Parachute silk					
Portable heating unit					
Two 45-caliber pistols					
One case dehydrated milk					
Two 100 lb. tanks oxygen					
Stellar map (of moon's constellations)					
Life raft					
Magnetic compass					
5 gallons of water					
Signal flares					
First aid kit containing injection needles					
Solar powered FM receiver–transmitter					

1. How did your individual ranking compare with the group ranking?

2. What group technique did you use to determine the group rankings? Was it effective? Why or why not?

3. Did any groupthink occur in your group? If yes, explain. If no, explain what strategies your group used to eliminate the factors associated with groupthink.

Endnotes

1. Evans, M. (n.d.). Pitfalls in decision making. Retrieved from https://exinfm.com/board/pitfalls_in_decision_making.htm

2. Moraiti, C. (29 October 2016). 4 most common pitfalls in decision making. Retrieved from https://www.alphagamma.eu/entrepreneurship/4-common-pitfalls-decision-making/

3. The Energy Project. (n.d.). Innovation as the status quo. Retrieved from https://theenergyproject.com/innovation-as-the-status-quo/

4. Dauvergne, J. (16 July 2012). Study of behavioral decision making: BP and the Deepwater Horizon disaster of 2010. Retrieved from https://www.slideshare.net/JeromeDauvergne/deepwater-horizon-oil-spill-29814608

5. Zwilling, M. (n.d.). There are 7 types of decision making. Retrieved from https://www.inc.com/martin-zwilling/there-are-7-types-of-decision-making-which-one-is-best-for-you.html

6. Frank, S. (n.d.). Difficult personal decision? 3 steps you need to make the right one. Retrieved from https://www.inc.com/stephanie-frank/difficult-personal-decision-here-are-the-3-steps-you-need-to-make-the-right-one-.html

7. Litemind. (n.d.). How to make great decisions in life. Retrieved from https://litemind.com/decision-insights/

8. Simons, T., Pelled, L.H., & Smith, K.A. (1999). Making use of difference: Diversity, debate, decision comprehensiveness in top management teams. *Academy of Management Journal, 42*, 662–73.

9. Janis, I.L. (1972). *Victims of groupthink*. New York: Houghton Mifflin.

10. Hoomans, J. (20 March 2015). 35,000 decisions a day. https://go.roberts.edu/leadingedge/the-great-choices-of-strategic-leaders

11. Hastie, R., & Kameda, T. (2005). The robust beauty of majority rules in group decisions. *Psychological Review, 112*, 494–508.

12. Roch, S.G. (2007). Why convene rater teams: An investigation of the benefits of anticipated discussion, consensus, and rater motivation. *Organizational Behavior and Human Decision Processes, 104*, 14–29.

13. Mohammed, S., & Ringseis, E. (2001). Cognitive diversity and consensus in group decision making: The role of inputs, processes, and outcomes. *Organizational Behavior and Human Decision Processes, 85*, 310–35.

14. Peterson, R. (1999). Can you have too much of a good thing? The limits of voice for improving satisfaction with leaders. *Personality and Social Psychology, 25*, 313–24.

15. NASA educational materials. (n.d.). http://www.nasa.gov/audience/foreducators/topnav/materials/listbytype/Survival_Lesson.html

CHAPTER 10

Managing Conflict and Understanding Unions

> *The only way to get the best of an argument is to avoid it.*
>
> —Dale Carnegie

> *During a negotiation, it would be wise not to take anything personally. If you leave personalities out of it, you will be able to see opportunities more objectively.*
>
> —Brian Koslow

Negotiation Breakdown

You are part of a team charged with negotiating the new collective bargaining agreement for your union. Your union is requesting profit sharing, a 10 percent raise for all union members, and an additional week of vacation time.

When you go into the meeting with management, they present their terms, which include a 5 percent pay cut due to lower product demand and greater responsibility to cover the cost of health care for union members, which would amount to about $50 per person, per paycheck.

The lead team member laughs at management's requests and tells them they have a long way to go in order to avoid a strike. You are uncomfortable with this comment, as you believe it doesn't set the right tone for the negotiation. In addition, the statement appears to be threatening, which you know is something to avoid during negotiation.

When your team presents their terms, management says there is no way they can meet those demands, so the union better get more realistic about the current economic state of the company.

As you leave the bargaining table with no progress, you know there is a long way to go before the union and management will be able to come to a resolution.

The focus of this chapter is to discuss conflict styles, and how to manage conflict in order to avoid situations such as this when negotiating.

10.1 What is Conflict?

In this chapter, you'll see that learning how to handle conflict and engaging in effective negotiation are key to successful human relations and to a successful career. Learning how to handle conflict confidently is a key component in your emotional intelligence toolkit—specifically, self-awareness and relationship management. Without the ability to deal with conflict, it is difficult to maintain healthy relationships.

Conflict can range from something small, such as a disagreement with a colleague, to something large such as violence in the workplace. In 2017, in fact, 18,400 workers reported being victims of workplace violence.[1]

conflict

A process that involves people disagreeing.

Conflict is defined as the difference between two or more beliefs, ideas, or interests. Conflict, if not addressed and resolved, can cause issues between friends, colleagues, and managers. There are several types of conflict which we will address next.

Types of Conflict

Intrapersonal Conflict

intrapersonal conflict

Conflict that arises within a person.

Intrapersonal conflict is a type of conflict that is internal. That is, the conflict takes place within someone's mind. It is a type of conflict that takes into consideration a person's values, thoughts, principles, and emotions. This type of conflict can be something small, such as deciding whether or not to walk the extra thirty steps to recycle your bottle, or something large, such as deciding which job to take. This type of conflict can be difficult to handle if one does not have the emotional intelligence skills of understanding one's own emotions.

Interpersonal Conflict

interpersonal conflict

Conflict that involves two individuals in disagreement.

Interpersonal conflict involves two individuals in disagreement. This is a natural thing, because everyone has a different personality, different beliefs, and different perspectives. An interpersonal conflict could be as simple as you and your friend wanting to go to two difference places for dinner, or something larger, such as a colleague and you disagreeing about the best way to handle a large project in your organization.

Intragroup Conflict

Intragroup conflict is when members of the same team (more than two) have a disagreement about something. This is similar to interpersonal conflict, in that it occurs because of different values, beliefs, and personalities. This type of conflict can be positive if managed correctly, because it gets team members to discuss issues and come to a resolution. If not handled appropriately, these types of conflicts can grow out of control and create issues among all of the team members. An example of an intragroup conflict might be two members of the marketing department disagreeing on the right approach for the new social media marketing campaign.

intragroup conflict

Conflict where members of a team (more than two) have a disagreement about something.

Intergroup Conflict

Intergroup conflict occurs when there are disagreements among different teams in an organization. For example, if the marketing department and the accounting department don't agree on a budget, this would be an example of intergroup conflict. This type of conflict occurs because of different interests and goals between the two teams.

Intergroup conflict

Occurs when there are disagreements among different teams in an organization.

Conflict Can Be Positive!

Often, when we think of conflict, we think of something negative. But conflict can actually be a way for people to be more productive! For example, if conflict is managed correctly, it can create several benefits in an organization, such as:

- Conflict can encourage new thinking;
- Conflict can raise important questions;
- Conflict can help beat stagnation;
- Conflict can build relationships;
- Conflict can cause people to have more open minds.

Based on these benefits, the next section will address how to manage conflict to make it productive.

 **WATCH THIS!**

This video demonstrates ways in which conflict can be positive.

View the video online at: http://www.youtube.com/embed/o97fVGTjE4w?rel=0

Key Takeaways

- Conflict, if managed correctly, can be beneficial to an organization.
- There are four types of conflict: intrapersonal, interpersonal, intragroup, and intergroup.
- Intrapersonal conflict refers to conflict that takes place within a person's mind. Interpersonal conflict takes place between two people. Intragroup conflict occurs when two or more members of a team don't agree, and intergroup conflict occurs when two different teams within an organization experience a conflict.

Exercise

1. Write a paragraph about the last conflict (big or small) you experienced. How did this conflict turn out? Are there ways you could have handled it better?

10.2 Conflict Styles and Managing Conflict

Learning Objectives

1. Identify your conflict-handling style.
2. Address advantages, disadvantages, and situations where each conflict-handling style might be used.
3. Implement strategies for effective conflict management.

As we addressed in the last section, conflict can be positive if managed correctly. We will first discuss styles of handling conflict, and the advantages and disadvantages to each style.[2]

Conflict-Handling Styles

Individuals vary in the way that they handle conflicts. There are five common styles of handling conflicts, as noted in the Thomas-Kilmann model for handling conflict.[3] Understanding how you handle conflict may make it easier to recognize how others handle conflict, resulting in better conflict management.

Competing

The **competing conflict style** is an approach where "I win, you lose." This style can come across as competitive, confrontational, and sometimes even aggressive. This type of style is best used when a quick decision needs to be made or when a manager needs to make an unpopular decision. This type of style can harm relationships, but can work if you need to stand up for your rights on an issue that is important to you. If you are dealing with an unreasonable customer, you might use this style to say, "I'm sorry, I can't give you a full refund on your meal."

competing conflict style

An approach to settling conflict with a statement where "I win, you lose" is utilized.

Accommodating

The **accommodating conflict style** is one where you give in to another's wishes, in other words, "I lose, you win." This approach is useful if you prefer to preserve the relationship rather than "win." Often, this style will be used when you see that someone cares deeply about an issue, and you know it doesn't matter to you that much. For example, if you and your roommate have a conflict over the temperature in your house, you might give in and keep it colder than you like because the issue just isn't that important to you. The downside to this approach is the fact it can give a false solution to a problem—because you give in and let the other person have what they want. With this approach, the goal is to please others to keep the peace.

accommodating conflict style

A style of conflict resolution where you give in to another's wishes, in other words, "I lose, you win."

Avoiding

An **avoiding conflict style** means withdrawal from the conflict or avoiding the conflict altogether. Because you are unwilling to face the conflict, it often results in an "I lose, you lose" situation. Use of this style can give the other person the perception you don't care. However, sometimes using this style is best if you need to really think about the situation and how to respond. For example, assume a friend texts you and says, "I'm angry because you always show up late when we are supposed to meet up at a certain time." You may use an avoiding conflict style initially because you need time to consider how you will respond. If this is a style you use often, though, you may find conflicts simmer and blow up all of a sudden over something small.

avoiding conflict style

A means of withdrawing from the conflict or avoiding the conflict altogether.

Conflict, if handled correctly, can actually be helpful to an organization.

© Shutterstock

compromising conflict style

"I win some, you win some." This can be an effective way to maintain relationships, but often means neither of you get what you want, since you are meeting somewhere in the middle.

Compromising

The **compromising conflict style** means, "I win some, you win some." This can be an effective way to maintain relationships, but often means neither of you get what you want, since you are meeting somewhere in the middle. Consider a conflict about where to go to dinner—you want sushi, your partner wants Italian food. So you decide, instead, to eat Thai food. It is a compromise—you both gave a little, but neither person is 100 percent satisfied with the decision.

Do you know your conflict-handling style? Knowing yourself may help to explain how you manage conflict, and give you ideas on how you can better manage conflict. Management of conflict is an emotional intelligence skill, which allows you to build relationships, and also create more self-awareness. Take this quiz to determine your preferred conflict-management style: http://www.blake-group.com/sites/default/files/assessments/Conflict_Management_Styles_Assessment.pdf

Collaborating

collaborating conflict style

"I win, you win." This style can be beneficial in most situations, because you spend time discussing the underlying issue.

The **collaborating conflict style** focuses on, "I win, you win." This style can be beneficial in most situations, because you spend time discussing the underlying issue. However, the downside is that often it can take time to get to that point. With this style, you do not give up your self interest, nor do you expect the other person to give up theirs. Instead, you focus on understanding another's view, and they do the same for you. An example of this style in action might be a conflict regarding budget issues between the marketing and accounting departments. The group may sit down together and discuss reasoning, then come to a conclusion where everyone gets what they want. As we stated, this style can take time, and may not be appropriate when a quick decision needs to be made.

WATCH THIS!

This video illustrates ways in which conflict can be resolved.

View the video online at: http://www.youtube.com/embed/KY5TWVz5ZDU?rel=0

 **WATCH THIS!**

Liz Kislik discusses why there's so much conflict at work and what you can do to fix it.

View the video online at: http://www.youtube.com/embed/2l-AOBz69KU?rel=0

Managing Conflict

We can all learn how to manage conflict better, utilizing the styles we addressed in the last section. It is important to note that no one style is best; rather, it is best to use a variety of styles, depending on the individual situation.

Identify Interests (Needs)

One of the best ways to manage conflict is to identify your needs, not your wants. What is critical, and why is it critical? This will help people better understand why you are asking for something. For example, telling your colleague, "I want those figures by Monday," is not nearly as effective as identifying your interests (needs). You can show your identification of needs by saying instead, "I'd like those figures by Monday so I have time to edit and add them into my report before our presentation on Wednesday." See how identifying the need actually works better? When people take a "hard stance" (competing style) such as, "The only choice is x and that's final," they will find it much more difficult to manage conflict, because they are only concerned about their own interest, not the interests of others.

Identifying your own interests (needs) is just as important as identifying the other person(s) interests. This way, you can frame your needs in a way that helps the other person meet their interests too. To determine what those interests are, you might ask open-ended questions, such as:

- What are you concerned about?
- What has worked for you before?
- Tell me your reasons for wanting x?
- What do you think about x?
- If you had your choice, what direction would you go and why?

Framing questions in this way can help you get to the root of the conflict, making a solution much easier to determine.

Steps to Conflict Resolution

There are several steps you can take to resolve a conflict.[4] The first step to resolving a conflict is determining what the disagreement is. Often, people are in agreement, and the real disagreement is how to accomplish the same goal. For example, two people working together may agree the report should be formatted the same way, but one person wants to use a Microsoft Word report template, while the other wants to manually input headings. The two are actually in agreement (the report needs to be formatted professionally) but have different ideas on how to go about accomplishing the goal. So, identifying what the actual disagreement is will help get to the heart of the matter.

The next step is to determine what the common goals are. As we discussed, often the end goal may be the same, but discussing the goals (and finding common goals) is an important step to determining what the next steps will be.

The third step, after determining common goals, is to brainstorm ideas on how to meet the common goal ideas and discuss any pitfalls or barriers that could prevent people from meeting the goal. By identifying (and being open to the other person's ideas), we are better able to see another side and, therefore, more willing to be creative in our thinking.

The fourth step is to determine what steps to take to meet the common goal. The individuals involved in the conflict should be able to agree on the best way to achieve the goal after discussion.

Finally, the last step is to address what each party's responsibilities will be in meeting the goal. What will each person need to do to resolve the conflict? What are the next steps to meeting the common agreed-upon goal?

Here are some other tips to consider when resolving conflict:

- Listen to the other party.
- Avoid overarching statements such as "you never" or "you always."
- Find the interests (needs) of all involved.
- Work together to come up with solutions.
- Avoid judgments.
- Share your strong feelings respectfully.
- Be willing to listen to other's strong feelings, even if you disagree.
- Do not react to emotional outbursts (e.g., "It looks like you are feeling emotional. Maybe we should take a break and talk about this in the morning?")
- Try to understand the other person's side.

Now that we've addressed the five common styles of handling, and managing conflict, we will address unions in organizations, and how conflict can be managed between unions and management.

Key Takeaways

- There are five main styles of handling conflict, with advantages and disadvantages to each.
- The five styles of handling conflicting include: competing, accommodating, avoiding, compromising, and collaborating.
- Identifying interests is an important aspect of resolving conflict.
- There are five steps to conflict resolution, which can be implemented to reduce conflict and come to a "win-win" resolution.

Exercise

1. Take the conflict style assessment in the "What's in it for me?" box in this section. After you've taken the quiz, address each of the following:

   a. What is your preferred conflict-management style?

   b. What is your least preferred conflict-management style?

   c. Give an example of when you've used your preferred conflict-management style. How did the conflict turn out?

   d. Identify three strategies you can implement to work on utilizing your least preferred conflict-management style.

   e. Using the steps identified in this section, outline each step and how you might use it to better resolve the conflict you identified in (c).

10.3 What are Labor Unions?

Learning Objectives

1. Be able to discuss the history of labor unions.
2. Explain some of the reasons for a decline in union membership over the past sixty years.
3. Be able to explain the process of unionization and laws that relate to unionization.

Since we are addressing conflict in this chapter, it makes sense to also address labor unions, and some of the conflicts that occur between labor unions and management.

> **labor union**
>
> A group of workers who band together to meet common goals, such as better pay, benefits, or promotion rules.

There is a good chance that, at some time in your career, you will join a labor union. The purpose of this section is to give you some background about unions. Oftentimes, depending on your union involvement, you may have to use a number of the human relations skills you have gained so far from reading this book. For example, the ability to work in a team and handle conflict are all aspects you may experience as a union member—or a member of any organization. A **labor union**, or union, is defined as workers banding together to meet common goals, such as better pay, benefits, or promotion rules. In the United States, 10.5 percent of workers belong to labor unions.[5] In this section, we will discuss the history of unions, reasons for decline in union membership, union labor laws, and the process employees go through to form a union. First, however, we should discuss some of the reasons why people join unions.

People may feel their economic needs are not being met with their current wages and benefits and believe that a union can help them receive better economic prospects. Fairness in the workplace is another reason why people join unions. They may feel that scheduling, vacation time, transfers, and promotions are not given fairly and feel that a union can help eliminate some of the unfairness associated with these processes. Let's discuss some basic information about unions before we discuss the unionization process.

History and Organization of Unions

Trade unions were developed in Europe during the Industrial Revolution, when employees had little skill and all the power was shifted to the employer. When this power shifted, many employees were treated unfairly and underpaid. In the United States, unionization increased with the building of railroads in the late 1860s. Wages in the railroad industry were low, and the threat of injury or death was high, as was the case in many manufacturing facilities with little or no safety laws and regulations in place. As a result, the Brotherhood of Locomotive Engineers and several other brotherhoods (focused on specific tasks such as conductors and brakemen), were formed to protect workers' rights. However, many workers were fired because of their union membership.

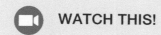 **WATCH THIS!**

A video from the AFL-CIO shows a history of labor unions, from its perspective.

View the video online at: http://www.youtube.com/embed/ublWyT7nGdU?rel=0

The National Labor Union (NLU), formed in 1866, paved the way for other labor organizations. The goal of the NLU was to form a national labor federation that could lobby the government for labor reforms on behalf of labor organizations. Its main focus was to limit the workday to eight hours. While the NLU garnered many supporters, it excluded Chinese workers and only made some attempts to defend the rights of African Americans and female workers. The NLU can be credited with the eight-hour workday, which was passed in 1862. Because of a focus on government reform rather than collective bargaining, many workers joined the Knights of Labor in the 1880s.

The Knights of Labor started as a fraternal organization, and when the NLU dissolved, the Knights grew in popularity as the labor union of choice. The Knights promoted the social and cultural spirit of the worker better than the NLU had. It originally flourished as a labor union for coal miners but also covered several other types of industries. The Knights of Labor initiated strikes that were successful in increasing pay and benefits, and membership increased. After only a few years, though, membership declined because of unsuccessful strikes, which were a result of an autocratic structure, lack of organization, and poor management. Disagreements between members within the organization also caused its demise.

The American Federation of Labor (AFL) was formed in 1886, mostly by people who wanted to see a change from the Knights of Labor. The focus was on higher wages and job security. Infighting among union members was minimized, creating a strong organization that still exists today. In the 1930s, the Congress of Industrial Organizations (CIO) was formed as a result of political differences in the AFL. In 1955, the two unions joined together to form the AFL-CIO.

Currently, the AFL-CIO is the largest federation of unions in the United States and is made up of fifty-six national and international unions. The goal of the AFL-CIO isn't to negotiate specific contracts for employees but rather to support the efforts of local unions throughout the country.

FIGURE 10.1 The Complicated Structure of AFL-CIO

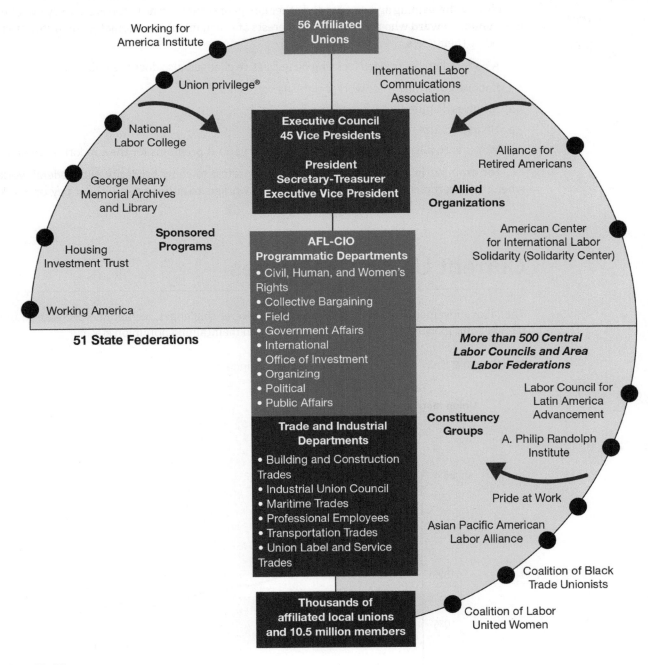

Data from: AFL-CIO

Currently in the United States, there are two main national labor unions that oversee several industry-specific local unions. There are also numerous independent national and international unions that are not affiliated with either national union:

1. AFL-CIO: local unions include Airline Pilots Association, American Federation of Government Employees, Associated Actors of America, and Federation of Professional Athletes.

2. CTW (Change to Win Federation): includes the Teamsters, Service Employees International Union, United Farm Workers of America, and United Food and Commercial Workers.

3. Independent unions: Directors Guild of America, Fraternal Order of Police, Independent Pilots Association, Major League Baseball Players Association.

The national union plays an important role in legislative changes, while the local unions focus on collective bargaining agreements and other labor concerns specific to the area. Every local union has a **union steward** who represents the interests of union members. Normally, union stewards are elected by their peers.

A national union, besides focusing on legislative changes, also does the following:

1. Lobbies government for worker rights laws;

2. Resolves disputes between unions;

3. Helps organize national protests;

4. Works with allied organizations and sponsors various programs for the support of unions.

For example, in 2018, Teamsters organized a protest to show solidarity with federal workers when the government shut down, forcing federal workers to either work without pay, or to take a leave of absence (furlough).[6]

union steward

An elected person with the organization who represents the interests of union members.

Current Union Challenges

The labor movement is currently experiencing several challenges, including a decrease in union membership, globalization, and employers' focus on maintaining nonunion status.

FIGURE 10.2 Union Membership has Declined Since 1983

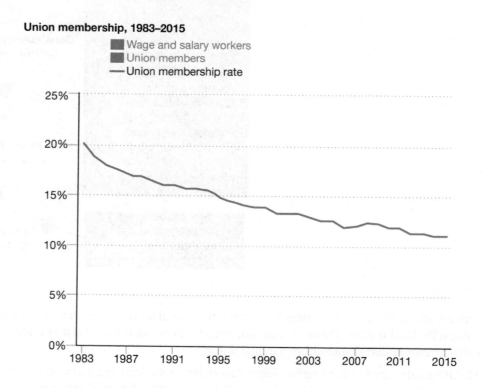

Union membership, 1983–2015
- Wage and salary workers
- Union members
- — Union membership rate

Data from: https://www.bls.gov/spotlight/2016/union-membership-in-the-united-states/pdf/union-membership-in-the-united-states.pdf

Research says the decline of unions is a result of globalization and the fact that many jobs that used to be unionized in the manufacturing arena have now moved overseas.[7] Other reasoning points to management's unwillingness to work with unions, which has caused a decline in membership. Others suggest that unions are on the decline because of themselves. Past corruption, negative publicity, and hard-line tactics have made joining a union less favorable.

Globalization is also a challenge in labor organizations today. As more and more goods and services are produced overseas, unions lose not only membership but also union values in the stronghold of worker culture. As globalization has increased, unions have continued to demand more governmental control but have been only somewhat successful in these attempts. Free trade agreements such as the North American Free Trade Agreement (NAFTA) have made it easier and more lucrative for companies to manufacture goods overseas. For example, La-Z-Boy and Whirlpool closed production facilities in Dayton and Cleveland, Ohio, and built new factories in Mexico to take advantage of cheaper labor and less stringent environmental standards. Globalization creates options for companies to produce goods wherever they think it best to produce them. As a result, unions are fighting the globalization trend to try and keep jobs in the United States.

There are a number of reasons why companies do not want unions in their organizations, which we will discuss in greater detail later. One of the main reasons, however, is increased cost and less management control. As a result, companies are on a quest to maintain a union-free work environment. In doing so, they try to provide higher wages and benefits so workers do not feel compelled to join a union. Companies that want to stay union free constantly monitor their retention strategies and policies.

Labor Union Laws

The **Railway Labor Act (RLA)** of 1926 originally applied to railroads and was amended in 1936 to cover airlines. The act received support from both management and unions. The goal of the act is to ensure no disruption of interstate commerce. The main provisions of the act include alternate dispute resolution, arbitration, and mediation to resolve labor disputes. Any dispute must be resolved in this manner before a strike can happen. The RLA is administered by the National Mediation Board (NMB), a federal agency, and outlines very specific and detailed processes for dispute resolution in these industries.

The **Norris-LaGuardia Act** of 1932 (also known as the anti-injunction bill) barred federal courts from issuing injunctions (a court order that requires a party to do something or refrain from doing something) against nonviolent labor disputes and barred employers from interfering with workers joining a union. The act was a result of common **yellow-dog contracts**, in which a worker agreed not to join a union before accepting a job. The Norris-LaGuardia Act made yellow-dog contracts unenforceable in courts and established that employees were free to join unions without employer interference.

Railway Labor Act (RLA)

Passed in 1926, the act applies to railroads and airlines. The goal of the act is to ensure no disruption of interstate commerce.

Norris-LaGuardia Act

Passed in 1932 (also known as the anti-injunction bill), this act barred federal courts from issuing injunctions against nonviolent labor disputes and barred employers from interfering with workers joining a union.

yellow-dog contracts

Before the Norris-LaGuardia Act, contracts in which a worker agreed not to join a union before accepting a job.

Wagner Act

A law passed in 1935 that changed the way employers can react to several aspects of unions and unionization.

National Labor Relations Board (NLRB)

The organization that oversees and enforces the Wagner and Taft-Hartley acts. It handles unfair labor practice complaints and facilitates unionization efforts.

Taft-Hartley Act

An act passed in 1947 that put several restrictions on unions. It amended the Wagner Act.

wildcat strikes

Strikes not authorized by the union and considered illegal according to the Taft-Hartley Act.

secondary actions

Made illegal by the Taft-Hartley Act, which disallowed a union from going on strike in sympathy for another union.

Landrum Griffin Act

An act passed in 1959 that is supposed to limit corruption in unions by requiring secret elections and reporting of financial information.

In 1935, the **Wagner Act** (sometimes called the National Labor Relations Act) was passed, changing the way employers can react to several aspects of unions. The Wagner Act had a few main points:

1. Employers must allow freedom of association and organization and cannot interfere with, restrain, or coerce employees who form a union.

2. Employers may not discriminate against employees who form or are part of a union or those who file charges.

3. An employer must bargain collectively with representation of a union.

The **National Labor Relations Board (NLRB)** oversees the Wagner Act, handling any complaints that may arise from the violation of this act.

The **Taft-Hartley Act** also had major implications for unions. Passed in 1947, Taft-Hartley amended the Wagner Act. The act was introduced because of the upsurge of strikes during this time period. While the Wagner Act addressed unfair labor practices on the part of the company, the Taft-Hartley Act focused on unfair acts by the unions. For example, it outlawed strikes that were not authorized by the union, called **wildcat strikes**. It also prohibited **secondary actions** (or secondary boycotts) in which one union goes on strike in sympathy for another union. The act allowed the executive branch of the federal government to disallow a strike should the strike affect national health or security. One of the most famous injunctions was made by President Ronald Reagan in 1981. Air traffic controllers had been off the job for two days despite their no-strike oath, and Reagan ordered all of them (over eleven thousand) discharged because they violated this federal law.

The **Landrum Griffin Act**, also known as the Labor Management Reporting and Disclosure (LMRDA) Act, was passed in 1959. This act required unions to hold secret elections, required unions to submit their annual financial reports to the US Department of Labor, and created standards governing expulsion of a union member. This act was created because of racketeering and corruption charges within unions. In fact, investigations of the Teamsters union found they were linked to organized crime, and the Teamsters were banned from the AFL-CIO. The goal of this act was to regulate the internal functioning of unions and to combat abuse of union members by union leaders.

FIGURE 10.3 Major Acts Regarding Unions, at a Glance

Railway Labor Act	• Covers railroads and airlines • Alternate dispute resolution methods instead of striking for these two industries
Norris-LaGuardia Act	• As a result of yellow-dog contracts • Barred federal courts from issuing injunctions against nonviolent labor disputes
Wagner Act	• Allowed for freedom to join a union without interference • May not discriminate against union employees • Set collective bargaining rules
Taft-Hartley Act	• Amends Wagner Act • Focus was on unfair practices by the union
Landrum-Griffin Act	• Required unions to hold secret elections • Financial reporting of unions required

The Unionization Process

There are one or two ways in which a unionization process can begin. First, the union may contact several employees and discuss the possibility of a union, or employees may contact a union on their own. The union will then help employees gather signatures to show that the employees want to be part of a union. To hold an election, the union must show signatures from over 30 percent of the employees of the organization.

FIGURE 10.4 The Unionization Process

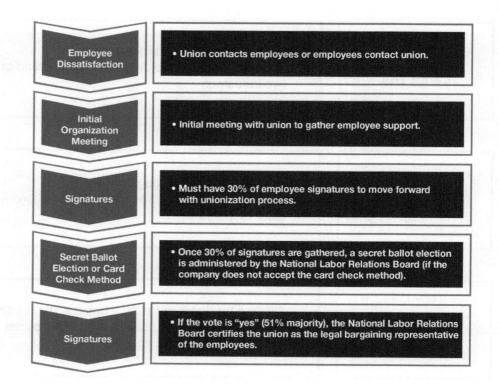

Once the signatures are gathered, the National Labor Relations Board is petitioned to move forward with a secret-ballot election. An alternative to the secret-ballot election is the card check method, in which the union organizer provides the company with authorization cards signed by a simple majority (half plus one). The employer can accept the cards as proof that the employees desire a union in their organization. The NLRB then certifies the union as the employees' collective bargaining representative.

If the organization does not accept the card check method as authorization for a union, the second option is via a secret ballot. Before this method is used, a petition must be filed by the NLRB, and an election is usually held two months after the petition is filed. In essence, the employees vote whether to unionize or not, and there must be a simple majority (half plus one). The NLRB is responsible for election logistics and counting of ballots. Observers from all parties can be present during the counting of votes. Once votes are counted, a decision on unionization occurs, and at that time, the collective bargaining process begins.

Once the NLRB is involved, there are many limits as to what the employer can say or do during the process to prevent unionization of the organization. It is advisable for HR and management to be educated on what can legally and illegally be said during this process. It is illegal to threaten or intimidate employees if they are discussing a union. You cannot threaten job, pay, or benefits loss as a result of forming a union. Figure 10.5 includes information on what should legally be avoided if employees are considering unionization.

FIGURE 10.5 Things That Shouldn't Be Said to Employees during a Unionization Process

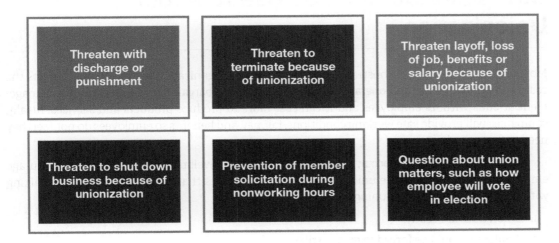

Threaten with discharge or punishment

Threaten to terminate because of unionization

Threaten layoff, loss of job, benefits or salary because of unionization

Threaten to shut down business because of unionization

Prevention of member solicitation during nonworking hours

Question about union matters, such as how employee will vote in election

Obviously, it is in the best interest of the union to have as many members as possible. Because of this, unions may use many tactics during the organizing process. For example, many unions are also politically involved and support candidates who they feel best represent labor. They provide training to organizers and sometimes even encourage union supporters to apply for jobs in nonunion environments to actively work to unionize other employees when they are hired. This practice is called **union salting**. Unions, especially on the national level, can be involved in corporate campaigns that boycott certain products or companies because of their labor practices. The United Food and Commercial Workers (UFCW), for example, has a "Wake Up Walmart Campaign" that targets the labor practices of this organization.

union salting

A union strategy that encourages union supporters to apply for jobs in nonunion environments to actively work to unionize other employees when they are hired.

▶ WATCH THIS!

Amid an ailing economy, labor unions find themselves struggling to compromise with employers on wages and benefits.

View the video online at: http://www.youtube.com/embed/g57Mg-489KQ?rel=0

Strategies Companies Use to Avoid Unionization

Most organizations feel the constraints of having a union organization are too great. It affects the cost to the organization and operation efficiency. Collective bargaining at times can put management at odds with its employees and it can cost more to produce products and services. Ideally, companies will provide safe working conditions, fair pay, and benefits so employees do not feel they need to form a union.

When a union vote may occur, most organizations will develop specific strategies to encourage employees to vote "no" for the union. Some of the arguments that might be used include talking with the employee and mentioning the following:

1. Union dues are costly.
2. Employees could be forced to go on strike.
3. Employees and management may no longer be able to discuss matters informally and individually.
4. Unionization can create more bureaucracy within the company.
5. Individual issues may not be discussed.
6. Many decisions within a union, such as vacation time, are based on seniority only.

But why would a company not want a union in their organization? We will address this in the next section.

The Impact of Unions on Organizations

You may wonder why organizations are opposed to unions. As we have mentioned, since union workers do receive higher wages, this can have a negative impact on the organization. Unionization also impacts the ability of managers to make certain decisions and limits their freedom when working with employees. For example, if an employee is consistently late for work, the union contract will specify the discipline, resulting in little management freedom to handle this situation on a case-by-case basis. For example, a Volkswagen plant in Chattanooga, TN, recently voted on adding a labor union due to scheduling issues, enforcing safety, and increasing pay. The vote was unsuccessful, which meant a labor union would not be part of this manufacturing plant's near future.[8]

Key Takeaways

- Union membership in the United States has been slowly declining. Today, union membership consists of only 10.5 percent of the workforce.
- The reasons for union decline are varied, depending on whom you ask. Some say moving jobs overseas is the reason, while others say unions' hard-line tactics put them out of favor.
- Besides declining membership, union challenges today include globalization and companies' wanting a union-free workplace.
- The United States began its first labor movement in the 1800s, the result of low wages, no vacation time, safety issues, and other problems.
- Many labor organizations have disappeared, but the *American Federation of Labor (AFL)* still exists today. However, it merged with the *Congress of Industrial Organizations (CIO)* and is now known as the AFL-CIO. It is the largest labor union and represents local labor unions in a variety of industries.

- Legislation has been created over time to support both labor unions and the companies that have labor unions. The *Railway Labor Act* applies to airlines and railroads and stipulates that employees may not strike until they have gone through an extensive dispute resolution process. The *Norris-LaGuardia Act* made *yellow-dog contracts* illegal and barred courts from issuing injunctions.

- The *Wagner Act* was created to protect employees from retaliation should they join a union. The *Taft-Hartley Act* was developed to protect companies from unfair labor practices by unions.

- The *National Labor Relations Board* is the overseeing body for labor unions, and it handles disputes between companies as well as facilitates the process of new labor unions in the developing stages. Its job is to enforce both the Wagner Act and the Taft-Hartley Act.

- The *Landrum Griffin Act* was created in 1959 to combat corruption in labor unions during this time period.

- To form a union, the organizer must have signatures from 30 percent of the employees. If this occurs, the National Labor Relations Board will facilitate a card check to determine more than 50 percent of the workforce at that company is in agreement with union representation. If the company does not accept this, then the NLRB holds secret elections to determine if the employees will be unionized. A collective bargaining agreement is put into place if the vote is yes.

- Companies prefer not to have unions in their organizations because it affects costs and operational productivity, and they will try to prevent a union from organizing in their workplace.

- Managers are impacted when a company does unionize. For example, management rights are affected, and everything must be guided by the union contract instead of management prerogative.

Exercises

1. Visit the National Labor Relations Board website. View the "weekly case summary" and discuss it in at least two paragraphs, stating your opinion on this case.
2. Do you agree with unionization within organizations? Why or why not? List the advantages and disadvantages of unions to the employee and the company.

10.4 Collective Bargaining

Learning Objectives

1. Describe the process of collective bargaining.
2. Understand the types of bargaining issues and the rights of management.
3. Discuss some strategies when working with unions.

When employees of an organization vote to unionize, the process for collective bargaining begins. **Collective bargaining** is the process of negotiations between the company and representatives of the union. The goal is for management and the union to reach a contract agreement, which is put into place for a specified period of time. Once this time is up, a new contract is negotiated. In this section, we will discuss the components of the collective bargaining agreement and how they relate to you as an employee and a manager.

collective bargaining

The process of negotiating an agreement between management and employees.

The Process of Collective Bargaining

The process of collective bargaining can be a lengthy one—lasting a year or more!

mandatory category

A collective bargaining topic, such as wages, that must be discussed in the agreement.

permissive topic

Topics in collective bargaining that are not mandatory but still topics of discussion, such as drug testing.

illegal topic

A bargaining topic that is illegal in both the bargaining agreement and within society, such as plans to discriminate against a specific group in employment.

In a collective bargaining process, both parties are legally bound to bargain in good faith; meaning they have a mutual obligation to participate actively in the deliberations and indicate a desire to find a basis for agreement. There are three main classifications of bargaining topics: mandatory, permissive, and illegal. Wages, health and safety, management rights, work conditions, and benefits fall into the **mandatory category**. **Permissive topics** are those that are not required but may be brought up during the process. An example might include the requirement of drug testing for candidates or the required tools that must be provided to the employee to perform the job, such as a cellular phone or computer. It is important to note that while management is not required by labor laws to bargain on these issues, refusing to do so could affect employee morale. Likewise, as we addressed in Section 2 on conflict management, using a competing approach is usually not effective in this situation. We can also classify bargaining issues as **illegal topics**, which are topics that aren't allowed to be discussed. These types of illegal issues may be of a discriminatory nature, or anything that would be considered illegal outside the agreement.

Examples of Bargaining Topics

- Pay rate and structure
- Health benefits
- Incentive programs
- Job classification
- Performance assessment procedure
- Vacation time and sick leave
- Health plans
- Layoff procedures
- Seniority
- Training process
- Severance pay
- Tools provided to employees
- Process for new applicants

The collective bargaining process has five main steps, and we will discuss each of these steps next. The first step is the preparation of both parties. The negotiation team should consist of individuals with knowledge of the organization and the skills to be an effective negotiator. An understanding of the working conditions and dissatisfaction with working conditions is an important part of this preparation step. Establishing objectives for the negotiation and reviewing the old contract are key components to this step. The management team should also prepare and anticipate union demands, and likewise, the union representatives should prepare and anticipate management requests to better prepare for compromises.

FIGURE 10.6 Steps in the Collective Bargaining Process

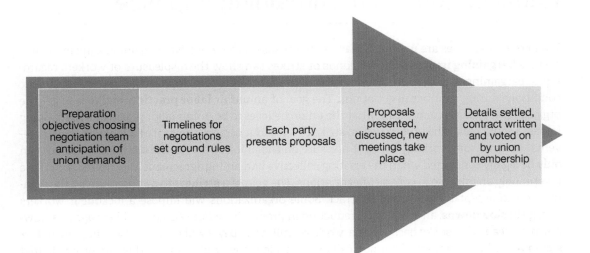

| Preparation objectives choosing negotiation team anticipation of union demands | Timelines for negotiations set ground rules | Each party presents proposals | Proposals presented, discussed, new meetings take place | Details settled, contract written and voted on by union membership |

The second step of the process involves both parties agreeing on the negotiation time lines. In addition, setting ground rules for how the negotiation will occur is an important step, as it lays the foundation for the work to come.

In the third step, each party comes to the table with proposals. It will likely involve initial opening statements and options to resolve any situations that exist. The key to a successful proposal is to come to the table with a "let's make this work" attitude. An initial discussion is had and then each party generally goes back to determine which requests it can honor and which it can't. At this point, another meeting is generally set up to continue further discussion.

Once the group comes to an agreement or settlement (which may take many months and proposals), a new contract is written and the union members vote on whether to accept the agreement. If the union doesn't agree, then the process begins all over again.

Ramifications of a Bargaining Impasse

bargaining impasse

Inability to agree on a contract.

economic strike

A strike based on unhappiness about economic conditions.

unfair labor practices strike

The goal is to get the organization to cease committing what the union believes to be an unfair labor practice; this kind of strike does not need to occur during negotiations.

lockout

When organizations do not allow workers to go to work.

strike

Workers protest and do not go to work as a result of contract disagreement.

slowdown

An alternative to a strike. Workers intentionally are less productive.

sick-out

When members of a union call in sick.

walk-out

An unannounced refusal to perform work; may be illegal.

jurisdictional strikes

Used to put pressure on an employer to assign work to members of one union versus another.

sympathy strikes

Work stoppages by other unions designed to show support for the union on strike.

When the two parties are unable to reach a consensus on the collective bargaining agreement, it is called a **bargaining impasse**. Various kinds of strikes can show the displeasure of workers regarding a bargaining impasse. An **economic strike** stems from unhappiness about the economic conditions during contract negotiations. The goal of an **unfair labor practices strike** is to get the organization to cease committing what the union believes to be unfair labor practices. A bargaining impasse could mean the union goes on strike or a lockout occurs. The goal of a **lockout**, which prevents workers from working, is to put pressure on the union to accept the contract. A lockout can only be legally conducted when the existing collective bargaining agreement has expired, and there is genuinely an impasse in contract negotiations. The goal of a **strike** is to put pressure on the organization to accept the proposed contract. Some organizations will impose a lockout if workers engage in **slowdowns**, an intentional reduction in productivity. Some unions will engage in a slowdown instead of a strike because the workers still earn pay—while in a strike they do not. A **sick-out** is when members of a union call in sick, which may be illegal since they are using allotted time, while a **walk-out** is an unannounced refusal to perform work. However, this type of tactic may be illegal if the conduct is irresponsible or indefensible, according to a judge. **Jurisdictional strikes** are used to put pressure on an employer to assign work to members of one union versus another (if there are two unions within the same organization) or to put pressure on management to recognize one union representation when it currently recognizes another. The goal of a sick-out strike is to show the organization how unproductive the company would be if the workers did go on strike. As mentioned under the Taft-Hartley Act, wildcat strikes are illegal, as they are not authorized by the union and usually violate a collective bargaining agreement. **Sympathy strikes** are work stoppages by other unions designed to show support for the union on strike. While they are not illegal, they may violate the terms of the collective bargaining agreement.

Now that we have addressed the collective bargaining process, do you see how you might use conflict styles and management of conflict techniques to help with the negotiation?

Key Takeaways

- *Collective bargaining* is the process of negotiating the contract with union representatives. Collective bargaining, to be legal, must always be done in good faith.
- There are three categories of collective bargaining issues. *Mandatory issues* might include pay and benefits. *Permissive bargaining* items may include things such as drug testing or the required equipment the organization must supply to employees. *Illegal issues* are those things that cannot be discussed, which can include issues that could be considered discriminatory.
- The collective bargaining process can take time. Both parties prepare for the process by gathering information and reviewing the old contract. They then set time lines for the bargaining and reveal their wants and negotiate those wants. A *bargaining impasse* occurs when members cannot come to an agreement.
- When a bargaining impasse occurs, a *strike* or *lockout* of workers can occur. An *economic strike* occurs during negotiations, while an *unfair labor practices strike* can occur anytime, and during negotiations. A *sick-out* can also be used, when workers call in sick for the day. These strategies can be used to encourage the other side to agree to collective bargaining terms.

Exercises

1. Research negotiation techniques, then list and describe the options. Which do you think would work best when negotiating with unions?
2. Of the list of bargaining issues, which would be most important to you and why?

10.5 Grievance Processes

Learning Objective

1. Be able to explain how a grievance process works.

A grievance procedure or process is normally created within the union and management's collective bargaining agreement. The **grievance procedure** outlines the process by which grievances over contract violations will be handled. As you have probably already identified, the grievance procedure is a formalized conflict, as we discussed in Chapter 10. Learning how to handle this type of conflict takes self-management skills—or the ability to avoid taking things personally—and relationship management skills. This will be the focus of our next section.

grievance procedure

Outlined in the contract; the process by which contract violations are handled.

Procedures for Grievances

A violation of the contract terms, or perception of violation, normally results in a grievance. The process is specific to each contract, so we will discuss the process in generalities. A grievance is normally initiated by an employee and then handled by union representatives. Most contracts specify how the grievance is to be initiated, the steps to complete the procedure, and identification of representatives from both sides who will hear the grievance. Normally, the human relations department is involved in most steps of this process. The basic process is shown in Figure 10.7.

FIGURE 10.7 A Sample Grievance Process

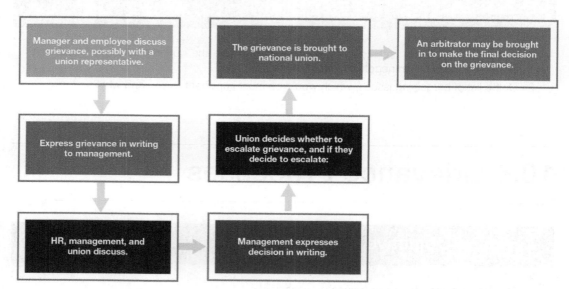

The first step is usually an informal conversation with the manager, employee, and possibly a union representative. Many grievances never go further than this step, because often the complaint is the result of a misunderstanding.

If the complaint is unresolved at this point, the union will generally initiate the grievance process by formally expressing it in writing. At this time, HR and management may discuss the grievance with a union representative. If the result is unsatisfactory to both parties, the complaint may be brought to the company's union grievance committee. This can be in the form of an informal meeting or a more formal hearing.

After discussion, management will then submit a formalized response to the grievance. It may decide to remedy the grievance or may outline why the complaint does not violate the contract. At this point, the process is escalated.

mediator

An impartial third party called in to help resolve a grievance. Any recommendation or decision is not binding.

Further discussion will likely occur, and if management and the union cannot come to an agreement, the dispute will normally be brought to a national union officer, who will work with management to try and resolve the issue. A **mediator** may be called in, who acts as an impartial third party and tries to resolve the issue. Any recommendation made by the mediator is not binding for either of the parties involved. Mediators can work both on grievance processes and collective bargaining issues. In Washington State (as well as most other states), a nonprofit organization is available to assist in mediations (either grievance or collective bargaining related) and arbitrations. The goal of such an organization is to avoid disruptions to public services and to facilitate the dispute resolution process. In Washington, the organization is called the Public Employment Relations Commission (PERC). You can review their mediation process utilizing the free PERC services at http://apps.leg.wa.gov/WAC/default.aspx?cite=391-55-020.

arbitrator

An impartial third party who is selected by both parties in a grievance and who ultimately makes a binding decision in the situation.

If no resolution develops, an arbitrator might be asked to review the evidence and make a decision. An **arbitrator** is an impartial third party who is selected by both parties and who ultimately makes a binding decision in the situation. Thus arbitration is the final aspect of a grievance.

Some examples of grievances might include the following:

1. One employee was promoted over another, even though he had seniority.
2. An employee doesn't have the tools needed to perform his or her job, as outlined in the contract.
3. An employee was terminated, although the termination violated the rules of the contract.
4. An employee was improperly trained on chemical handling in a department.

Most grievances fall within one of four categories. There are **individual/personal grievances**, in which one member of the union feels he or she has been mistreated. A **group grievance** occurs if several union members have been mistreated in the same way. A **principle grievance** deals with basic contract issues surrounding seniority or pay, for example. If an employee or group is not willing to formally file a grievance, the union may file a **union or policy grievance** on behalf of that individual or group.

The important things to remember about grievances are that they should not be taken personally and, if used correctly, can be a fair, transparent process to solving problems within the organization.

In order for unions and management to avoid conflict, strong communication is necessary.

© Thinkstock

individual/personal grievances

When one member of the union feels he or she has been mistreated and files a grievance.

group grievance

Occurs if several union members have been mistreated in the same way and file a grievance.

principle grievance

A grievance that deals with basic contract issues surrounding contract items, such as pay or seniority.

union or policy grievance

A grievance initiated by the union if an employee or group is not willing to formally file a grievance.

 WATCH THIS!

This video shows a philosophical perspective of the grievance process for the Association of Flight Attendants union.

View the video online at: http://www.youtube.com/embed/agMgB9y7k3w?rel=0

Key Takeaways

- The *grievance process* is a formal process to address any complaints about contract violations.
- The grievance process varies from contract to contract. It is an important part of the contract that ensures a fair process for both union members and management.
- The grievance process can consist of any number of steps. First, the complaint is discussed with the manager, employee, and union representative. If no solution occurs, the grievance is put into writing by the union. Then HR, management, and the union discuss the process, sometimes in the form of a hearing, in which both sides are able to express their opinion.
- Management then expresses its decision in writing to the union.
- If the union decides to escalate the grievance, the grievance may be brought to the national union for a decision. At this point, *an arbitrator*, suitable to both parties, may be brought in to make the final binding decision.

- There are four main types of grievances. First, the *individual grievance* is filed when one member of the union feels mistreated. A *group grievance* occurs when several members of the union feel they have been mistreated and file a grievance as a group. A *principle grievance* may be filed on behalf of the union and is usually based on a larger issue, such as a policy or contract issue. A *union or policy grievance* may be filed if the employee does not wish to file individually.

- Grievances should not be taken personally and should be considered a fair way in which to solve problems that can come up between the union and management.

Exercise

1. What are the advantages of a grievance process? What disadvantages do you see with a formalized grievance process?

10.6 Chapter Summary and Case

Chapter Summary

- Conflict can run the gamut from minor annoyances to physically violent situations. At the same time, conflict can increase creativity and innovation or it can bring organizations to a grinding halt.

- There are many different types of conflict, including interpersonal, intrapersonal, intragroup, and intergroup.

- Within organizations, there are many common situations that can spur conflict.

- Certain organizational structures, such as a matrix structure, can cause any given employee to have multiple bosses and conflicting or overwhelming demands. A scarcity of resources for employees to complete tasks is another common cause of organizational conflict, particularly if groups within the organization compete over those resources.

- Of course, simple personality clashes can create intrapersonal conflict in any situation.

- Communication problems are also a very common source of conflict, even when no actual problem would exist otherwise.

- When conflict arises, it can be handled by any number of methods, each with varying degrees of cooperation and competitiveness. Different situations require different conflict-handling methods, and no one method is best.

- Negotiations occur during many important processes, and possessing astute negotiation skills can be an incredible tool.

- A key component to negotiations involves having a BATNA, or "best alternative to a negotiated agreement."

- Negotiations typically move through five phases, including investigation, determining your BATNA, presentation, bargaining, and closure.

- During a negotiation, it is important not to make any number of common mistakes. These mistakes can include accepting the first offer, letting ego get in the way, having unrealistic expectations of the outcome of the negotiation, becoming too emotional during the process, or being weighed down by previous failures and letting the past repeat itself.

- It is important to keep in mind that many cultures have preferential methods for handling conflict and negotiation. Individuals should understand the cultural background of others to better navigate what could otherwise become a messy situation.

Chapter Case

A Case of Listening: When Silence Is Golden[9]

Listening can be an effective tool during negotiations. William Devine was representing a client on a land purchase. "The owner and I spent two hours on the phone horse-trading contract issues, then turned to the price," Devine explained. "We were $100,000 apart." The owner then said, "The price your client proposes will leave us well short of our projections. That makes it very tough on us." The line went silent.

"My impulse was to say something in response to the silence, and I started to speak, then stopped. As I hesitated, I sensed that if I said, 'My client can pay all cash,' or 'It's still a good deal for you,' then the owner would take my comment as an invitation to joust, we would battle over the hundred grand, and my client would end up having to pay some or all of that sum. The owner had not asked a question or proposed a compromise, so no response was required from me at that moment. I decided to remain silent. After what felt like days but was probably less than 30 seconds, I heard, 'But I guess it's good for us [i.e., his company] to just get this deal done, so we'll do it.'"

Devine saved his client $100,000 by staying silent.

1. What does this case suggest about the role of silence in negotiations?
2. Have you ever had a similar experience when saying nothing paid off?
3. Are there times when silence is a bad idea? Explain your answer.

Endnotes

1. National Safety Council. (n.d.). Assaults fourth leading cause of workplace death. Accessed from https://www.nsc.org/work-safety/safety-topics/workplace-violence

2. Thomas, K.W. & Kilmann, R.H. (n.d). An overview of the Thomas-Kilmann conflict mode instrument. Retrieved from https://kilmanndiagnostics.com/overview-thomas-kilmann-conflict-mode-instrument-tki/

3. Thomas, K.W. & Kilmann, R.H. (n.d). An overview of the Thomas-Kilmann conflict mode instrument. Retrieved from https://kilmanndiagnostics.com/overview-thomas-kilmann-conflict-mode-instrument-tki/

4. Benjamin, K.A. (24 June 2013). 6 steps to conflict resolution. Retrieved from https://hrdailyadvisor.blr.com/2013/06/24/6-steps-to-conflict-resolution-in-the-workplace/

5. U.S. Bureau of Labor Statistics. (18 January 2019). Union members summary. Retrieved from https://www.bls.gov/news.release/union2.nr0.htm

6. Teamsters website. (19 January 2019). Teamsters take part in government shutdown protest on Capitol Hill. Retrieved from https://teamster.org/news/2019/01/teamsters-take-part-government-shutdown-protest-capitol-hill

7. Ingraham, C. (19 January 2019). Union membership remained steady in 2017: That trend may not hold. Retrieved from https://www.washingtonpost.com/news/wonk/wp/2018/01/19/union-membership-remained-steady-in-2017-the-trend-may-not-hold/?noredirect=on&utm_term=.d8f77f231bd1

8. Anzilotti, E. (14 June 2019). This major unionization vote at a Volkswagen plant could be a turning point for organized labor. Retrieved from https://www.fastcompany.com/90364513/this-major-unionization-vote-in-the-south-could-be-a-turning-point-for-organized-labor

9. Devine, W. (2002, September 30). Anatomy of a deal-maker. *California Real Estate Journal*. Retrieved November 14, 2008, from http://www.wdesquire.com/pages/dealmaker.html.

CHAPTER 11
Embracing Diversity, Multiculturalism, and Cultural Intelligence

We all live with the objective of being happy; our lives are all different and yet the same.

—Anne Frank

Differences challenge assumptions.

—Anne Wilson Schaef

Multicultural Hiring

On a Tuesday afternoon, as you are getting ready to go to lunch, you receive an e-mail from your human resources (HR) manager about the need to hire a new project manager, and there is a $500 bonus for referring a friend who successfully joins the company. Immediately, you e-mail your friend Daniel, because you know he would be great for the job. Daniel is eventually hired for the position, and a few months later a new e-mail goes out asking for friend recommendations for a new position. You and Daniel both recommend someone, and eventually that person gets hired. Over the next year, hiring notices are not advertised externally as the organization has had good luck with this hiring practice. Seems like a great way to recruit new people, doesn't it? It can be, but it also can be a detriment to the diversity and multiculturalism of the workplace. How, you might wonder?

While not true across the board, people tend to spend time with others like themselves in race, income level, and other aspects of diversity, such as sexual orientation. In fact, according to the National Institute of Child Health and Human Development and a study published in the *American Journal of Sociology*, it is much more likely that someone will name a person of their own race as a friend than someone of a different race.[1] Likewise, even from a young age, people tend to choose friends who are of the same race. As a result, when you recommend Daniel for a position, it is highly likely that Daniel is similar, from a diversity perspective, to you. Then, when Daniel recommends someone for a job, it is highly likely that he, too, is recommending someone with similar characteristics as you both. This obviously creates a lack of multicultural diversity in the workplace, which can mean lost profits for companies. In addition, it is important for us to be able to function effectively in a multicultural work environment, as multicultural understanding improves our ability to engage in positive human relations with others.

11.1 Diversity and Multiculturalism

diversity

The real or perceived differences between individuals.

multiculturalism

Looks at power and privilege differences in society.

Many people use the terms *diversity* and *multiculturalism* interchangeably, when in fact there are major differences between the two. **Diversity** is defined as the differences between people. These differences can include race, gender, sexual orientation, religion, background, socioeconomic status, and much more. Diversity, from the workplace perspective, tends to focus more on a set of policies to meet compliance standards.

Multiculturalism goes deeper than diversity by focusing on inclusiveness, understanding, and respect, and also by looking at unequal power in society.

This chapter focuses on the advantages of a diverse workplace and discusses multiculturalism at work. In addition, we will address how you can develop cultural intelligence skills necessary for success in the global workforce today.

Advantages to Diversity in the Workplace

While there may be no "money fairy," diversity has proven to result in higher profits for companies.

© Thinkstock

When people look at diversity and multiculturalism, they think that someone's gender, skin color, or social class shouldn't matter. So, while diversity can help companies create policies to prevent discrimination, multiculturalism can help us gain a deeper understanding of the differences between people—elevating our emotional intelligence skills.

For companies, having a diverse workforce can create competitive advantage, which can include:

1. Diverse perspectives can drive innovation.
2. The more different the backgrounds, the greater variety of experience, which results in greater creativity in teams.
3. Customers are better served by being offered a broader range of services, such as being able to speak a variety of languages and understanding other cultures.
4. We can better communicate with one another (saving time and money) and with customers.
5. With a multicultural perspective, teams have greater functionality, which in turn means they are more productive.

Diversity in the workforce does benefit companies greatly. Companies that have gender diversity outperform companies who don't by 15 percent, and those that have ethnic diversity outperform those that don't by 35 percent.[2] For example, companies with higher diversity in the executive board achieved 53 percent more profit than those in the lower percentile for executive board diversity.[3]

Now that you have an understanding of the meaning of diversity and multiculturalism, and the advantages of a diverse workforce, let's address them in depth.

Power and Privilege

As defined in this chapter, diversity focuses on the "otherness" or differences between individuals and has a goal of making sure, through policies, that everyone is treated the same. While this is the legal and the right thing to do, multiculturalism looks at a system of advantages based on race, gender, and sexual orientation called **power and privilege**. In this system, the advantages are based on a system in which one race, gender, and sexual orientation is predominant in setting societal rules and norms.

> **power and privilege**
>
> A system of advantages based on race, gender, sexual orientation, and other components of diversity.

The interesting thing about power and privilege is that if you have it, you may not initially recognize it, which is why we can call it an invisible privilege. Here are some examples:

1. **Race privilege.** Let's say you (a Caucasian) and your friend (an African American) are having dinner together, and when the bill comes, the server gives you the check. While this may not seem like a big issue, it assumes you (being Caucasian) are the person paying for the meal. This type of invisible privilege may not seem to matter if you have that privilege, but if you don't, it can be infuriating.

2. **Social class privilege.** This relates to the economic ability of an individual. For example, if you can to go to the grocery store and buy just about anything you wish, you may have social class privilege. Social class privilege can also be seen in the educational system, where individuals who can afford to pay to go to prestigious colleges and universities tend to have more financial resources, because the gap in financial aid and the ability of families to help with college is too large.

3. **Gender privilege.** This refers to privileges one gender has over another—for example, the assumption that a female will change her name to her husband's when they get married. In addition, gender privilege relates to the fact that there is acceptance surrounding your assigned gender. For those who may be androgynous, bi-gender, transsexual, and transgender, they do not experience the same privilege as those who have been assigned a gender they accept and conform to at birth (e.g., identified as female because born with female "parts.")

4. **Sexual orientation privilege.** This refers to privilege related to one's sexual and/or gender identity. For example, if I am heterosexual, I can put a picture of my partner on my desk without worrying about what others think. I can talk about our vacations together or experiences we've had without worrying what someone might think about my relationship. This is not the case for many gay, lesbian, and transgender people and their partners.

Oftentimes the privilege we have is considered invisible, because it can be hard to recognize one's own privilege based on race, gender, or social class. Many people utilize the color-blind approach, which states, "I treat everyone the same" or "I don't see people's skin color." In this case, the person is showing invisible privilege and thus ignoring the privileges he or she receives because of race, gender, or social class. While it appears this approach would value all people equally, it doesn't, because people's different needs, assets, and perspectives are disregarded by not acknowledging differences.[4]

 **WATCH THIS!**

This video demonstrates the effects of societal privileges.

View the video online at: http://www.youtube.com/embed/hD5f8GuNuGQ?rel=0

Another important aspect of power and privilege is the fact that we may have privilege in one area and not another. For example, I am a Caucasian female, which gives me race privilege but not gender privilege. It's important to note here that the idea of power and privilege is not about "white male bashing" but understanding our own stereotypes and systems of advantage so we can be more inclusive with our coworkers, and managers.

So what does this all mean in relation to you? It means we can combine the understanding of certain systems that allow for power and privilege, and by understanding we may be able to eliminate or at least minimize these issues, creating a better workplace for ourselves and others..

What's in it for me?

Seventy-one percent of companies say they aspire to be inclusive and diverse.[5] Therefore, it is likely that an understanding of diversity and multiculturalism can help you when you are interviewing for that next job! Many companies ask interview questions regarding diversity, and having an understanding of it will help you nail that interview question!

Key Takeaways

- *Diversity* is important to the success of organizations. Many studies have shown a direct link between the amount of diversity in a workplace and the company's success.
- *Diversity* is the real or perceived differences between individuals. This can include race, gender, sexual orientation, size, cultural background, and much more.
- *Multiculturalism* is a term that is similar to diversity, but it focuses on development of a greater understanding of how power in society can be unequal due to race, gender, sexual orientation, and privilege.
- *Power and privilege* is a system of advantages based on one's race, gender, and sexual orientation. This system can often be invisible (to those who have it), which results in one race

or gender having unequal power in the workplace. Of course, this unequal power results in unfairness, which may be of legal concern.

Exercises

1. Perform an Internet search to find a diversity policy for an organization. What is the policy? From what you know of the organization, do you believe they follow this policy in reality?
2. Visit the website http://www.diversityinc.com and find their latest "top 50 list." What criteria are used to appear on this list? What are the top five companies for the current year?

11.2 Multiculturalism and the Law

Learning Objectives

1. Define the role of the Equal Employment Opportunity Commission (EEOC).
2. Explain the various types of laws covered by the EEOC.

As we already know, it is in an organization's best interest to have a multicultural and diverse workforce. Sometimes though, people are still discriminated against at work. As a result, a federal agency has been established to ensure employees have a place to file complaints should they feel discriminated against. That will be the focus of this section.

The Equal Employment Opportunity Commission (EEOC)

The **Equal Employment Opportunity Commission (EEOC)** is a federal agency charged with enforcing federal employment discrimination laws. The agency was created in 1964, as part of Title VII of the Civil Rights Act. As early as 1941, however, a movement began to prohibit discrimination in work settings. Franklin D. Roosevelt signed into law an executive order to prohibit government contracts from engaging in employment discrimination on the basis of race, color, or national origin. This was the first-ever action taken by a president to prohibit discrimination.

> **Equal Employment Opportunity Commission (EEOC)**
>
> A federal agency charged with enforcing federal employment discrimination laws.

The EEOC set of laws includes those that protect people from discrimination in all areas of employment, such as race, color, religion, sex, national origin, age, and disability. People who have filed a discrimination charge are also protected against discrimination under the EEOC. Employers with at least fifteen employees (twenty for age discrimination) are covered under the EEOC. This agency covers not only discrimination in hiring but also discrimination in all types of work situations such as firing, promotions, harassment, training, wages, and benefits. The EEOC has the authority to investigate charges of discrimination against employers. The agency investigates the claims, makes a finding, and then tries to settle the charge. If they are unsuccessful in settling the charge, the EEOC has the right to file a lawsuit on behalf of the complainants. The EEOC has headquarters in Washington, DC, with fifty-three field offices throughout the United States.

If a company has more than one hundred employees, a form called the EEO-1 must be filled out yearly. This form confirms the demographics of an organization based on different job categories.[6] An organization that employs more than fifty people and works for the federal government must also file an EEO-1 yearly, with the deadline normally in September. In addition, organizations must post the EEOC notice, which you have probably seen before, perhaps in the company break room. Finally, organizations should keep records such as hiring statistics on file in the event of an EEOC investigation.

It is necessary to mention here that while there are multiple laws to protect people from discrimination, the focus of a company should be to hire a diverse workforce because it is good for the company and for profitability, not just to meet the requirements of the law.

TABLE 11.1 How the EEOC Process Works and Requirements for Employers

Requirements by EEOC	Process for Investigation
• Post Federal and State EEOC notices • File yearly report called EEO-1 • Keep copies of documents on file	1. The EEOC complaint is filed. 2. The EEOC notifies the organization of the charges. 3. The EEOC acts as a mediator between the employee and the employer to find a solution. 4. If Step 3 is unsuccessful, the EEOC will initiate an investigation. 5. The EEOC makes a determination, and then the employer has the option of remedying the situation or facing a potential lawsuit.

EEOC Federal Legislation

Title VII of the Civil Rights Act

This act, passed in 1964 and enforced by the EEOC, covers several areas of discrimination, including age, race, and sex.

bona fide occupational qualification (BFOQ)

A quality or attribute employers are allowed to consider when making decisions during the selection process.

While the EEOC is the larger governing body, many pieces of legislation relating to multicultural practices are part of the EEOC family of laws. Many of these laws began with **Title VII of the Civil Rights Act** in 1964, as mentioned earlier. This act, enforced by the EEOC, covers several areas in which discrimination was rampant. However, a **bona fide occupational qualification (BFOQ)** is a quality or attribute employers are allowed to consider when making decisions during the selection process. Examples of BFOQs are a maximum age limit for airline pilots for safety reasons and a Christian college's requirement that the president of the college be Christian.

The set of EEOC laws protects the following groups:

1. Age
2. Disability
3. Equal pay/compensation
4. Genetic information
5. National origin
6. Pregnancy
7. Race/color
8. Religion
9. Retaliation
10. Sex
11. Sexual harassment

We will address each of these next.

Age

Age discrimination involves treating someone less favorably because of his or her age. The **Age Discrimination in Employment Act (ADEA)**, created in 1967, is enforced by the EEOC. This law covers people who are age forty or older. It does not cover favoring an older worker over a younger worker if the older worker is forty years or older. The law covers any aspect of employment, such as hiring, firing, pay, job assignments, promotions, layoffs, training, fringe benefits, and any other condition or term of employment.

The law also goes deeper by forbidding harassment of someone based on age. While simple teasing or offhand comments are not covered, more serious offensive remarks about age are covered by this EEOC law.

Disability

The **Americans with Disabilities Act (ADA)** prohibits discrimination against those with disabilities and is enforced by the EEOC. Discrimination based on disability means treating a qualified person unfavorably because of a disability. For example, if someone has AIDS that is controlled, the employee cannot be treated unfavorably. The law requires an employer to provide **reasonable accommodation** to an employee or applicant with a disability, unless this accommodation would cause significant difficulty or expense for the employer. A reasonable accommodation is defined by the EEOC as any change in the work environment or in the way things are customarily done that enables an individual with a disability to enjoy equal employment opportunities. A reasonable accommodation might include making the workplace accessible for wheelchair use or providing equipment for someone who is hearing or vision impaired.

This law does not mean that organizations are required to hire unqualified people. The law specifically states the person must be qualified for the job and have a disability defined by the law, which can include the following:

1. Physical or mental condition that limits a major life activity (walking, talking, seeing, hearing, or learning).

2. History of a disability (e.g., cancer that is in remission).

3. Physical or mental impairment that is not transitory (lasting or expected to last less than six months).

The law places limits on employers when it comes to asking job applicants questions about medical history or asking a person to take a medical exam.

Equal Pay/Compensation

The basis of this law is that people are paid the same for the same type of work, and the law explicitly addresses gender pay differences. Rather than job title, job content is used to determine if the jobs are the same. In addition to covering salary, the law deals with overtime pay, bonuses, stock options, profit sharing, and other types of bonus plans such as vacation and holiday pay. If inequality in pay is found, the employer cannot reduce the wages of either sex to equalize the pay.

An employee who files an equal pay charge has the option to go directly to court rather than to the EEOC.

Age Discrimination in Employment Act (ADEA)

Created in 1967 and enforced by the EEOC, this law prohibits discrimination based on age and covers people who are age forty or older.

Americans with Disabilities Act (ADA)

Prohibits discrimination against those with disabilities and is enforced by the EEOC.

reasonable accommodation

A change in the work environment or the way things are customarily done that enables an individual with a disability to enjoy equal employment opportunities.

Genetic Information

This is one of the newer EEOC laws, which took effect in November 2009. The EEOC's definition of genetic information includes family medical information or information about the manifestation of a disease or disorder in an individual's family. For example, an employer cannot discriminate against an employee whose family has a history of diabetes or cancer. This information could be used to discriminate against an employee who has an increased risk of getting a disease and may make health care costs more expensive for the organization.

In addition, the employer is not allowed to seek genetic information by requesting, requiring, or purchasing this information. However, there are some situations in which receiving this information would not be illegal:

1. A manager or supervisor overhears an employee talking about a family member's illness.
2. Information is received based on wellness programs offered on a voluntary basis.
3. If the information is required as documentation to receive benefits for the Family and Medical Leave Act (FMLA).
4. If the information is commercial, such as the appearance of information in a newspaper—as long as the employer is not specifically searching those sources for the purpose of finding genetic information.
5. If genetic information is required through a monitoring program that looks at the biological effects of toxic substances in the workplace.
6. For those professions that require DNA testing, such as law enforcement agencies. In this case, the genetic information may only be used for analysis in relation to the specific case at hand.

This law also covers how information about genetics should be kept. For example, genetic information must be kept separate from an employee's regular file.

National Origin

It is illegal to treat people unfavorably because they are from a particular country or part of the world, because of their accent, or because they appear to be of a particular descent (even if they are not). The law protecting employees based on national origin refers to all aspects of employment—hiring, firing, pay, job assignments, promotions, layoffs, training, and fringe benefits. An employer can require an employee to speak English only if it is necessary to perform the job effectively. An "English-only policy" is allowed only if it is needed to ensure the safe or efficient operations of the employer's business. For example, Forever 21 in San Francisco was sued by three employees who claimed they were subjected to discipline, severe scrutiny, and threatened with termination when speaking Spanish at work.[7] California law states an "English-only policy" can only be used if there is "an overriding legitimate business purpose," such as being "necessary to the safe and efficient operation of the business." As a result, a policy such as this could be considered discriminatory and should be used only when absolutely necessary.

Pregnancy

Family and Medical Leave Act (FMLA)

This law gives twelve weeks of unpaid leave for childbirth, adoption, or caregiving of sick family members.

This section of the EEOC refers to the unfavorable treatment of a woman because of pregnancy, childbirth, or a medical condition related to pregnancy or childbirth. The Pregnancy Discrimination Act of 1978, added to the Civil Rights Act of 1964, is enforced by the EEOC. The female who is unable to perform her job owing to pregnancy must be treated the same as other temporarily disabled employees. For example, modified tasks or alternative assignments should be offered. This law refers not only to hiring but also to firing, pay, job assignments, promotions, layoffs, training, and fringe benefits. In addition to this law against discrimination of pregnant women, the **Family**

and Medical Leave Act (FMLA) is enforced by the US Department of Labor.[8] The FMLA requires companies with fifty or more employees to provide twelve weeks of unpaid leave for the following:

1. Birth and care of a newborn child;
2. Care of an adopted child;
3. Care for immediate family members (spouse, child, or parent) with a serious health condition;
4. Medical leave for the employee who is unable to work because of a serious health condition.

In addition to the company size requirement, the employee must have worked at least 1,250 hours over the past 12 months.

Race/Color

This type of discrimination refers to treating someone unfavorably because he or she is of a certain race or because of specific characteristics associated with race. These characteristics might include hair texture, skin color, or facial features. Discrimination can occur when the person discriminating is the same race or color of the person who is being discriminated against. EEOC law also protects people who are married to or associated with someone of a certain race or color. As with the other types of antidiscrimination laws we have discussed, this law refers not only to the initial hiring but also to firing, pay, job assignments, promotions, layoffs, training, and fringe benefits.

Religion

This part of the EEOC refers to treating a person unfavorably because of their religious beliefs. This law requires a company to reasonably accommodate an employee's religious beliefs or practices unless doing so would burden the organization's operations. For example, allowing flexible scheduling during certain religious time periods might be considered a reasonable accommodation. This law also covers dress and grooming accommodations, such as a headscarf, religious dress, or uncut hair and a beard in the case of a Sikh. Ideally, the employee or applicant would notify the employer that he or she needs such an accommodation for religious reasons, and then a discussion of the request would occur. If it wouldn't pose a hardship, the employer should honor the request. If the request might cause a safety issue, decrease efficiency, or infringe on the rights of other employees, it may not be honored.

An accommodation for religion, such as allowing turbans, would be considered a reasonable accommodation in work dress.

© Shutterstock

Sex and Sexual Harassment

quid pro quo

A type of sexual harassment in which the victim is asked for favors of a sexual nature in exchange for a workplace benefit, such as a pay raise or promotion.

hostile work environment

A sexual harassment situation in which the victim is subjected to unwelcome and inappropriate sexual behavior.

Sex discrimination involves treating someone unfavorably because of their sex. As with all EEOC laws, this relates to hiring, firing, pay, job assignments, promotions, layoffs, training, and fringe benefits. This law directly ties into sexual harassment laws, which include unwelcome sexual advances, requests for sexual favors, and other verbal or physical harassment of a sexual nature. There are two main types of sexual harassment: quid pro quo and hostile work environments. In a **quid pro quo** situation, the victim is asked for sexual favors in return for a raise, promotion, or other workplace-related benefit. In a **hostile work environment** sexual harassment situation, the victim is subjected to unwelcome and inappropriate sexual behavior. For example, a supervisor constantly asking the victim on a date, even when he or she says no. It can be more extreme in some cases, such as sexual-based physical advances, pictures, or comments. The victim can be male or female, and sexual harassment can occur female to female, female to male, male to female, and male to male.

Examples of Sexual Harassment

Follow this link to see additional examples of sexual harassment.

http://burro.cwru.edu/women/harassment/examples.html

📹 WATCH THIS!

Female founders of IT organizations discuss sexual harassment they've experienced.

View the video online at: http://www.youtube.com/embed/PsM5rl82Hug?rel=0

Retaliation

In all the laws mentioned, the EEOC laws make it illegal to fire, demote, harass, or retaliate against people because they filed a charge of discrimination, complained about discrimination, or participated in employment discrimination proceedings. For example, the Veterans Administration of Central Alabama was accused of retaliation. There were claims that senior leadership allegedly subjected employees who spoke up to patterns of punishment including physical isolation and verbal abuse, bullying and counter-investigations that blamed the employees for creating a "hostile work environment." In addition, those involved in the case stated there was an entrenched management culture that used fear and intimidation to prevent potential whistleblowers from talking.[9]

 **WATCH THIS!**

A VA whistleblower tells his story in this video.

View the video online at: http://www.youtube.com/embed/6VTfd0Sx_wc?rel=0

Military Service

The Uniformed Services Employment and Reemployment Rights Act (USERRA) protects people who serve or have served in the armed forces, Reserves, National Guard, or other uniformed services. The act ensures these individuals are not disadvantaged in their civilian careers because of their service. It also requires that they are reemployed in their civilian jobs upon return to service and prohibits discrimination based on past, present, or future military service.

As you've read about in this chapter, the law focuses on fair hiring and other practices. However, as you remember from earlier in this chapter, having a diverse workforce isn't about meeting the requirements of the law, but can create competitive advantages for the organization.

Key Takeaways

- The *Equal Employment Opportunity Commission (EEOC)* is a federal agency charged with the development and enforcement of laws relating to multiculturalism and diversity in the workplace.
- The EEOC covers discrimination based on several areas. Companies cannot discriminate based on age—against people who are forty years or older.
- Employers cannot discriminate against people with disabilities and must provide reasonable accommodations, such as the addition of a wheelchair ramp to accommodate those with disabilities.
- Equal pay refers to the fact people should legally be paid the same amount for performing the same type of work, even if the job title is different.
- The newest addition to EEOC law prohibits discrimination based on genetic information, such as a family history of cancer.
- Unfavorable treatment of people because they are from a particular country or part of the world or have an accent is covered by the EEOC. An organization cannot require people to speak English, unless it is a requirement for the job or needed for safety and efficient operation of the organization.
- Women can't be discriminated against because they are pregnant. The inability to perform certain tasks due to pregnancy should be treated as a temporary disability; accommodation can be in the form of modified tasks or alternative assignments.

- The EEOC protects people from discrimination based on their race or color.
- Religion is also an aspect of the EEOC family of laws. The protection of religion doesn't allow for discrimination; accommodations include modifications of work schedules or dress to be made for religious reasons.
- Discrimination on the basis of sex is illegal and covered by the EEOC. Sexual harassment is also covered by the EEOC and states that all people, regardless of sex, should work in a harassment-free environment.
- Retaliation is also illegal. An organization cannot retaliate against anyone who has filed a complaint with the EEOC or filed a discrimination lawsuit.
- The US Department of Labor oversees some aspects of EEOC laws, such as the *Family and Medical Leave Act (FMLA)*. This act requires organizations to give twelve weeks of unpaid leave in the event of an adoption, birth, or to provide care to sick family members.

Exercises

1. Visit the EEOC website at http://www.eeoc.gov and explain the methods you could use if you needed to file a complaint with the EEOC.
2. If an employer is found to have discriminated, what are some "remedies" listed on the EEOC website?

11.3 Cultural Intelligence

Learning Objectives

1. Define cultural intelligence.
2. Implement strategies to enhance your cultural intelligence.

cultural intelligence (CQ)

The ability to relate to and work effectively with people from different cultural backgrounds.

Cultural intelligence (CQ) is defined as the ability to relate to and work effectively with people from different cultural backgrounds. It goes beyond simple awareness of other cultures but focuses on how to actually harness other cultural backgrounds to create innovative solutions within the workplace.

Emotional intelligence is similar to EQ, but not exactly the same. CQ takes emotional intelligence to the next level, in that having this skill allows us to understand and accept social norms in cultural situations which are not familiar to us. For example, in the United States, we tend to smile using our entire mouth, while in Japan this might be considered too emotional, as Japanese tend to shy away from overt displays of emotions on one's face. Learning CQ would allow us to recognize this different way of expressing oneself. This can be an important skill in today's workplace! Let's next discuss the importance of CQ and then address how we can get better at our CQ skills.

Why is Cultural Intelligence (CQ) Important?

There are many reasons personally and professionally that make CQ important. First, learning CQ allows us to have higher quality interactions with others, thereby expanding our ability to relate to a variety of people.

Ninety percent of executives in companies are looking to hire people who exhibit cultural intelligence skills,[10] which means by developing an understanding of other cultures, you will be more likely to get hired for your dream job!

Similar to a diverse and multicultural workforce, having employees with CQ allows organizations to be more effective in their problem solving, innovation, and creativity. This is because having a culturally diverse workforce brings about new and different ideas.

How to Develop Cultural Intelligence (CQ)

Now that we have addressed the importance of CQ, let's talk about ways we can develop our own CQ. Similar to emotional intelligence, this skill can be developed over time.

Here are some ways you can develop greater CQ:[11]

- Continue to develop your interaction skills with others.
- Be tolerant of uncertainty.
- Be adaptable and willing to change your behavior based on the culture of others.
- Show empathy—understand a situation from a different cultural perspective.
- Be aware of subtle meanings in words, facial expressions, and actions.

Consider Masaki Yuki, a behavioral scientist at Hokkaido University in Japan. When doing work with American colleagues, he was very confused at the use of emoticons in e-mails such as a happy face :-) or a sad face :-(. The happy face (^_^) and the sad face (;_;) are depicted very differently in Japanese culture than in the United States. After discovering this, he performed research on the topic to find Japanese people focus more on the expressions of the eyes than of the mouth (hence the difference in use of emoticons).[12] When understanding these types of subtle differences, we can begin to obtain higher CQ skills.

Body language isn't the only part of CQ we should be aware of when improving our CQ. Things like punctuality, task or relationship focuses, table manners, and negotiation styles are all examples of aspects of CQ that are important to understand.

While it might be impossible to understand the differences between every culture you will encounter, there is a model that can assist us in developing greater CQ. The model consists of four stages, which include:[13]

1. CQ Drive. The motivation to learn about other cultures.
2. CQ Knowledge. Developing knowledge about cultural norms and values.
3. CQ Strategy. Addresses what you've learned in the knowledge stage, and focuses on how you can apply it. For example, regularly thinking about cultural differences and their impacts is a good way of asking "why" someone from a different culture might write an e-mail in a certain way, or react helps build your CQ.
4. CQ Action. Refers to how you implement all you have learned in your behaviors and actions when working with other cultures.

FIGURE 11.1 Cultural Intelligence Model
The model for building cultural intelligence includes: Drive, Knowledge, Strategy, and Action.

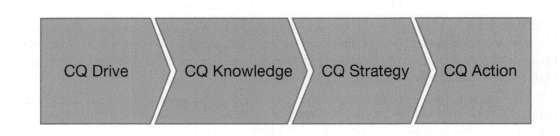

CQ Drive > CQ Knowledge > CQ Strategy > CQ Action

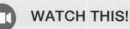 **WATCH THIS!**

Research from more than thirty countries reveals four capabilities that consistently emerge among those who can be described as culturally intelligent (CQ).

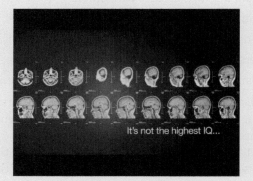

It's not the highest IQ...

View the video online at: http://www.youtube.com/embed/x2C7Mfft9OY?rel=0

In this chapter we have addressed the importance of diversity, multiculturalism, and CQ. After reading this chapter, what strategies do you plan on implementing to gain a better understanding of these topics and to help propel you in your career?

Key Takeaways

- Cultural Intelligence (CQ) is defined as the ability to relate to, and work effectively with, people from different cultural backgrounds.
- CQ, like diversity and multiculturalism, is important to a successful and productive workplace.
- The CQ model shows us how we can develop higher CQ using four stages: Drive, Knowledge, Strategy, and Action.

Exercises

1. Using the strategies outlined in this section, discuss at least five specific strategies you intend to implement to improve your CQ.
2. Take the CQ quiz located at https://commonpurpose.org/knowledge-hub-archive/all-articles/what-is-cultural-intelligence/cq-test/. Do you feel the results are accurate? Why or why not?

11.4 Chapter Summary and Case

Chapter Summary

- *Diversity* is the real or perceived differences between individuals. Diversity can include race, gender, sexual orientation, size, cultural background, and many other differences. *Multiculturalism* is similar to diversity but focuses on the development of a greater understanding of how power in society can be unequal because of race, gender, sexual orientation, power, and privilege.
- *Power and privilege* is a system of advantages based on one's race, gender, and sexual orientation. This system can often be invisible (to those who have it), which results in one race or gender having unequal power in the workplace. Of course, this unequal power results in unfairness, which may be a legal concern.
- *Diversity* is important to the success of organizations. Many studies have shown a direct link between the amount of diversity in a workplace and the success of the company.
- The *Equal Employment Opportunity Commission (EEOC)* is a federal agency charged with development and enforcement of laws relating to multiculturalism and diversity in the workplace.
- The EEOC covers discrimination based on several areas. Companies cannot discriminate based on age—that is, against someone who is forty or older. They also can't discriminate against people with disabilities or on the basis of race, genetic information, national origin, gender, or religion.
- Retaliation is also illegal, based on EEOC laws. An organization cannot retaliate against anyone who has filed a complaint with the EEOC or filed a discrimination lawsuit.
- The US Department of Labor oversees some aspects of EEOC laws, such as the *Family and Medical Leave Act (FMLA)*. This act requires organizations to give twelve weeks of unpaid leave in the event of an adoption, birth, or caregiving of sick family members.
- Cultural Intelligence (CQ) is defined as the ability to relate to, and work effectively with, people from different cultural backgrounds.
- CQ, like diversity and multiculturalism, is important to a successful and productive workplace.
- The CQ model shows us how we can develop higher CQ using four stages: Drive, Knowledge, Strategy, and Action.

Chapter Case

You are an employee in a fifty-person company that specializes in the development and marketing of plastics technologies. When you were hired, you felt the company had little idea of what you should be paid and just made up a number, so you easily negotiated a higher salary than some who have been on the job for over a year. While you have been on the job for three months, you have noticed a few concerning things in the area of multiculturalism, besides the way your salary was offered. The following are some of those items:

1. You know that some of the sales team, including the sales manager, get together once a month to have drinks at the local pub.

2. A Hispanic worker left the organization, and in his exit interview, complained of not seeing a path toward promotion.

3. The only room available for breast-feeding mothers is the women's restroom.

4. The organization has a policy of offering $200 to any employee who refers a friend, as long as the friend is hired and stays at least six months.

5. The manufacturing floor has an English-only policy.

6. You have heard managers refer to those wearing turbans in a derogatory way.

What do you think needs to be done to create a more inclusive environment, taking into account diversity, multiculturalism, and CQ? What suggestions would you make to management, and what reasons would you give for wanting to create an environment that welcomes diversity?

Endnotes

1. Moody, J. (2001). Race, school integration, and friendship segregation in America. *American Journal of Sociology 107*(3), 679–719.

2. Parsi, N. (16 January 2017). Workplace diversity and inclusion gets innovative. Retrieved from https://www.shrm.org/hr-today/news/hr-magazine/0217/pages/disrupting-diversity-in-the-workplace.aspx

3. Parsi, N. (16 January 2017). Workplace diversity and inclusion gets innovative. Retrieved from https://www.shrm.org/hr-today/news/hr-magazine/0217/pages/disrupting-diversity-in-the-workplace.aspx

4. Plaut, V.C., Thomas, K.M., & Goren, M.J. (2009). Is Multiculturalism or Color Blindness Better for Minorities? *Psychological Science 20*, no. 4 (2009): 444–46.

5. Moutsos, K. (11 May 2017). 4 honest questions and answers about diversity and inclusion in the workplace. Retrieved from https://www.goodhire.com/blog/4-honest-answers-on-diversity-and-inclusion

6. Equal Opportunity Employment Commission. (n.d.). EEO-1 Survey. Retrieved from http://www.eeoc.gov/employers/eeo1survey.

7. Bell, J. (21 June 2017). English-only rules can be a minefield in the workplace. Retrieved from https://www.shrm.org/resourcesandtools/legal-and-compliance/state-and-local-updates/pages/english-only-rules-in-the-workplace-can-be-a-minefield.aspx

8. US Department of Labor. (n.d.). Retrieved from https://www.dol.gov/whd/fmla/

9. Westervelt, E. (21 June 2018). For VA Whistleblowers a culture of fear and retaliation. Retrieved from https://www.npr.org/2018/06/21/601127245/for-va-whistleblowers-a-culture-of-fear-and-retaliation

10. Cultural Intelligence Center. (n.d.). About CQ. Retrieved from https://culturalq.com/about-cultural-intelligence/

11. IESE Business School. (24 March 2015). Why you need cultural intelligence. Retrieved from https://www.forbes.com/sites/iese/2015/03/24/why-you-need-cultural-intelligence-and-how-to-develop-it/#1f4a2e917d68

12. Wenner, M. (10 May 2007). Americans and Japanese read faces differently. Retrieved from https://www.livescience.com/1498-americans-japanese-read-faces-differently.html

13. Mind Tools. (n.d.). Cultural Intelligence. Retrieved from https://www.mindtools.com/pages/article/cultural-intelligence.htm

CHAPTER 12
How to Be a Leader

> *Leadership is action, not position.*
> —Donald H. McGannon

> *Leaders don't create followers, they create more leaders.*
> —Tom Peters

The Biggest Challenge

Casey is the Human Resources manager at your company. You make an appointment with him because of some issues you are having with your supervisor.

"Casey," you say, "I really need to vent. Can I sit down and talk with you?" Casey offers you a seat. You begin to tell him about Sam, your supervisor, and the way he has been managing your team lately.

You say, "Sam was a really great manager when he started here three months ago. He had individual meetings with all of us, and he asked a lot of questions. We were all really excited to have him as our new boss, because he really seemed to care, and implemented some of our ideas.

"Lately, though, he seems to be short-tempered and seems to want to make all of the decisions. I have talked with him about it, but he doesn't seem to notice that it has become a problem. In fact, I know of two people who are looking for other jobs because of it."

Casey thinks about the situation and asks you if the timing of Casey's behavior change was around the same time corporate people had come to visit.

"I hadn't thought of that before, but yes, the timing would be about right."

Casey explains that many of the managers have been told they need to make some changes in the organization, and these changes must be done without feedback from employees.

Casey says that he knows it is different than the usual management style of the department and asks you if you can hang on for a little longer. He believes once the changes are made, Sam will be back to his old self. In the meantime, Casey suggests you talk with your manager about your concerns.

Although you feel a bit nervous to do so, you feel talking with Sam might be the best thing for your department.

12.1 Management Styles

Learning Objectives

1. Define the various types of management styles.
2. Explain how we can determine which management style to use in a variety of situations.

Management style ties in very closely with leadership style; however, they are different, which we will address in the next section. There isn't necessarily one management style that is better than another; they are simply different and might be used in a variety of situations. Let's look at some of the common management styles. As we discuss this, consider managers you've had in your past and what style they used. This will help you gain a better understanding of how the different styles work "in action."

Task-Oriented Style versus People-Oriented Style

task-oriented style

A management style that tends to focus on the details of what must get done.

people-oriented style

A management style mostly concerned with the interpersonal relationships within the organization.

When we look at the styles of management, we see that most styles fall into one of two categories—a task-oriented management style or a people-oriented style.

A manager with a **task-oriented style** will focus on the technical or task aspects of the job. The concern for this manager is that employees know what is expected of them and have the tools needed to do their job.

A **people-oriented** style is more concerned with the relationships in the workplace. The manager emphasizes interpersonal relations as opposed to the task. The manager is most concerned about the welfare of the employee and tends to be friendly and trusting.

Now that we've addressed these two main differences in management styles, we will look at other possible styles a manager might use.

Participatory, Directing, or Teamwork Styles

participatory management style

A management style that focuses on task-oriented and people-oriented styles. This style is supportive.

directing management style

A management style in which the manager tends to direct rather than allow for feedback.

Utilization of a **participatory management style** involves both a task-oriented style and a people-oriented style. This style emphasizes how the employee's assigned task fits into the bigger picture. This style will provide support and input where needed. As a result, the focus is on the task but also on the person and the relationships required to get the task done. This style might be used when the employees are experienced and the deadlines reasonable enough to provide the time needed to focus both on the task and the person. If more hands-on management is required,[1] a **directing management style** might be appropriate. Consider a very tight deadline or an emergency situation in which someone needs to be calling the shots. For example, assume you make baked dog treats and sell them in your town. You have one other employee, and just received an order for one hundred dog cookies to be made by later that afternoon. When you manage your employee, using a directing style might be best to make sure the order gets complete. This style doesn't focus on the person, but rather focuses on getting the task done; hence it tends to be more of a task-oriented style.

A manager who uses a **teamwork management style** believes there is a value (or necessity) in having people work in teams. As a result, this style tends to require a people-oriented approach. Relationships are most important with this style, and assuming the individuals work well together, the task will be successfully accomplished. The advantage to this style, given the type of task and situation, is that as a manager you are able to pool resources and abilities from several different people. Use of a team style can also provide big benefits for the company. For example, Google uses a teamwork approach it calls "**grouplets**." Google believes that individuals should be able to spend time on something that interests them but is also company related. Engineers at Google spend 20 percent of their time on this endeavor. As a result, grouplets are formed, and the grouplet works on their idea with no specific budget. Some of the best ideas from Google have come through this teamwork process. Gmail, in fact, was developed using a grouplet.[2]

teamwork management style

A highly people-oriented approach to management in which relationships are most important.

grouplets

A teamwork management style used by many organizations.

Autocratic, Participative, and Free-Rein Styles

An **autocratic style** of management involves the task-oriented style. The focus is on getting things done and relationships are secondary. This type of manager tends to tell people what to do and takes a "my way or the highway" approach. Another description for this type of manager is a taskmaster. This person uses his or her authority and makes all the decisions as to who does what, how it is done, and when it should get done.

On the other hand, a **participative style** constantly seeks input from the employees. Setting goals, making plans, and determining objectives are viewed as a group effort, rather than the manager making all the decisions.

At the other extreme, a **free-rein style** gives employees total freedom to make decisions on how things will get done. The manager may establish a few objectives, but the employees can decide how those objectives are met. In other words, the leader tends to be removed from the day-to-day activities but is available to help employees deal with any situation that may come up.

autocratic style

A management style that takes a task-only focus and tends to make most of the decisions for the department.

participative style

A management style that seeks input from employees.

free-rein style

A management style that gives employees freedom to make decisions.

Path Goal Model for Leadership

The path goal theory says that the role of a leader is to define goals and lay down the path for the employees to meet those goals. Aspects include clarification of the task and scope of the process. Clarification of the employee's role and clarification around how the success of the task will be measured are key aspects of this model. The leader is also involved in guidance and coaching surrounding the goal and removes obstacles that might affect the completion of the task. The path goal theory says that if employees are satisfied by the leadership style, they will be motivated toward the goals of leadership. Part of the model also stresses that the skills, experience, and environmental contingencies of the job play a role in the success of the leader.

FIGURE 12.1 Path Goal Model for Leadership

Applying Management Styles

It is great to talk about management style, but application of that management style, especially in an HR environment, is just as important as knowing the management styles. In this section, we will discuss how and when you might use each style when managing people.

Another way we can view leadership is through the **situational leadership model**.[3] This model, developed by Ken Blanchard (author of the *One Minute Manager* series of books), does a good job explaining how we might use one type of management style over another.

The model looks at three areas: the relationship behavior of the manager, the task behavior of the manager, and the readiness of employees. The relationship behavior means how supportive the manager needs to be in helping employees. Task behavior refers to the type of style the manager should use when managing employees, based on their readiness level. Readiness includes the willingness and skills to perform the task at hand. Depending on where the employees fall in each of these areas, you might use a different management style:

- D4—High Competence, High Commitment—Experienced at the job and comfortable with their own ability to do it well. May even be more skilled than the leader.

- D3—High Competence, Variable Commitment—Experienced and capable, but may lack the confidence to go it alone or the motivation to do it well/quickly.

- D2—Some Competence, Low Commitment—May have some relevant skills but won't be able to do the job without help. The task or the situation may be new to them.

- D1—Low Competence, High Commitment—Generally lacking the specific skills required for the job at hand but has the confidence and/or motivation to tackle it.

Based on the readiness and commitment of the employee, the leader can see what management style and level of support the employee should experience:[4]

- S1—Telling/Directing—High Task Focus, Low Relationship Focus—Leaders define the roles and tasks of the "follower" and supervise them closely. Decisions are made and announced by the leader, so communication is largely one way. This style can be used with people who lack competence but are enthusiastic and committed and who need direction and supervision to get them started.

- S2—Selling/Coaching—High Task Focus, High Relationship Focus—Leaders still define roles and tasks but seek ideas and suggestions from the follower. Decisions remain the leader's prerogative, but communication is much more two-way. This approach can be used with people who have some competence but lack commitment and who need direction and supervision because they are still relatively inexperienced. These individuals may also need support and praise to build their self-esteem and involvement in decision making to restore their commitment.

- S3—Participating/Supporting—Low Task Focus, High Relationship Focus—Leaders pass day-to-day decisions, such as task allocation and processes, to the follower. The leader facilitates and takes part in decisions, but control gives to the follower. This style can be used with people who have the necessary competence but lack confidence or motivation. These individuals may need little direction because of their skills, but support is required to bolster their confidence and motivation.

- S4—Delegating—Low Task Focus, Low Relationship Focus—Leaders are still involved in decisions and problem solving, but control is with the follower. The follower decides when and how the leader will be involved. This style would work with people who have both competence and commitment and who are able and willing to work on a project by themselves with little supervision or support. Consider the immense amount of changes that can happen during a crisis, such as the COVID-19 pandemic. A follower who normally prefers a S4, Delegating Approach, may need or want more help. The leader might change their style to telling/directing or participating/supporting, until the employee feels more comfortable with the changes the crisis has created.

The bottom line when discussing management style is that no style works best in all situations. We may be more comfortable with one style versus another, but we need to change our management style depending on the person and task we are working with. For example, if you have an employee who is brand new, you will likely work with that person using a more directive style. As she develops, you might change to a participative style. Likewise, someone who does good work and has lots of experience may prefer a free-rein style. Many managers make the mistake of trying to use the same style with every person in every situation. To be a great manager, we must change our management styles based on the situation and the individual involved.

FIGURE 12.2 Blanchard's Situational Leadership Model

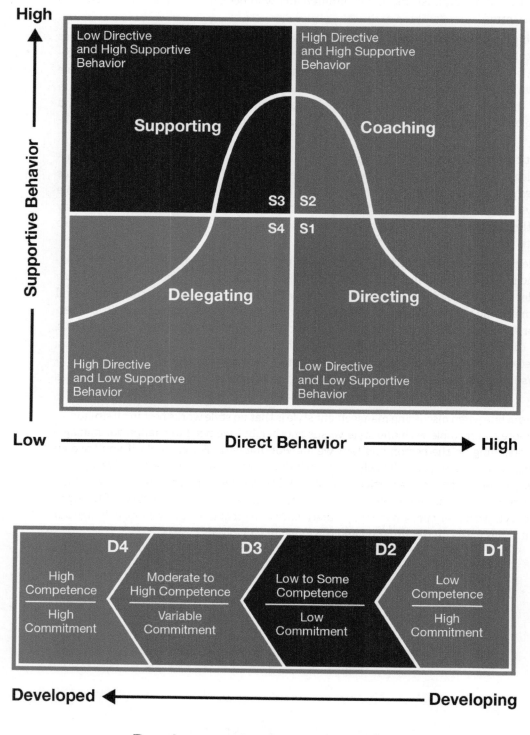

How does this relate to human relations? Understanding your own tendencies for management styles can add to your emotional intelligence skills, and make you more aware of what styles managers use with you.

 **WATCH THIS!**

This video discusses several ways to deal with a poor manager.

View the video online at: http://www.youtube.com/embed/uW6oJ988OJ8?rel=0

Key Takeaways

- Just as with communication, a different management style should be used depending on the employee.
- *Task-oriented styles* focus on getting the job done, while *people-oriented styles* focus on relationships.
- A *participatory* style involves both task-oriented and people-oriented styles. A *directing style* is focused on the task and doesn't allow for employee participation. A *teamwork style* focuses on teamwork and is a people-oriented style. The advantage of this style is the ability to use strengths from everyone on the team.
- An *autocratic* style doesn't allow much room for employee decision making; the focus is on getting the task done. A *participative* style constantly requires input from employees. The *free-rein* style gives employees freedom to make decisions on how things will get done.
- The *situational leadership model*, which looks at relationship behavior, task behavior, and the readiness of employees, is used to recommend different management styles.
- No one management style works in all situations. The approach should be varied based on a variety of factors.

Exercises

1. Why is it important to understand management style as a manager? Why is it important to understand management style as an employee? Discuss three points for each.
2. What combinations of management style might you use in each of these situations and why?
   a. You are considering a major change in the way your company does business. Your staff has an excellent record of achieving goals, and your relationship with them is trusting and supportive.
   b. Your employees do a great job. A situation has developed in which you need to make quick decisions and finish a project by the end of the week.
   c. Your employees are having trouble getting the job done. Their performance as a whole is less than expected.
   d. You have an employee who is very motivated but has little experience.

12.2 Leadership versus Management

Leadership

Many people use the term leadership and management interchangeably, but the two terms are actually quite different. The term management implies someone has a position or title, and through that position or title, they have power to guide others. Leadership, on the other hand, does not require specific titles. Consider the last group project you worked on for school. It was likely that someone took on the leadership role for this project, such as coordinating schedules, e-mailing the team, and so forth. This person did not have a formal title but lead the group anyway; this is an example of leadership. To be successful at our jobs, we must show leadership skills. These leadership skills can come from our emotional intelligence skills—for example, self-awareness, self-management, relationship management, and social awareness. All emotional intelligence skills are needed to be a successful leader. For example, if you are the informal leader for your group project and feel frustrated with response times, you must have the ability to be aware of this emotion and manage it by not taking your frustration out on your team members when you see them!

Getting the team to work better together requires social awareness skills, or the ability to understand how actions of one team member may affect another. Finally, relationship management is necessary to manage group conflict and maintain good relationships with your team. As you can see, leadership encompasses all of the emotional intelligence skills we have been discussing throughout the book. Do you think leadership comes naturally to some and not to others?

Whether or not there is a "natural leader," born with a combination of talents and traits that enable a person to lead others, has been a subject of debate across time. In a modern context, we have come to recognize that leadership comes in many forms and representations. Once it was thought that someone with presence of mind, innate intelligence, and an engaging personality was destined for leadership, but modern research and experience show us otherwise. Just as a successful heart surgeon has a series of skill sets, so does a dynamic leader. A television producer must both direct and provide space for talent to create, balancing control with confidence and trust. This awareness of various leadership styles serves our discussion, as groups and teams often have leaders, and they may not always be the person who holds the title, status, or role.

appointed leader

Individual designated by an authority to serve in the leadership capacity.

Leaders take on the role because they are appointed, elected, or emerge, and group members play an important role in this process. An **appointed leader** is designated by an authority to serve in that capacity, irrespective of the thoughts or wishes of the group. They may serve as the leader and accomplish all the designated tasks, but if the group does not accept their leadership role, it can prove to be a challenge. As Bruce Tuckman[5] notes, "storming" occurs as group members come to know each other and communicate more freely, and an appointed leader who lacks the endorsement of the group may experience challenges to his or her authority.

A **democratic leader** is elected or chosen by the group but may also face serious challenges. If individual group members or constituent groups feel neglected or ignored, they may assert that the democratic leader does not represent their interests. The democratic leader involves the group in the decision-making process and ensures group ownership of the resulting decisions and actions. Open and free discussions are representative of this process, and the democratic leader acknowledges this diversity of opinion.

An **emergent leader** contrasts the first two paths to the role by growing into the role, often out of necessity. The appointed leader may know little about the topic or content, and group members will naturally look to the senior member with the most experience for leadership. If the democratic leader fails to bring the group together or does not represent the whole group, subgroups may form, each with an informal leader serving as spokesperson.

Types of Leaders

Thomas Harris and John Sherblom[6] specifically note three leadership styles that characterize the modern business or organization and reflect our current economy. We are not born leaders but may become them if the context or environment requires our skill set. A **leader-as-technician** role often occurs when we have skills that others do not. If you can fix the copy machine at the office, your leadership and ability to get it running again are prized and sought-after skills. You may instruct others on loading the paper or changing the toner, and even though your pay grade may not reflect this leadership role, you are looked to by the group as a leader within that context. Technical skills, from Internet technology to facilities maintenance, may experience moments where their particular area of knowledge is required to solve a problem, and their leadership will be in demand.

The **leader-as-conductor** involves a central role of bringing people together for a common goal. In a familiar analogy, a conductor leads an orchestra and integrates the specialized skills and sounds of the various components the musical group comprises. In the same way, a leader who conducts may set a vision, create benchmarks, and collaborate with a group as they interpret a set script. Whether it is a group of teams that comes together to address a common challenge or a smaller team of two, the leader-as-conductor keeps the time and tempo of the group.

Coaches are often discussed in business-related books as models of leadership, with good reason. A **leader-as-coach** combines many of the talents and skills we've discussed here, serving as a teacher, motivator, and keeper of the goals of the group. A coach may be autocratic at times, give pointed direction without input from the group, and stand on the sidelines while the players do what they've been trained to do. The coach may look out for the group and defend it against bad calls and may motivate players with words of encouragement. We can recognize some of the behaviors of coaches, but what specific traits have a positive influence on the group? Thomas Peters and Nancy Austin[7] identify five important traits that produce results:

1. Orientation and education;
2. Nurturing and encouragement;
3. Assessment and correction;
4. Listening and counseling;
5. Establishing group emphasis.

Coaches are teachers, motivators, and keepers of the group goals. There are times when members of the team need to remember it is a group effort, and coaches serve to redirect the attention and energy of the individuals to the overall goals of the group. They conduct the group with a sense of timing and tempo and, at times, relax and let the members demonstrate their talents. Through their listening skills and counseling, they come to know each member as an individual but keep the team focus for all to see. They set an example. Coaches, however, are human and by definition are not perfect. They can and do prefer some players over others and can display less-than-professional sideline behavior when they don't agree with the referee, but the style of leadership is

democratic leader

Individual elected by a group to serve as its leader.

emergent leader

Individual who grows into the leadership role, often out of necessity.

leader-as-technician

Occurs when the leader has skills that others do not.

leader-as-conductor

Central role of bringing people together for a common goal.

leader-as-coach

Individual serving as a teacher, motivator, and keeper of the goals of the group.

worthy of your consideration in its multidisciplinary approach. Coaches use more than one style of leadership and adapt to the context and environment in which they are working. A skilled business communicator will recognize that this approach has its merits.

 **WATCH THIS!**

This short video provides ten clear distinctions to help understand the differences between a manager and a leader.

View the video online at: http://www.youtube.com/embed/8ubRzzirRKs?rel=0

Since we have discussed both leadership and management styles in this chapter, you can see where the difference between the two is not altogether clear. Either way, looking toward future careers it can be valuable to understand both leadership and management styles as well as the process of leader development over time.

What's in it for me?

As we have discussed in this chapter, you do not need a fancy title to be a leader. **To be an effective leader, you must exhibit all aspects of emotional intelligence skills.** For example, good leaders will know themselves well and understand their strengths and weaknesses. Good leaders also know their feelings from moment to moment and they have learned how to handle those emotions. Good leaders have many similar qualities, such as empathy, ethics, understanding, and patience. These skills are also emotional intelligence skills—specifically, social awareness and relationship management skills.

Social awareness skills are crucial in leadership, including reading and interpreting social cues and body language, setting goals, resolving conflict, understanding the perspectives of others, and having a positive attitude. A leader is someone people want to be around because they have a certain charisma that draws us to them! Leaders are also excellent at relationship management in that they handle relationships with others well.

Remember, you do not need a fancy title to be a leader, but showing emotional intelligence skills in the workplace can not only make you a happier person but also show your supervisor you are ready to move up within your organization—resulting in higher salaries, promotions, and excelling in your chosen career!

Key Takeaways

- Leadership is a bit different than management in that management includes a "title" while leadership and the leadership development process can occur without a title.
- Leaders can be appointed, elected, or emerge into the role of leader.
- There are three types of leaders. The first is leader-as-technician—meaning the person taking the leadership role has skills we may not have.
- The second, leader-as-conductor role, involves bringing people together to reach a common goal.
- The third, leader-as-coach, combines many talents and skills, such as teacher and motivator.
- Many leaders will use a variety of approaches, depending on the situation.

Exercise

1. Think of a leader you admire and respect. How did this individual become a leader—for example, by appointment, democratic selection, or emergence? How would you characterize this leader's style—is the leader autocratic or laissez-faire, a technician or a coach? Write three paragraphs and describe.

12.3 Chapter Summary and Case

Chapter Summary

- Just as in communication, a different management style should be used depending on the employee.
- *Task-oriented styles* focus on getting the job done, while *people-oriented styles* focus on relationships.
- A *participatory style* involves both task-oriented and people-oriented styles. A *directing style* is focused on the task and doesn't allow for employee participation.
- A teamwork style focuses on teamwork and is a people-oriented style. The advantage of this style is the ability to use strengths from everyone on the team.
- An *autocratic style* doesn't allow much room for employee decision making; the focus is on getting the task done. A *participative style* constantly requires input from employees. The *free-rein style* gives employees freedom to make decisions on how things will get done.
- The *situational leadership model*, which looks at relationship behavior, task behavior, and the readiness of employees, is used to recommend different management styles.
- No one management style works in all situations. Just like with communication, you will likely want to vary your approach based on the situation to get the best results.
- Leadership and management are similar, although management implies a specific title. Leaders can be appointed, elected, or emerge into a leadership role. Some people may be excellent leaders, although they may not have a formal title within an organization.
- Depending on the situation, a leader may take on a variety of roles to solve challenges.

Chapter Case

You own a regional gift store in your town. The store opened in 2018 and the same four people have worked together since that time. Recently, the manager left and you need to hire a new manager. You have decided that one of the four people currently working for you would definitely be great for the job, but you need to create a list of criteria for the job and then compare it with the skills of your existing employees. Your task is to develop specific criteria or a "wish list" of skills and abilities for this job based on three different aspects:

1. Skills needed for the job,
2. Human relations skills,
3. Leadership skills.

Once you have created the criteria, rank the skills in each category and provide a written description as to why you ranked them as you did.

Endnotes

1. Cardinal, R. (13 January 2015). 6 management styles and when to use them. Retrieved from https://www.huffingtonpost.com/rosalind-cardinal/6-management-styles-and-when-to-use-them_b_6446960.html
2. Robinson, A. (12 March 2018). Want to boost your bottom line? Encourage your employees to work on side projects. Retrieved from https://www.inc.com/adam-robinson/google-employees-dedicate-20-percent-of-their-time-to-side-projects-heres-how-it-works.html
3. Blanchard, K., Zigarmi, P., & Zigarmi, D. (2000). *Leadership and the One Minute Manager.* HarperCollins Entertainment. New York: NY
4. The Center for Leadership Studies. (n.d.). The situational leadership grid. Retrieved from https://www.situational.com/the-cls-difference/situational-leadership-what-we-do/
5. Tuckman, B. (1965). Developmental sequence in small groups. *Psychological Bulletin, 63,* 384–99.
6. Harris, T., & Sherblom, J. (1999). Small group and team communication. Boston, MA: Allyn & Bacon.
7. Peters, T., & Austin, N. (1985). A Passion for Excellence: The Leadership Difference. New York, NY: Random House.

CHAPTER 13

Building Career Success

> *I long to accomplish a great and noble task, but it is my chief duty to accomplish small tasks as if they were great and noble.*
>
> —Helen Keller

> *A journey of a thousand miles begins with a single step.*
>
> —Lao-Tzu

A Shining Star

In the morning, Jackson gives a lot of thought to what he is going to wear to work. Not only does he want to look nice, but he also finds that clients respect him more and look to him for answers when he dresses up. His company has a casual policy, but Jackson always wears at least dress pants and a button-up shirt. The program director wears a similar outfit, and Jackson wants a promotion, so he assumes it is best to look the part.

Another thing Jackson does for career success is to have an awareness of his power position. To create a stronger power position, Jackson is helpful to his colleagues, has a positive attitude, shows his problem-solving ability, handles conflicts with people well, and rarely complains. These are all human relations skills he has learned over his ten-year career. Jackson is a positive, upbeat person who others like to be around. He is polite, friendly, and confident, but not in an egotistical way.

Jackson's manager says he is a prime candidate for a promotion. He is dedicated, commits himself to client satisfaction, and tries to learn new things continuously. When a deadline is looming, Jackson stays late to help his colleagues finish projects, and always recognizes people's contributions to the organization. Jackson epitomizes someone who is emotionally intelligent, which creates better relationships and, thus, more career opportunities.

Like Jackson, you can do many things to achieve career success, no matter what career you choose, but it is impossible to achieve career success without human relations skills. This chapter will discuss some of the strategies, such as understanding power positions, dealing with change, dressing, and networking skills, that can help propel anyone to have positive human relations and high emotional intelligence, which are both ingredients for career success.

13.1 Career Growth: Power Positioning and Power Sources

Learning Objective

1. Be able to apply power positioning techniques to your career.

Throughout this book, we have discussed the factors that create good human relations with our work and personal relationships. When you started reading this book, you learned how your personality, attitude, and self-esteem could impact your human relations with other people. We also talked about the following:

- The importance of emotional intelligence when relating to other people, both professionally and personally.
- Understanding diversity, and how our diversity and that of others could impact our human relations.
- How to work in teams, as working on a team is a mainstay of the workplace, and working with others is required in most jobs and careers.
- Communication styles—both ours and others—can impact how we relate to people and how they relate to us.
- Handling conflict in the workplace. The ability to handle conflict in a constructive manner ensures our ability to manage our relations with others.
- People respect others who are ethical; therefore, making ethical decisions can assist us in creating good relationships with others.
- Having an understanding of human motivation can give us perspective into how others "tick," allowing us to handle our relationships better.
- Knowing what it means to have personal success can create happiness—which leads to better human relations skills.
- The ability to make sound decisions relates to human relations, in that these skills can help us think logically and not emotionally, which can improve how we relate to others in group decision making. Knowing how to make sound decisions also relates to conflict management and the ability to handle conflict in group decision-making processes.
- Managing stress so it doesn't create negative human relations with others.

FIGURE 13.1 Emotional Intelligence Skills
Remember our ongoing discussion on emotional intelligence skills and their necessity for career success? Here is how emotional intelligence skills tie into our chapter on career success.

Self-Management	• Coping with change • Controlling emotions
Self-Awareness	• Personality traits • Understanding your own communication style • Using our POWER behaviors
Social Awareness	• Dining etiquette • Handshake, introduction etiquette • Technology etiquette • Thank-you notes • Clothing choices
Relationship Management	• Handling change • Using power positioning appropriately • Having social awareness can help improve relationships • Find a mentor

With an understanding and practice in all of these areas, we can become successful people in our careers. This is the focus of the chapter—the skills it takes to be productive individuals through positive human relations. The first step is developing an understanding of how we can use power both at work and in our personal life.

Understanding power and power structure in our organizations can assist us in being more successful in our careers. **Power** refers to our ability to influence others and convince them to do what we want them to do. Power is different than influence, in that **influence** is the application of the power we have to get people to do what we want them to do. Although it may seem this only applies to managers, we all use power in a variety of ways, both in our personal and professional lives. For example, Abbey may use her power to convince Amy they should have sushi for dinner tonight, but that doesn't mean that Amy thinks it is the right thing to do. It isn't until Abbey uses her influence that Amy agrees to eat sushi. Please keep in mind that power is not a negative thing if used properly. Power and influence, ultimately, are what allows things to get done in our organizations.[1] Whether or not we are leaders in our organization, power can come in many forms. A study by John French and Bertram Raven in 1959 identified the ways leaders can influence others.[2] They include the following:

1. **Reward power.** Refers to a person's ability to present the receiver some form of reward, should they do something in return. For example, a manager may use raises or praise. If John wants to reward his employees, he might use reward power by offering them a bonus if they meet specific sales goals. John, as a parent, may promise dessert if his son finishes his dinner.

2. **Coercive power.** Refers to the power to punish someone should they not do something the person wants them to do. For example, John may say, "If you don't meet the sales goal, you will have to look for another job." This type of power focuses on punishment rather than rewards. As a parent, John may tell his son he will be grounded if his son does not do as asked.

3. **Legitimate power.** Refers to the ability to make another feel obligated or responsible. Because John's title is manager, for example, he has the power or the right to make certain decisions. This can be powerful at first, but over time it can become less important if trust does not exist. Have you ever heard your Mom say, "Because I said so," without further explanation? This is an example of legitimate power. The mother has the power simply because she is the mother.

power

Refers to our ability to influence others and convince them to do what we want them to do.

influence

The application of the power we have to get people to do what we want them to do.

4. **Expert power.** Sometimes people have power because they have a lot of knowledge or are known as experts in a particular field. John, for example, might use expert power by saying, "I know you can meet the sales goal because I was able to meet this same sales goal last year." Because John is an expert salesperson, his employees respect his abilities, and this respect gives him power. If John is using expert power with his son when teaching him to play baseball, he might tell his son about the years of experience he has had playing the sport—therefore, John's son is motivated to listen to him.

5. **Referent power.** Referent power is often referred to as charisma, charm, or appeal. This type of power comes from one person respecting and liking another, so they are willing to do what the leader says. For example, if John's employees really like and respect him, his source of power is the fact that people want to do what he says. If John is a convincing person with charisma, he may also use his power to convince his friends to go to the movie he wants to see.

Again, we feel it is important to point out there is nothing wrong with utilizing power to make things happen; the concern is when an individual is power-compulsive. **Power compulsive** means the person's personality has a lust for power and they may use it for personal gain. This is the opposite of the **power-shy** personality, who prefers not to be in charge of things and is not comfortable using power. Power-shy individuals may not be positive either, in that at some point, people must be willing to use power to make decisions. Keep in mind, we all use power, no matter what title we hold at work.

power-compulsive

A person's personality has a lust for power and may use power for personal gain.

power-shy

A personality characteristic of someone who prefers not to be in charge of things and is not comfortable using power.

FIGURE 13.2 Influence Strategies

Managers may use various types of power depending on the person they are trying to influence. This figure shows some of the strategies used for influence from most-to-least popular strategies in all countries.

Most-to-Least Popular Strategies Used in All Countries

	When Managers Influenced Superiors	When Managers Influenced Subordinates
Most Popular to Least Popular	Reason Coalition Friendliness Bargaining Assertiveness Higher authority	Reason Assertiveness Friendliness Evaluation Bargaining Higher authority Sanction

Source: David Kipnis et al., "Patterns of Managerial Influence: Shotgun Managers, Tacticians, and Bystanders," *Organizational Dynamics* 12, no. 3 (New York: American Management Association, 1984), 62.

power position

The use of power in an appropriate way when getting ahead in an organization.

As mentioned earlier, the idea of "power" often seems negative, but we can appropriately use power when getting ahead in our organizations—this is called **power position**. Power position comes from the concept of feng shui, where the power position is the physical position in the room for a business meeting. In this position, the person can see all entrances to the room and is seated against a wall. Because of this, they are said to be the center of attention and thus in the power position. Our meaning here refers to your ability to use conscientious techniques that can lead to personal and professional organizational growth; these also happen to be the characteristics needed for career success, and we can tie into emotional intelligence. Techniques that may help increase your power position at work include the following:

1. **Be authentic.** Be yourself. Stay true to your values and those things you find important.

2. **Refuse to let people push your buttons.** This can result in conflict, which does not increase your power position. Make an effort to try and get along with others.

3. **Develop esteem and confidence.** Esteem and confidence will give you the ability to take on difficult tasks, help others, and contribute to the organization.

4. **Be a team player.** Do all the things necessary to be part of a team. Get along with and help others. Helping others shows leadership, ability, and good citizenship. It can put you in a position of not only earning the respect of others but also showing your value to the organization.

5. **Be someone that makes others feel good.** Make others feel good when they are around you—for example, by being genuinely interested in them.

6. **Develop your communication skills.** Work on your written, oral, and nonverbal language skills. Learn to read and understand others' body language.

7. **Be visible in the workplace.** Don't take credit for others' work, but do take credit for your own work. Choose high-profile projects that can put you in a position where others see your work.

8. **Don't complain.** Unless you can also provide a solution, don't offer a complaint!

9. **Be goal-oriented and willing to take risks.** Focus on goal-setting personally and professionally, and show managers and colleagues how you can help them meet goals.

10. **Have positive psychological capital.** There are four aspects to positive **psychological capital**: hope, self-efficacy, optimism, and resiliency. Self-efficacy refers to belief in your own abilities, while optimism means to have a positive outlook. Resiliency is the ability to make it through difficult circumstances. In a study by the Leadership Institute[3] on psychological capital, there was a clear relationship between positive psychological capital and job performance/job satisfaction—two very important components for good human relations!

> **psychological capital**
>
> Four aspects to positive psychological capital include hope, self-efficacy, optimism, and resiliency.

🎥 WATCH THIS!

This somewhat silly (with typos) video shows the types of power.

View the video online at: http://www.youtube.com/embed/-MxSNrtRouM?rel=0

In addition to these techniques, we can think about power position as a set of behaviors we exhibit on a daily basis. These five behaviors can help us increase our power position at work, and we can remember these behaviors by using the acronym POWER:

- **P**ositive approach. Having a positive approach to everything can help increase your power position. Avoiding rumors, gossip, and other negative behaviors can gain others' trust.

- **O**pen. Being open to others, new ideas, and people can help increase your power position.

- **W**illingness. The willingness to do things differently, trying something new, and taking risks can increase your power position.

- **E**mploying. Employing tact, common courtesies, humor, patience, and emotional intelligence skills can increase your power position.
- **R**emembering. Know your purpose, set goals, and always do your best.

Having an understanding of the types of power and how to improve your own power position at work can increase your human relations skills at work and, therefore, your success—and probably make work more enjoyable, too!

Key Takeaways

- Power refers to our ability to influence others and convince them to do what we want them to do. This is different from influence, which is the application of our power to get people to do what we want them to do. In other words, power is our ability, while influence allows us to move someone to action.
- Someone who is power-compulsive may lust for power, while someone who is power-shy may try to avoid situations where he or she might have to exert power.
- Our power position can help us achieve career success, and refers to the use of our own power to get ahead in organizations.
- Power positioning can be done using a variety of methods, but specific techniques and behaviors can be used. For example, the POWER method refers to behaviors we can exhibit to increase our power position. They include positive approach, openness, willingness, employing things like tact and social skills, and remembering our purpose and goals.

Exercise

1. In a small group, discuss examples you or your team members have experienced relating to each of the sources of power. These can be examples from past or present work experiences, school, or home life. Compile a list and then present to the rest of the class.

13.2 Career Growth: Negotiation

Learning Objective

1. Be able to explain some of the strategies you can use with negotiation.

We already know we can negotiate the price of a house or a car, but did you know there are many other things that can be negotiated? Negotiating can occur on a daily basis, from negotiating with your roommate about who does the dishes, to negotiating salary at a new job. This section will cover some basics of negotiation, and ways you can be successful at negotiating.

Persuading others is a learned skill, but one that also takes practice. Here are some of the top tips for negotiating:[4]

- Be prepared to show the other party how they can benefit from your offer. For example, if you are negotiating salary, you can say, "I understand the salary is x amount, but given my skills in x, I believe I can save you x dollars in the long run." Or, "I understand the car is priced at x, but I am willing to buy it today if you can sell it to me for x."

- Maintain your human relations skills. You can still negotiate yet be respectful of the other party.

- Try to foster a collaborative environment while negotiating.

- Know what you want before the negotiation. Know what you will not accept, what you would consider, and what would make you say "yes" right away. Knowing your own goals before the negotiation will set you up for success.

- Listen to the other party to fully understand their needs and wants. This allows you to better negotiate a win for them and a win for you.

- Be aware of the power of a **negotiation anchor**, which is the first offer, and usually the starting point for most negotiations. Suppose you wish to buy a car where the sticker price is $24,999. If you make an offer of $22,999, this is the negotiation anchor, and all negotiations will be based on this offer. However, if you'd made an offer of $18,999, this might be on the low side, but anchors the negotiations from that starting point instead. The trick is to determine an anchor offer that is not too low but gives you a negotiating advantage.

- Keep expectations realistic. If you are offered a job paying $40,000 per year, but ask for $65,000, this unrealistic figure will likely hinder or even stop the negotiations.

Remember that negotiation is ultimately about problem-solving and creating value for both parties. Maintaining relationships when negotiating is obviously very important, and this is done with mutual respect and using your emotional intelligence skills.

> **negotiation anchor**
>
> In negotiations, usually is the first offer, the anchor is the starting point for most negotiations.

Key Takeaways

- Many things in life can and will be negotiated, from salary to large purchases.
- There are many things to consider when negotiating. Respecting the other party, communicating well, and being aware of your needs and wants before going into the negotiation can make it smoother.
- A negotiation anchor is a starting point for negotiations, and usually, all negotiations are based around this first figure. Because of this, it is important to understand the right anchor to start the negotiations with.

Exercise

1. Perform a self-assessment of your negotiation skills by answering the following questions:
   a. What have you recently negotiated?
   b. How did you feel the negotiation went? If it was successful, what made it successful? If it wasn't, why wasn't it successful?
   c. What negotiation skills would you like to work on?
   d. Discuss specific strategies to work on the negotiation skills you mention in question c.

13.3 Career Growth: Behaviors and Change

Since this chapter is all about professional growth, it makes sense to discuss planning strategies used by people who want to further their careers. Each of these involves and requires emotional intelligence skills discussed in Chapter 2 and throughout the book. Having emotional intelligence skills, as you may recall, is even more important than having a high IQ.[5] Knowing ourselves and the ability to manage ourselves is the core of this section in the form of a discussion on what kinds of human relations behaviors are necessary to achieve career success.

How to get promoted must be one of the questions managers are asked the most. Often, earning a promotion or moving into a higher pay level is dependent not only on one's skills and abilities but also certain behaviors. According to Long Yun Siang of Career Success for Newbies,[6] there are several characteristics people have that can help them earn a promotion, and these fall into one of three categories: plan, attitude, and action. They are as follows:

1. **Perform self-analysis.** Where are you, and why are you there? Is there a key strength that has gotten you to where you are now? What skills can you continue to leverage to get that promotion? Likewise, are there weaknesses you must resolve before moving to the next level?

2. **Keep your eye on the goals.** Where do you want to be, and how do you get there? Remember our chapter on goal setting? Now is the time to apply those ideas! Using SMART objectives (Chapter 2), determine where you want to be in the short, medium, and long term. Then create objectives that will help you meet those goals.

3. **Put pride, passion, and belief into everything you do.** People who get promoted have pride in their work; they enjoy what they are doing and have genuine enthusiasm. They work toward their own goals but also those of the company and the department.

4. **Back it up with skills, knowledge, and direction.** Do your best to acquire skills—take seminars, workshops, and attend conferences. Make sure you continually update your skills.

5. **See challenges as opportunities.** Avoid complaining and look at problems to overcome as ways to improve your skills, but also to show others you are capable of solving problems.

6. **Understand your role in helping the organization achieve goals.** Be a team player to understand what you must do to help the rest of the department and organization achieve success.

7. **Do your best, and do more than necessary.** Volunteer for more work or projects, and take the initiative. Look at how you can solve problems for the manager.

8. **Do work from the next level up.** Continue to do your own work, but try to take on assignments that may be "above your pay grade" or above your normal expected workload. This shows you are capable of the position you want.

9. **Understand the importance of networking.** Much of the business done today happens through networking.[7] Networking events are where we can meet new clients, friends, and employers. They might include events through your local chamber of commerce, charity functions, and professional organization conferences and events. The ability to stay in touch with people we meet at events has never been easier through the use of technology. Building relationships with others takes time but is also worthwhile. People you meet today may be a

future employer or client. Networking can also help us find mentors and gain new insights into our industry.

Besides understanding the skills, attitudes, and abilities needed for a promotion, learning how to handle change is a great way to earn a promotion and obtain career success. We discussed change in Chapter 2; because it's necessary both from a personal and career perspective, it is good to discuss it here from a career approach. Often, people get too comfortable in their jobs, which does not allow them to move upward within the organization. We know that change is a continual process, and the more comfortable we can get, the better, especially to experience continued success at work. But why do people avoid change in their careers or jobs, and why would they avoid taking on more responsibility to obtain a promotion? Figure 13.3 gives some examples.

FIGURE 13.3 Career Change Avoidance
When considering making a career change, whether it be to move to a different company or to earn a promotion, there are many reasons why people may be afraid of such a change.

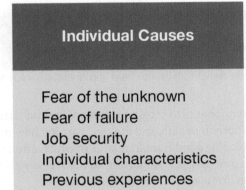

Individual Causes

Fear of the unknown
Fear of failure
Job security
Individual characteristics
Previous experiences

It's important to identify the reasons why you may avoid change. When we identify them and our behaviors, we can begin to understand why we behave the way we do, which is a key component to self-knowledge and emotional intelligence skills. Another aspect of career success is knowing basic etiquette, which we will discuss next.

Key Takeaways

- Part of career success is making sure you know how to increase your power position and having an awareness of your attitude and personality.
- There are three main behavioral aspects to optimizing career success—planning, attitude, and action. Examples include being willing to go above and beyond your job description and having a specific goal you want to reach. Besides goal setting, having a positive, can-do attitude can help improve chances for promotion.
- Besides attitude and personality, career promotion means being comfortable with possible changes. People resist change because of fear of job security, the unknown, and failure; their individual personality; and bad past experiences with change.

Exercises

1. Go to http://images.barnesandnoble.com/pimages/resources/pdf/Change_Quiz.pdf and take the quiz on change. Then answer these questions:

a. Based on your results, what are some things you could do to improve your resistance to change?

b. Why do you think the abilities to deal with change and job promotion are so closely tied?

2. Discuss each of the personality characteristics to obtaining a promotion. If you were a manager, how important do you think these are? Which would be the most important to you?

13.4 Career Growth: Impression Management

Learning Objective

1. Be able to explain etiquette aspects that can help you achieve career success.

Perhaps the most important components to career success are how we manage our reputation and the impression we give others, both in person, and online. Learning how to manage our reputation can be a key ingredient to developing good human relations, which often results in career success. Although much of this may be a review, it is important to discuss key elements to making a good impression in a professional environment.

Introductions

An introduction to a person is possibly one of the most important aspects of etiquette. This nonverbal behavior can send positive or not-so-positive messages to a person with whom you want to make a good impression.[8] Here are the components to a good handshake and introduction:

1. **Firm handshake.** A firm handshake shows self-confidence. Try not to make it too firm or too soft. Do not place your other hand on top of the other person's hand while shaking. There may be times, such as during a pandemic, where handshaking is not appropriate. If this is the case, instead of a handshake, look the other person in the eye as you introduce yourself.

2. **Web-to-web handshake.** When you shake someone's hand, extend your right hand, and the web of skin between your thumb and pointer finger should touch the same area of the other persons hand. Try to avoid grabbing someone's fingers when shaking hands, as this could send a negative message.

3. **Eye contact.** As you shake the person's hand, make direct eye contact. This can be challenging for some people who grew up in a culture where direct eye contact would be considered rude. Be sure to smile.

A handshake should be firm but not too firm. The web of the other person's hand should touch yours, as to avoid shaking someone's fingers!

© Thinkstock

4. **Say your name and repeat the other person's name.** As you are making eye contact and shaking hands, you might say something like, "Hi, my name is Laura Portolese. It is a pleasure to meet you." When they say their name, be sure to repeat it, which will make it easier to remember. In fact, if they give you a business card, perhaps write down some of the things you discussed. This way, when you meet again, you are more likely to connect their name with a personal or professional interest.

5. **Introducing two people.** If you are introducing two people, say both people's names and try to tell them something they have in common that they can discuss. For example, "Casey, meet Ms. Robins. Both of you went to Central Washington University." This gives them a starting point to begin their conversation.

Good handshakes and introductions are important, but they also take practice. Often, people are too worried about the impression they are making to focus on their handshake, eye contact, and other aspects. The more comfortable you can get with this, the more second nature it will become and the better your human relations skills will be!

WATCH THIS!

This video discusses the importance of handshakes.

View the video online at: http://www.youtube.com/embed/IHUAJA2t_NA?rel=0

Dining Out

Often, a time will come when you must attend a business dinner with your supervisor or colleagues. When we dine alone or with our family, sometimes we do not pay as much attention to table manners as we should. Exhibiting proper table manners in a business setting not only conveys high emotional intelligence but also can create positive relationships with others. Let's discuss this as if we are starting a dinner from the beginning.

FIGURE 13.4 Place Settings
Sometimes the amount of dinnerware can be overwhelming! For forks, use the last one out and work your way in. Make sure the napkin goes on your lap. Also be aware, your bread and butter plate will always be on your left, while your glasses will be on your right.

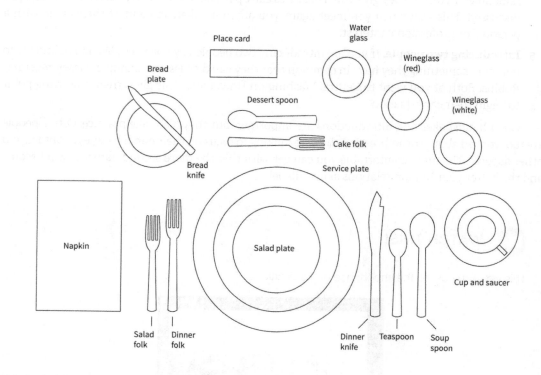

© Shutterstock, Inc.

First, it would be proper to make sure the host is seated before you sit. Unless the host is male, in which case he may wait until all females are seated to take his seat (although this practice is becoming less and less common). Likewise, in any situation such as a job interview, you should never sit unless invited. Next, you will want to put the napkin on your lap. Avoid wiping your nose with the napkin. If you need to get up, leave the napkin on either side of your plate.

Try to order within the same price range as your host. Never order the most expensive menu item. Also, avoid ordering alcohol unless the host is ordering it, and even then never drink more than your limit in a business situation. When food is served, you should not begin eating until everyone has received their food, unless, of course, they tell you to go ahead and start.

Any food dish on the left is yours; any glass that is yours is on the right. Most silverware is arranged so the first-used is on the outside, and you work your way in. For example, the appetizer fork might be on the outside, then the salad fork, and the dinner fork. When you are finished with your meal, rest the silverware crosswise on your plate to indicate you are done.

If you are in a situation where food should be passed around the table, always pass from left to right. Avoid reaching past people's plates to get something. If someone asks you for salt and pepper, always pass both together, even if both were not requested. It goes without saying, but don't talk with your mouth full or play with food on your plate. If you don't like something, try to take a few bites, but it is ok to leave food. If you have special dietary restrictions—for example, if you are a vegetarian—don't make a big deal out of it and just avoid eating those things you wouldn't normally eat.

Always say please and thank you to anyone who does something for you, such as refilling your water or removing your plate. These basic manners can go a long way in showing politeness to the wait staff.

When the check comes and there is no obvious host, reach for it. If there is an obvious host, such as if your supervisor had told everyone he was going to take the department to dinner, it is fine not to reach for the check. If people are splitting the check, it is normal to split it evenly, unless people had significantly differently-priced items. For example, if one person had only a salad and another person had the porterhouse steak, splitting might not be appropriate.[9] Likewise, if you had an adult beverage but someone else didn't, offering to pay more would be appropriate. It is also customary to tip 20 percent, as not doing so would be considered in poor taste. Please note that dining etiquette discussed here is specific to the United States. Before you travel, consider doing research on proper etiquette at your destination, as we discussed in Chapter 11 Section 3.

Silverware resting together indicates to the server that you are finished with your meal.

© Thinkstock

Clothing

Dress is another etiquette consideration, and will vary greatly from region to region. For example, in the Seattle area, it is normal for many people to wear jeans to work, while in other parts of the country, this would be considered inappropriate. When deciding what to wear, it is always best to be a bit overdressed rather than underdressed. For job interviews, jeans or shorts would rarely, if ever, be acceptable. Typically, in job interviews, dressing one "step up" from what people wear at the company is a good rule of thumb.

Showing too much skin in some work environments may prevent upward movement in a company, as it sends the wrong message to your boss or future boss (fair or not). In a study by Peter Click, women in high-level positions who dress in what is seen as sexy attire are viewed as less competent, regardless of their skill sets.[10] Fair or not, there are many unspoken rules about what is appropriate and what is not. The best thing to do is to look at what the successful people around you are wearing. For example, if all of the men in the workplace wear suit jackets and rarely take them off, this is an indicator of expected workplace dress. If all of the women in the office wear closed-toed shoes and leave the flip flops at home, it might be a good idea for you to do the same. Personal style and individuality are important, but in some professions it makes sense to err on the side of caution when choosing a work wardrobe.

Technology

Another important thing to mention is the use of technology. Although technology has made our lives easier in many ways, to succeed in your career, there are some basic technology etiquette rules to consider:

- Don't look at your phone while talking with someone else.
- Don't text while at the dinner table.
- Don't talk loudly on the phone in a public space.

- Avoid letting "text speak" cross over into e-mails (i.e., "tho" is OK for texts, but spell it out—"though"—for e-mails).
- Try to avoid multitasking with your phone in inappropriate places, such as in the restroom.
- When sending e-mails, avoid clogging up peoples' e-mail boxes with "reply all" messages.
- Use spellcheck for e-mails.
- Try to answer e-mails within twenty-four hours, even if it is to say, "I am not sure about this but I will get back to you."

Another note related to technology is the use of social media. Be sure not to post anything you wouldn't want your boss or future boss to see. For example, never bash your workplace or boss on social media or allow pictures to be posted that show questionable behavior, and try to stay positive.

Reputation Management

Many companies pay hundreds, even thousands of dollars every month, to monitor and clean up their online reputations. The process of monitoring your online reputation is called reputation management. Reputation.com, one of hundreds of firms that specializes in "fixing" online reputations, has become popular for companies looking to enhance their online image. Reputation management isn't just for companies—individuals are using these services to make unflattering things on the Internet about them disappear.[11]

Anything posted on the Internet—from a picture on Facebook to a comment on a blog—will be in cyberspace indefinitely. Considering how and what you post is very important, especially for the job seeker. Seventy percent of companies, in fact, will look at a candidate's social media sites before making a hiring decision![12]

So how exactly can you monitor your online reputation? Here are some tips:

- Google yourself often and see what the search results return.
- Consider changing your privacy settings on social media, so people you are not "friends" with cannot view your profile.
- Change your social media settings so you must approve posts that "tag" you.
- Be aware of your company's policy on posting resumes on websites like LinkedIn.
- Do not talk about work on social media sites.
- Never mention your company name on social media sites.

Managing your online reputation can make sure that when an employer or potential employer sees your online persona, they are seeing the side you want them to see. It will show them that you represent the company in a positive light, which can enhance career success.

 **WATCH THIS!**

This video discusses the importance of managing your online reputation.

View the video online at: http://www.youtube.com/embed/JtC_ulXkvJA?rel=0

General Etiquette for Career Success

We should discuss other parts of etiquette that would be considered general politeness and show professionalism—both skills that create positive relationships with others. Some of these include the following:

- Be on time for appointments. If you can't be on time, call if you will be more than five minutes late.
- RSVP when people send an invitation.
- Always use please and thank you.
- Always send thank you notes (handwritten is best!) when someone goes out of their way for you.
- Apologize if you make a mistake.
- Always bring a gift like wine or flowers to the host when dining at another person's home.
- Hold the door—whether you are male or female—if you get to the door first.
- Make eye contact.
- When given a business card, always look at it before tucking it away. Do not put it in a pocket.
- Avoid hoarding a conversation. Learn how to ask questions and be interested in what others have to say.
- Don't use swear words in a professional environment.
- Don't interrupt people.

Understanding and following general etiquette rules can help boost your career. People who do not have manners may not be as respected, and as a result, they may not be promoted or experience career growth. Etiquette is part of social intelligence skills, which—as we discussed in Chapter 2—are proven to help people attain career success. Speaking of career growth, how does one actually grow in their career? That will be the topic of Section 5.

Key Takeaways

- To ensure career success, there are a few main things to be noted. First impressions are important, so having a firm handshake that is web to web is important.
- When meeting someone, shake their hand, look them in the eye, and repeat their name to help you remember it.
- When dining, there are many etiquette rules. For example, place the napkin on your lap and use the correct forks and glasses. Generally speaking, the first forks you will use are farthest from the plate, and then you work your way in. Dinnerware, such as a bread plate, is always on the left and glasses are always on your right.
- Basic commonsense etiquette, such as not using the napkin on your face or nose, and waiting to begin eating until everyone has their food, would be important to consider in dining etiquette.
- The use of technology has increased and so has the rudeness, some studies show. Basic etiquette for phones includes not texting while you are having a face-to-face conversation with someone and avoiding speaking loudly.
- Other things to consider regarding technology might include not copying everyone on an e-mail, making sure to use spellcheck, and using proper grammar.
- Make sure to engage in careful consideration before posting comments on social media. This is called reputation management.
- Other tips for etiquette include sending thank you cards (not e-mails), being on time, keeping commitments, and making sure to involve others in a conversation.

Exercises

1. Shake the hands of five people you know well. Ask them to give you feedback on your handshake, and then write at least two to three paragraphs about it.
2. Visit a public place such as a mall or restaurant. Observe how people use technology when they are alone and when others are around them. What did you observe? What would be considered rude and what would be considered acceptable and normal behavior? Write four paragraphs on your observations and bring to class to discuss.

13.5 Career Growth: Resumes, Interviews, and Personality

Learning Objectives

1. Be able to discuss resume writing and interviewing tips.
2. Be able to explain the personality characteristics that can increase the chances for your personal career growth.
3. Be able to explain why having a mentor can be an important part of your career growth.

This section will address resumes, interviewing, and also personality traits to continue working on to make your career a success. First, let's talk about resumes and interviews.

Land That Job: Resumes!

Most people will need to create a resume in order to land that perfect job. A few tips on writing your resume:

- Use active verbs in your resume. Instead of stating what you did in a job, use words like managed, handled, collaborated, or analyzed. This makes your resume more interesting to read. If you google "resume action verbs," there are many resources that could give you ideas.

- Always be honest on your resume. All of the technologies available today make it easy to determine if someone has been dishonest on their resume.

- Consider the job description. Use key words from the job posting to include in your resume since many companies use resume parsing software, which automatically pulls out resumes that appear to meet the criteria.

- Focus on what you can do for the company. For example, instead of saying, "I want a job where I can grow with the company" say, "I see potential for career growth, given the x, y, and z skills I possess."

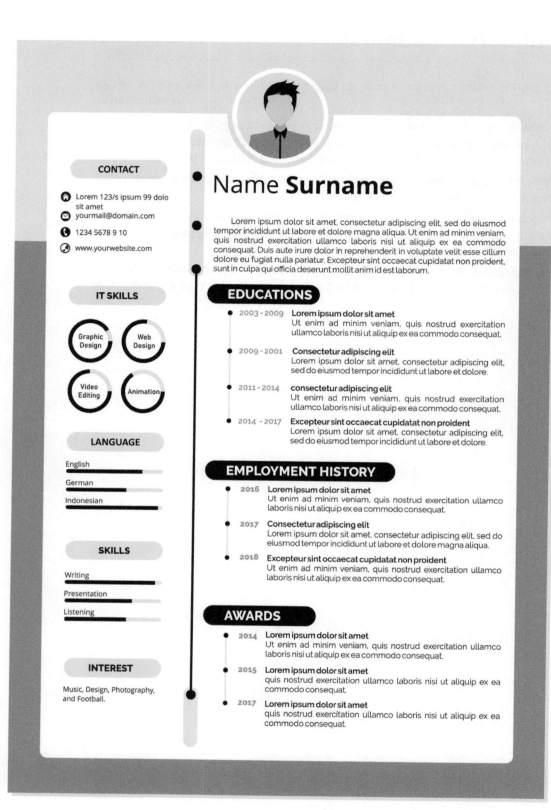

CV / RESUME   COVER LETTER

WATCH THIS!

Suggestions on how to write an effective resume.

View the video online at: http://www.youtube.com/embed/-JIFZBYp0jE?rel=0

Land That Job: Interviewing!

So your perfect resume landed you an interview! Congratulations! The next step is to prepare for the interview. Interviewing is most certainly a nerve-wracking experience, but by being prepared, you can nail that interview! Here are some tips on interviewing:

- Prepare! Do research on the company and come up with 2–3 good questions you can ask.
- Avoid talking about salary, unless directly asked.
- Role play with a friend for practice. Have them ask you interview questions and prepare your responses.
- Every answer to an interview question should include an example. For instance, if you are asked how you've handled working in a difficult team, you might say, "I work very well in teams and have strong emotional intelligence skills. For example, at a previous employer, there was a team member . . ." and show how you handled the difficult situation. Providing examples will not just tell the potential employer, but actually show them your abilities.
- Make sure your phone is turned off.
- Make eye contact.
- Make sure the potential employer knows what skills you would bring to the position.
- Arrive 10–15 minutes early. If it is a virtual meeting, make sure to test the technology ahead of time to ensure you are comfortable with it prior to your interview.
- Even if the interview is virtual, make sure to dress appropriately. Depending on the type of job, a button-up shirt and slacks for men, and slacks, skirt or dress for women, is appropriate. Tank tops, T-shirts, or sleeveless shirts generally are not appropriate for a job interview, whether it be in person or virtually.

Finally, there are literally thousands (if not hundreds of thousands) of websites dedicated to sample interview questions and answers, complete with lots of tips. Make sure to also spend some time before your interview learning all you can about interviewing.

Dressing appropriately for an interview, whether the interview is virtual or in person, can show the employer you are the right person for the job!

© Shutterstock

 **WATCH THIS!**

These interview questions and answers can help prepare you for any job interview.

View the video online at: http://www.youtube.com/embed/Csl2ccBpo4g?rel=0

Now that we have addressed resumes and interviews let's assume you've landed that job! Now, we will discuss tips for developing a career after you already have the job. First, we already know there are some personality characteristics that tend to be required for career success. Please note that this is different than behaviors, which we discussed earlier. Personality is a stable set of traits, while behavior is an expression of those traits in different circumstances. Although personality traits tend to be stable over time, we can change our personality traits. For example, Phil's personality may typically not be career-driven and motivated, and this could come out in the way he relates to others in his organization. But suppose Phil finds a job he really likes. His behavior can change in that his satisfaction makes him confident, relaxed, and able to work well in teams. So sometimes when we change our behavior, our personality can change—and our human relations can change, as well.

Some of the personality characteristics for success might include the following:

- Motivated
- Driven
- Good social skills
- Listening
- Reading body language
- Written communication
- Verbal communication
- Ability to make good decisions
- Ability to work with a diverse workforce
- Teamwork
- Handling conflict
- Managing emotions
- Managing stress
- Being ethical
- Positive attitude
- Goal oriented
- Informing your supervisor that you want to grow your career

Of course this list is not exhaustive, but we have discussed many of these characteristics throughout the book. But how do you develop these skills? First, being aware of your own need for self-improvement can go a long way to improving these skills. Assume Steve isn't a very good listener, and he identifies this as an area for improvement. Steve then needs to make a conscious effort to improve his listening skills. Having an awareness of this need and then putting together an improvement plan is a step in the right direction. But, until we are able to recognize our strengths and weaknesses, we are not able to improve upon them. In another example, assume Duana realizes she gets very stressed at work, and that stress causes her to be short with people. Learning how to manage stress better can create better relations with others.

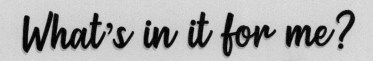

Human relations skills allow us to better deal with situations and people (us included) who are imperfect. Human relations—and emotional intelligence—has shown to be twice as important to determine excellent performance at work.[13] Not every work situation will be great. **Bosses will be difficult to work for, we will have colleagues who we don't enjoy working with, and personal relationships will have their ups and downs. How we handle these situations is the true measure of our human relations skills.** How well can we handle situations that are difficult or learn to make decisions that may be challenging? By employing the human relations information throughout the book, we can begin to analyze our own strengths and weaknesses in each of these areas. If we have an "I'm fine" attitude, we are not able to improve, limiting our potential for positive human relations, and limiting our career success.

To get better at human relations, we need to hone our strengths and weaknesses (self-awareness skills) and understand what human relations skills we should and could improve on. Those areas we identify as our strengths are what we need to continue to develop.

Sample assessment of strengths and weaknesses:

- I want to improve e-mail communication (Chapter 5), so I am more focused and clear, resulting in the receiver understanding my message more clearly.

- I tend to be impatient and protective of my time. Because of this personality trait (Chapter 1), I can sometimes come across as too demanding to others.

- I want to improve the way I deal with difficult team or group situations (Chapter 8), so I don't get so angry when things don't go the way I want.

- Improve conflict management skills. My emotions run too high when there is conflict and disagreement. I want to improve this skill, because I know effective skills will allow me to resolve situations and move forward in my relationships (Chapter 10).

- A strength is my ability to solve problems (Chapter 9) in a logical manner. I will continue to employ logical thinking in the decisions I make and teach others to do the same through the example I set.

- A strength is my understanding and appreciation of cultural differences. I understand people may behave differently from me based upon their background (Chapter 11). Because I know this, I am comfortable in a wide variety of work environments. I will continue to develop this skill by reading about other cultures and traveling to experience the culture firsthand.

- A strength is my willingness to help team members. I try to always go above and beyond to assist someone who may lack skills that I have (Chapter 8). I will make an effort to continually do this, even if it isn't convenient.

These examples shows how you might assess your own strengths and weaknesses in relation to your own human relations. As we know from this chapter, acknowledging the need to further develop skills, then making efforts to improve the skills, are the first steps to a positive human relations—and a successful career.

Soon, you will be taking final exams, working on final projects, and moving on to the next set of classes—or maybe a new career. **Don't think of your journey for improving emotional intelligence skills as ending; really, it is just beginning.** Continuing to improve these skills you've developed will propel you to success with your relationships and in your career!

 **WATCH THIS!**

Stone-cold millionaire Larry Beachham explains why having a mentor can help your career.

View the video online at: http://www.youtube.com/embed/wBT8u5RwsXE?rel=0

One of the ways we can develop the skill of recognizing your strengths and weaknesses is to utilize a mentor. A **mentor** is someone who is a trusted counselor or teacher. Sometimes, companies have formal mentorship programs. Often, though, the best mentorships come from relationships that form over time. For example, when Paul started working at Ascent Corporation, he knew he wanted to move up the company ranks but didn't know how. When Paul was assigned a project with Beth, a managing director, he knew that he wanted to talk with her to find out how she made it to that position. Paul felt nervous approaching Beth at first because she was so busy. But he decided to take the risk and invited her to have coffee after their meeting. After that, they began to speak weekly, and Beth took an interest in helping Paul in his career. Together, the two worked to develop strategies and objectives for Paul's career. When he had questions about his career path, she helped him. When a position opened up, Beth coached Paul on the interview, and he was promoted.

Make sure you continue learning. Taking seminars and courses can help make you more marketable in your field. Since most fields change on a regular basis, we must continually update our skills to build upon what we already know and learn new things.

mentor

Someone who is a trusted counselor or teacher.

Key Takeaways

- Writing a resume is the first step to landing that dream job! Use all of the resources available to you to write the perfect resume.
- Similar to resume writing, there are many resources available to you on how to nail that interview. Take advantages of all of the resources available online once you've landed that interview.
- There are many personality characteristics that can help someone be successful at work. They include learning how to manage emotions, being ethical, and learning how to deal with stress.
- Other factors to career success might include the ability to set goals, make decisions, and deal with conflict.
- Knowing which of these things you are good at and which need work is an important part to making sure you continually grow professionally and personally.

- Getting a mentor, that is, someone who can guide you through your career, is also a valuable tool for making sure you experience career growth.
- Continually learning is another way to grow in your career. Make sure you stay updated on new technologies and discoveries in your field. This can happen through formal training courses or reading publications from your industry.

Exercises

1. Draft a resume. Have at least five people review it for use of action words, and general editing.
2. Looking at the list of personality characteristics for success in this section, rate yourself on a scale from one to ten, with ten being your strongest areas. Once you rate yourself, look at the three lowest areas. Create specific goals and objectives that will help you overcome these weaknesses.
3. List at least three possible mentors for you, and then discuss how you might approach each one to ask about his or her availability to mentor you.

13.6 Chapter Summary and Case

Chapter Summary

- Power refers to our ability to influence others and convince them to do what we want them to do. This is different from influence, which is the application of our power to get people to do what we want them to do. In other words, power is our ability, while influence allows us to move someone to action.
- Someone who is power-compulsive may lust for power, while someone who is power-shy may try to avoid situations where he or she might have to exert power.
- Our power position can help us achieve career success, and refers to the use of our own power to get ahead in organizations.
- Power positioning can be done using a variety of methods, but specific techniques and behaviors can be used. For example, the POWER method refers to behaviors we can exhibit to increase our power position. They include positive approach, openness, willingness, employing things like tact and social skills, and remembering our purpose and goals.
- Learning how to negotiate effectively can assist you in all aspects of your career.
- Part of career success is making sure you know how to increase your power position and having an awareness of your attitude and personality.
- There are three main behavioral aspects to optimizing career success—planning, attitude, and action. Examples include being willing to go above and beyond your job description and having a specific goal you want to reach. Besides goal setting, having a positive, can-do attitude can help improve chances for promotion.
- To ensure career success, there are a few main things one should be noted. First impressions are important, so having a firm handshake that is web to web is important.
- When meeting someone, shake their hand, look them in the eye, and repeat their name to help you remember it.
- When dining, there are many etiquette rules—for example, placing the napkin on your lap and using the correct forks and glasses. Generally speaking, the first forks you will use are

farthest from the plate, and then you work your way in. Dinnerware, such as a bread plate, is always on the left and glasses are always on your right.

- Basic commonsense etiquette, such as not using the napkin on your face or nose, waiting to begin eating until everyone has their food, and others would be considered important things to consider in dining etiquette.

- The use of technology has increased and so has the rudeness, some studies show. Some basic etiquette rules for phones include not texting while you are having a face-to-face conversation with someone and avoiding speaking loudly.

- Other things to consider regarding technology might include not copying everyone on an e-mail, making sure to use spellcheck, and proper grammar.

- Other tips for etiquette include sending thank you cards (not e-mails), being on time, keeping commitments, and making sure to involve others in a conversation.

- Many personality characteristics can help someone be successful at work. They include topics discussed throughout this book, such as learning how to manage emotions, being ethical, and learning how to deal with stress.

- Other factors to career success might include the ability to set goals, make decisions, and deal with conflict.

- Knowing which of these things you are good at and which need work is an important part to making sure you continually grow professionally and personally.

- Getting a mentor, that is, someone who can guide you through your career is also a valuable tool for making sure you experience career growth.

- Continually learning is another way to grow in your career. Stay updated on new technologies and discoveries in your field. This can happen through formal training courses or reading publications from your industry.

Chapter Case

Robert is a supervisor at a large bottling company and has career goals with the organization. His job includes managing safety and breaks and setting schedules for his twenty-five employees who use forklifts and other machinery to package and move filled bottles onto trucks for delivery. First, he would like to become the bottling manager, which is one step up from his current job. In five years, Robert would like to become the director of operations and oversee the entire factory floor.

Robert is an excellent, well-liked manager by his employees, but when it comes to his supervisors, he is very quiet. He never mentioned the fact that his shift had one hundred accident-free days in a row or that productivity had increased 10 percent since he took over the shift. Robert is also a bit shy, so he avoids any kind of social interaction, such as the holiday party.

While Robert wants to be promoted in the organization, he knows he lacks some of the skills needed to do the job, such as the ability to put together budgets. Because of this, he has identified two courses he would like to take to improve his financial skills.

Robert was recently asked to review the operational processes during his shift and excelled at it. In fact, because of the shifts' awareness, Robert motivated his staff to change some of the procedures to be more cost-effective. Since Robert would like a promotion, he knows he should assess his strengths and weaknesses.

1. Consider each of the following topics examined in this chapter and discuss Robert's strengths and weaknesses in each of the following areas (making reasonable assumptions is fine). Then create a plan addressing what Robert can do to improve in each area:

    a. Power positioning

    b. Planning, action, and attitude

    c. Etiquette

    d. Personality characteristics

   e. Mentoring

   f. Continual learning

2. Once you complete some ideas for Robert, think about your strengths and weaknesses in each area. Make a plan on how you can improve on each point.

Endnotes

1. Mind Tools Website. (n.d.). French and Raven's five forms of power. Retrieved from http://www.mindtools.com/pages/article/newLDR_56.htm

2. French, J.R.P., & Raven, B. (1959). The bases of social power. In D. Cartwright & A. Zander (Eds.). *Group dynamics*. New York: Harper & Row.

3. Luthans, F., Avolio, B.J., Avey, J.B., & Norman, S.M. (2007). Positive psychological capital: Measurement and relationship with performance and satisfaction. *Leadership Institute Faculty Publications*. Paper 11. http://digitalcommons.unl.edu/leadershipfacpub/11

4. Kelchner, L. (12 March 2019). Top ten effective negotiation skills. Retrieved from https://smallbusiness.chron.com/top-ten-effective-negotiation-skills-31534.html

5. Goleman, D. (n.d.). Emotional intelligence. Retrieved from http://www.nytimes.com/books/first/g/goleman-working.html

6. Siang, L.Y. (2006). How to get promoted. Career Success for Newbies. Retrieved from http://www.career-success-for-newbies.com/how-to-get-promoted.html

7. Fox News. (3 June 2008). The importance of networking. Retrieved from http://www.foxnews.com/story/0,2933,362704,00.html

8. Lorenz, K. (9 September 2009). Six tips for a perfect handshake. Retrieved from http://www.careerbuilder.com/Article/CB-431-Getting-Hired-Six-Tips-for-a-Perfect-Handshake/

9. United States dining etiquette Guide. (n.d.). Retrieved from http://whatscookingamerica.net/Menu/DiningEtiquetteGuide.htm

10. Sinberg, L. (22 July 2009). What not to wear to work. Retrieved from http://www.forbes.com/2009/07/22/office-fashion-sexy-forbes-woman-style-clothes.html

11. Tozzi, J. (30 April 2008). Do reputation management services work? *Businessweek*, accessed May 22, 2012, http://www.businessweek.com/smallbiz/content/apr2008/sb20080430_356835.htm

12. Driver, S. (7 October 2018). Keep it clean: social media screenings gain in popularity. Retrieved from https://www.businessnewsdaily.com/2377-social-media-hiring.html

13. Goleman, D. (January 2004). What makes a leader? *Harvard Business Review*, accessed May 23, 2012, http://hbr.org/2004/01/what-makes-a-leader/ar/1

Index